AF560682

GODS, MEN AND TERRITORY
Society and Culture in Kathmandu Valley

GODS, MEN AND TERRITORY

Society and Culture in Kathmandu Valley

Anne Vergati

CENTRE DE SCIENCES HUMAINES
2002

First published 1995
Reprinted 2002

ISBN 81-7304-078-8

Published by
Ajay Kumar Jain for
Manohar Publishers & Distributors
4753/23, Ansari Road, Daryaganj
New Delhi - 110002

Distributors in Nepal
Mandala Book Point
G.P.O. Box 528, Kanti Path
Kathmandu, Nepal

Ratna Pustak Bhandar
Post Box No. 98, Bhotahity
Kathmandu, Nepal

Typeset by
A J Software Publishing Co. Pvt. Ltd.
New Delhi - 110005

Printed at
Rajkamal Electric Press
Delhi - 110033

Acknowledgements

It was at the suggestion of Professor T.N. Madan, who had taken an interest in my work over the last fifteen years, that I decided to group together the articles which comprise this volume. These, along with the Introduction, represent some facets of my work in Nepal; those dealing with Rajasthan are being published elsewhere. In Nepal, I received much help and encouragement from Professors M. Witzel, B. Kölver, A.W. Macdonald, Dr. N. Gutschow, Dr. David Gellner and other colleagues.

In France, I am particularly indebted to the Centre National de la Recherche Scientifique (C.N.R.S.) in Paris and to the Laboratoire d'Ethnologie et de Sociologie Comparative at the Université de Paris X, Nanterre. I was trained at the latter institution, and it also gave me travel money for several trips to Nepal and India. In particular, I wish to thank Professor Éric de Dampierre for his patience and his good counsel. At the Collège de France, Professor Gérard Fussman and the team of Dr. André Padoux helped me to grasp the importance of written texts and historical documents pertinent to my fieldwork in Nepal. Some of my articles were also discussed by members of other C.N.R.S. research teams such at CEIAS (Centre d'Etudes Indienness et d'Asie du Sud) URA 118, whose former director Professor Madeleine M. Biardeau and Professor M.L. Reiniche were always a source of encouragement. With problems involved in the translation into English of some of the articles that were originally published in French, Professor A.W. Macdonald was very helpful. During my stay in Delhi I enjoyed the kind hospitality of Mr. Michel Postel to whom I express my grateful thanks.

The publication of this book in India was facilitated to

some extent by a subvention from the French Foreign Ministry and by the Centre de Sciences Humaines in New Delhi and its Director, Dr. O. Guillaume. Finally, I wish to thank Mr. Ajay Jain who accepted this volume for publication. My hope is that it will contribute to a better understanding of the orientation of French research in South Asian studies, particularly in India.

The author and the publisher would like to thank the editors and publishers of the following journals and books for their permission to reprint the articles in the present volume.

'*Digu Dyo:* A Lineage Deity of the Newars', in *Bulletin de l'Ecole Française d'Extrême-Orient,* LXVI, 1979, pp. 115-27

'The Image of the Divinity in the Lineage Cult among the Newars', in *L'image divine. Culte et méditation dans l'hindouisme.* Ed. A. Padoux, 1991, Paris, C.N.R.S., pp. 133-43.

'Social Consequences of Marrying Viṣṇu Narayana: Primary Marriage among the Newars of Kathmandu Valley', in *Contributions to Indian Sociology,* No. 2, 1982, pp. 271-87.

'Taleju, Sovereign Deity of Bhaktapur', in *Asie du Sud. Traditions et Changements,* Colloques Internationaux du C.N.R.S., No. 582, Paris, Editions du C.N.R.S., 1979, pp. 162-69.

'The Religious Associations (*Guṭhi*) of Kathmandu Valley Temples', in *Puruṣārtha,* ed. J.C. Galey, L'espace du temple II, Les sanctuaires dans le Royaume, Paris, 1986, No. 10, pp. 97-123.

'Śaivite Temples in Bhaktapur', in *Newar Art, Nepalese Art during the Malla Period,* Warminster, Aris and Phillips, 1979, pp. 83-107.

'Ritual Planning of the Bhaktapur Kingdom', in A.Dallapiccola, ed., *Shastric Traditions in Indian Art,* Wiesbaden, F. Steiner Verlag, 1989, pp. 261-69.

'The Killing of the Snakes or the Founding of the Town of Bhaktapur' in *Tracés de foundation,* M. Detienne, ed., Peters, Louvain-Paris, 1990, pp. 223-48.

'The Worship and Iconography of Dipankara Buddha in the Valley of Kathmandu', in *Arts Asiatiques*, 37, 1982, pp. 22-27.

'The King as Rainmaker: A New Version of the Legend of Red Avalokitesvara', in *Bulletin de l'Ecole Française d'Extrême-Orient*, 74, 1985, pp. 267-303.

Contents

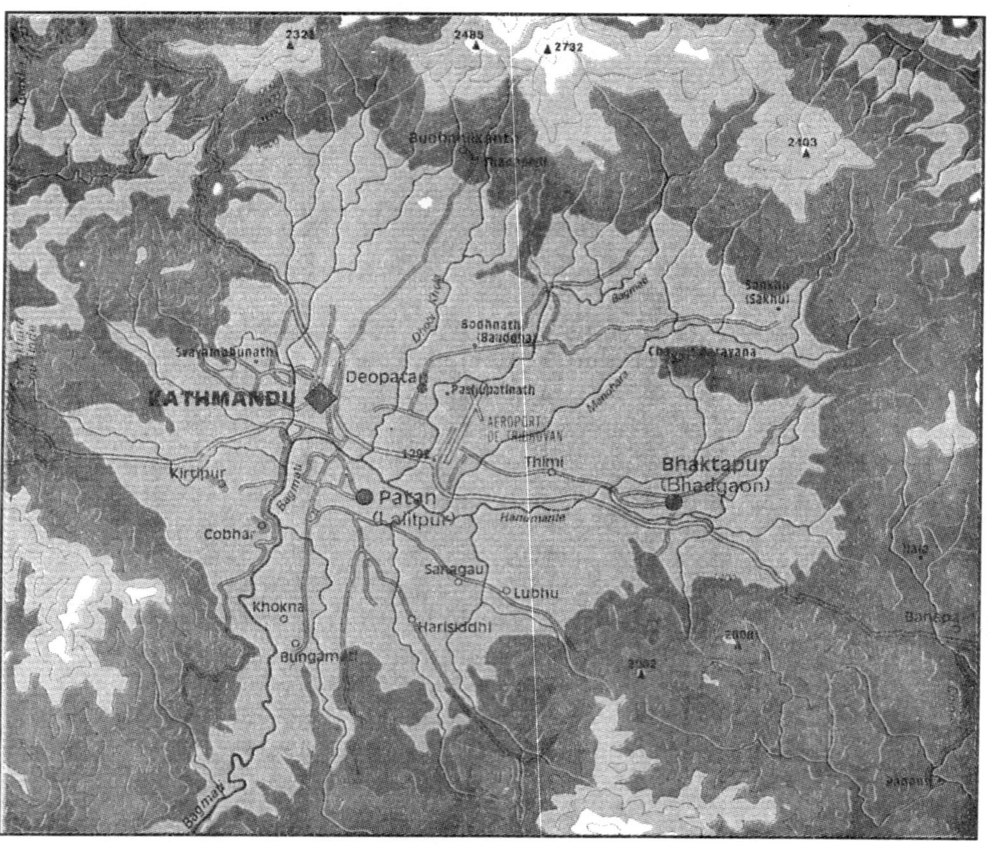

Map of Kathmandu Valley

Introduction: An Approach to Newar Society

In the introduction which follows I describe briefly my fieldwork experience in Nepal and then introduce a set of research papers that were the result of this fieldwork. Published one by one over fifteen years they have been brought together here, because, when read as a whole, they present, I think, an overall picture of some of the essential features of Newar society. They highlight some of the basic themes of Newar culture.

Shortly after completing my doctoral dissertation at the University of Paris X, at Nanterre, I went to Nepal, for the first time, in 1974. I went to Kathmandu to teach at the newly created Department of Sociology at Tribhuvan University, at Kirtipur. I went to Nepal with enthusiasm because I had read the writings of the great French orientalist Sylvain Lévi and those of A. David Neel and I was anxious to see the country. At that time I had little knowledge of the intellectual life of Kathmandu and it was only much later that I realized to what extent the creation of a department of sociology at the University of Kirtipur represented an innovation in the life of the country. The department had in fact been created in 1973 under the impetus of the British Council, the cultural section of the local British Embassy. Teaching was in English and those who came to my lectures belonged to a certain intellectual élite and most of them were members of the higher castes. They had the impression that sociology was a very abstract subject and their questions were almost always focused on its practical uses: in what way could sociology further development? Did it offer a livelihood or grants for travel abroad? Later, I realized that there was a considerable difference in the academic scenes between India and Nepal, between the two capitals, Delhi and Kathmandu. In India, since the beginning of the twentieth century or even earlier there had been a tradition of teaching and research work on social matters.[1] In Nepal, such research had begun only twenty years or so before I arrived there. After 1950 quite a number of Nepalese scholars were indeed trained in social sciences and economics in Indian universities and some went to America and Great Britain. In Nepal, as in many other Asian countries, it was only the sociology of development which provoked the interest of local scholars. For members of a caste society the analysis of the concept of social hierarchy proved difficult: that sociology is only interesting if it can be applied is an attitude which exists in Nepal even today.

I was immersed at once in my work at the University. This put me in contact immediately with a considerable number of very helpful and courteous young Nepalese from differing social backgrounds. If, to me, everybody was new, I was new to most people. In this new world everything was different: the climate, the food, the combination of mountain scenery and tropical vegetation, the way of life of the local people. On their side as well as mine, there were therefore innumerable questions to be asked: and the answers were not always easy to formulate in terms which could be grasped by both parties to the dialogue which ensued. It was only twenty years ago that Nepal had been "opened" up to the outside world. If, for centuries, commercial and cultural links had opened Nepalese eyes to Indian civilization, Russia, Japan, the United States of America and Europe were little known to the students I met at Kirtipur.

I was impressed by the natural beauty of the Kathmandu Valley. I was also fascinated by the architecture and art of the

Valley's monuments and buildings. So I wanted to learn more about the people who had created them. However, there were few publications concerning the Newars, the principal inhabitants of this Valley, whose ancestors had raised these buildings. Fortunately, among my students was a young Newar called Bal Gopal Baidya. Sociology was new to him as he had previously studied economics abroad. He answered my inquisitive questions about his family by taking me to his house in Bhaktapur from where his family originated and by introducing me to several family members and even distant relatives. I remember very clearly that, when he began to tell me about his family, he led me to the site of his lineage's deity. There he explained its importance and how necessary it was that it should remain in the same place. From my first contact with him I realized Bal Gopal was atypical. As he had been trained in economics outside Nepal and belonged to a family whose members were traditionally doctors, his outlook was much less parochial than that of many of his contemporaries.

In those days, Bhaktapur was still relatively sheltered from the deluge of social and administrative change which was falling with increasing force on all the Valley. To me, its narrow paved streets, its large public squares and its old brick buildings were a reminder of what I had read about the towns of medieval Europe. Life was still lived at Bhaktapur in a traditional and fairly leisurely manner. It is true that many foreign tourists arrived by bus or taxi every morning from Kathmandu but they never stayed in Bhaktapur for more than a few hours. They always wandered around the same places taking photographs: and by four o'clock in the afternoon most of them had already left the town. Even in the eastern part of Bhaktapur, where the Germans were repairing and renovating some building in the Dattātreya area, there were few foreigners who stayed over night. The atmosphere was completely different from that in Kathmandu where Freak Street was still, in those days, a mythical heaven for Western hippies.

In Newar culture there is not so marked a difference

between a village and a town as there is in India. Every Newar village has something of an urban character: the houses have two or three storeys and the population density is considerable. The three main towns in the Valley are clearly the consequence of the aggregation in each case of previously extant villages or smaller settlements. In Newari the word used by local inhabitants to designate a small or a large settlement is invariably *des* which, in Sanskrit or in Hindi, has a different meaning. Perhaps the most satisfactory English word for Newari *des* is "locality". Several authors have recently emphasized this urban character of Newar civilization. Sylvain Lévi, the first Western scholar to draw attention to it, and to compare Newar houses with those of Parisians, wrote: "The outstanding trait in the character of the Newar is his liking for society. A Newar never lives in isolation whether in town or village, he likes to lodge, somewhat in the manner of the Parisian, in several-storeyed houses, even if this means living in cramped conditions. He knows how to enjoy all the pleasures which nature offers; he sings, he chants, he laughs, he is a shrewd judge of country; he likes to picnic in gay company in some shady spot near a spring or a stream, in the shadow of an aged sanctuary facing a friendly or a grandiose landscape."[2]

Besides getting to know Bal Gopal's family, I had also met Thakurlal Manandhar, an erudite Newar scholar who lived near Bhimsen's Tower in Kathmandu and who came often to the University. As his name indicates, his family were traditionally oil-pressers. So, for Manandhar, knowledge and its acquisition were not only a personal quest but also a means of social climbing. His learning enabled him to discuss on an equal footing with *Vajrācārya* and Brahmins. Few citizens of Nepal could read and understand fifteenth or sixteenth century texts as he was able to do. He was much pre-occupied with the education of his sons so that they too, by their training, would maintain a certain social prestige. It was only slowly that I realized that, in Bhaktapur, Manandhars are considered to be of lower rank than they are in Kathmandu: Thakurlal often came to see me in Bhaktapur but he did not introduce me to his relatives who lived there. Both Bal Gopal and Thakurlal spoke English but I knew that to study Newar society I must learn Newari. My attempts to learn Newari's rudiments must have exasperated Thakurlal because he himself was preoccupied with etymological problems and his own theories on Newar History and culture. I was later to edit, with the help of Professor Jean Filliozat and the Ecole Française d'Extrême Orient his Newari-English Dictionary.[3]

When I returned to Nepal, in 1975, after a six-month interval in Europe, I rented the upper part of a house at Bhaktapur. I was lucky enough to find as teacher a Newar Brahmin, Ramapati Raj Upadhyaya. He had a real gift for teaching, a veritable passion for it, but he knew no English. The beginnings were difficult but, even from the start, he managed to make himself understood: he explained many things to me which I did not know. For some weeks he was very much on his guard and did not wish me to come to see him in his own house. He manifested a constant fear of being polluted and this made me understand what ritual purity really meant to him. Later on, however, I was very hospitably welcomed in his house by his wife and children. By then I had become accustomed to living on the floor and the absence of furniture had ceased to worry me. Once I had got past the cow which lived in the ground-floor stable, and as soon as I had climbed the ladder to the first floor, I was, as an honoured guest, given a cushion to sit on. When I stepped into the house I entered a new cultural world—from observing Hinduism I moved inside it.[4]

However Ramapati Raj has never yet eaten in my presence. He was very strict in observing carefully the obligations imposed on a Hindu at meal times. He used to classify people according to what they ate. On one occasion, when he came to visit me at "my" house, he met a low-caste person who was already in the room: Ramapati Raj muttered that in his lifetime habits had changed and that such a meeting would have been impossible a few years previously.

Often, local people asked me why I was staying in Bhaktapur and what I was doing there. As they talked between themselves about me, I became the object of gossip if not of scandal, so I had to give a clear-cut reason for my presence and repeat it to everybody. I told the simple truth: I was there to study Newar lineage deities known as *digu dyo.* What made me choose this subject? In every-day conversations names and stories about deities were frequently mentioned; and I was particularly intrigued by references to kinship links between individuals and a certain category of deity: *digu dyo.* It seemed to me that all Newars with the same deity must have kinship links with one another. The name of the deity was kept secret but the site at which it was located was not. Obviously it was an extremely complex society and it was not easy to isolate a "social fact".

In my early days in Bhaktapur, I experienced many difficulties because I did not know the Hindu and Buddhist pantheons in any detail. So I had to make considerable efforts to learn them. Often, when I was standing in front of statues in different parts of the town, I was questioned by children about their identity, and when I made mistakes the children who surrounded me burst out laughing. I feel therefore that in courses at European Universities for Western students intending to work later on in Nepal, it would be useful to incorporate lectures on the iconography of Hinduism and Buddhism. Such lectures at present are mainly addressed to art students. A solid grounding in iconography also helps considerably towards the study of rituals. I am very grateful indeed to Ramapati Raj for his explanations of local statues and his comment on the functional roles of different deities. In 1981 when I showed him the book *Newar Art* he immediately leafed through the illustrations and questioned me on the content of each caption. *Newar Art* is a study, from an anthropological perspective, of the social and cultural conditions in which the art of the Valley was created.[5] He commented on the statues and monuments of Bhaktapur, showing little interest in the illustrations of Newar edifices outside the town and no special aesthetic appreciation.

In Nepal each festival is linked to a temple or temples: in the refined and sophisticated civilization of the Newars, each temple is decorated with sculpted wooden window-frames and is often surrounded by sculpted struts figuring local deities under the over-hang of the roof; it encloses and is surrounded by statues. The links between festivals, localities and buildings are clearly manifested: a festival occurs in honour of a certain god or goddess. The locality in which it takes place is often situated within the territorial limits of an ancient kingdom.

Many festivals are of considerable complexity: that is to say, they complicate the domestic and social life of the community. Such festivals are also a source of anxiety to the anthropologist who has great difficulty describing what is going on, even to his own satisfaction let alone that of his informants. Many events occur simultaneously in different places and one cannot be everywhere at once. It is true that for some short rituals one is helped because there exist manuals which prescribe which steps should be executed and in what order. They are not always followed exactly. For large festivals one can only consult oral traditions and commentaries: thus one is led inevitably to accord a greater degree of confidence to some informants and less to others. One often hears that it is only by making lengthy stays in a given locality that one can hope to understand what occurs there. This is true but even a lengthy stay is not a solution to every problem. For instance, between the celebration of each festival of *Bisket jātrā* at Bhaktapur there is an interval of one year: and, even if one observes the festival several times, one also has to watch over its preparation and the packing up afterwards. The itineraries followed by the gods' and goddesses' chariots occupy several days: one cannot follow one procession from start to finish and, at the same time, oversee what ceremonies and *pūjā* are taking place in other parts of the town. Patience, though necessary, is not enough. One must first find out when a given ceremony is due to start: and one must be present on the spot before and after that time because few ceremonies begin and end "on time". Complex ceremonies never develop twice in exactly the same manner any more than an actor or a bard's performance is exactly similar two times running. Participants fall ill or are hurt and are not there where they should be "according to the book". Wheels get broken; ropes split; chariots, like cars, break down. To analyse the pattern of a simple *pūjā* is a far easier task than to abstract the structure of a complex festival, although large festivals do, of course, combine certain ritual sequences which are constant. It is quite a different matter for a solitary individual to observe one fire-offering and then to compare that experience with his general perception of a festival in which tens of thousands participate. Perhaps teamwork and division of labour are the only ways of working by which anthropologists can control the latter situation.

It is certain that Newars accord great importance to their festivals, which are different from those of the Indo-Nepalese. I often heard the complaint from Newars, who like to stress their separate identity from that of the Indo-Nepalese by emphasizing the difference between their respective festivals, that the present-day dynasty no longer gives enough money for the correct conduct of Newar festivals. I was even asked by a Citrakar, a painter who was responsible for the conservation of paintings in different temples in Bhaktapur, to petition the government authorities so that certain paintings and monuments be properly renovated before festival periods.[6] Care is constantly taken to maintain statues and temples in good repair. Artisans and others explain to you that a statue which is not in perfect condition should be replaced or repaired.[7]

The Newars have a veritable passion for secrets. Some anthropologists, for instance M. Allen, had noted the difficulty of talking with Newars about religion and tantric rituals.[8] They had attributed this to the influence of Tantrism on Newar culture. It took me some time to realize this: for I had never imagined that to reveal the name of a god was to risk being abandoned by that god's protection. This is, I suppose, a very Tantric way of looking at life which is still held with great conviction. A number of Western anthropologists have worked in Nepal but none has ever had access to the inner sanctuaries (*āgam*) of certain temples. The *dīkṣā* ritual of Tantric initiation which is supposed to take place in the inner sanctuaries has not yet, as far as I am aware, been observed by foreign scholars.[9]

I must admit that, as a well-intentioned scholar, I found it a hindrance to my work, after having worked for months with Ramapati Raj and his cousin Kedar Raj, not to be able to go up to the first floor of the Taleju temple in Bhaktapur and take part in or at least watch certain rituals. Crushed in a large crowd I could watch what was happening in the Main Chowk at the time of *Bisket jātrā*: but I was never able to see the box which reputedly contains the *yantra* of the goddess Taleju. I write this today, fifteen years later, after having visited in the interim many other sites in different parts of North India: now I realize that, in religious matters, the behaviour of Nepal's population is, in many respects, much stricter and more orthodox than that of other Hindus in India.

The anthropologist, in any country, even when he shares the local language, remains something of an intruder. His knowledge of a society will and can be only partial. I clearly understood that, in a Hindu context, to speak to a woman who is also a foreigner is fraught with much greater danger of pollution than is a conversation with a man.

"Anthropology" remarked C. Geertz, "inevitably involves an encounter with the Other. All too often, however, the ethnographic distance that separates the reader of anthropological texts and the anthropologist himself from the Other is rigidly maintained and at times even artificially exaggerated. In many cases this distancing leads to an exclusive focus on the Other as primitive, bizarre, and exotic. The gap between a familiar 'we' and the exotic 'they' is a major obstacle to a meaningful understanding of the Other, an obstacle that can only be overcome through some form of participation in the world of the Other".[10]

While still a student, I had, like many of my generation, come under the spell of the writings of Louis Dumont, in particular of his book *Homo Hierarchicus.* The intellectual coherence of his work attracted me. Éric de Dampierre, Professor of Comparative Sociology at the University of Paris, had warmly encouraged me to read and re-read Dumont's writings before I went to Nepal.

Certain descriptions in the writings of L. Dumont remained present in my mind when I was confronted with situations in the field. For instance, the behaviour of Ramapati Raj at meal-times provided a living illustration of Dumont's description of the dangers which surround and may assail a Hindu when he eats.[11] It seemed to me that Dumont had described such a situation in a definitive manner and that there was little else I could add to complete the picture he drew. There is however a world of difference between reading and approving theoretical texts and establishing good working relationships with individuals " in the field". It is relatively easy to observe agrarian techniques or the building of houses: it is quite another matter when it comes to discussing religion and rituals. This is seldom admitted in the writings of field anthropologists—for my part, I found it much easier to talk about kinship in Bhaktapur than to talk about religion. To converse with Newars on the subject of religion is just as difficult as is talking about money with the French.

When the Newars talk about their language, they emphasize the differences between dialects spoken in the three principal towns of the Valley. At the beginning of my stay, I myself was somewhat disconcerted because I wondered if I was in the presence not of three different dialects but of three different languages.

In conversation with foreigners, Newars constantly drew

attention to the superiority as well as to the specificity of their own culture, comparing their customs in the first place with those of the Indo-Nepalese and then with those of other ethnic groups such as Tamangs, Gurungs, Bhotias, etc.[12] All cultural comparisons concerning Newar identity or social hierarchy are based, in the first place, on local comparisons: one situates oneself, one's identity vis-à-vis the neighbours.

They are very conscious of the fact that they belong to an ancient civilization and in conversation they stress that they are the only ethnic group in Nepal which has built monuments such as Royal Palaces, temples, etc.

Members of different Newar castes speak about their caste's Indian origins. Often they say that their ancestors came from India "long ago", often with a king who is usually Hari Simha Deva (fourteenth century)—but the precise date is never mentioned.[13] In the background of all Newar oral traditions are "real" historical events. However, as in the case of India, historical events are taken out of their context and linked to mythical personages.

When Newars speak of themselves, in their own context, they also emphasize that Buddhist priests, *Vajrācārya*, as well as Newar Brahmins, because they are tantric, may eat meat and drink alcohol but are nevertheless from a hierarchical point of view on an equal footing with the Brahmins of other ethnic groups. This is not however the view expressed in the Nepalese Code *Mulukī Ain* of 1854 where Newar Brahmins and the *vajrācārya* are placed lower in the social hierarchy than other Brahmins because unlike the latter they drink alcohol.[14]

For the Newars, whether they be Hindus or Buddhists, the distinctive features of Newar society are not only religious but also social. For instance the ritual such as *ihi*—the group marriage of young girls to a god, before puberty— confers a relatively high status on Newar women who have certainly much more freedom than Indo-Nepalese women, even those of high caste. The ritual *bura jyanko,* when a person, at the age of seventy-seven leaves the world of men for that of gods, has never been the object of detailed study.

Tantrism has an important impact on the notion of ritual purity among the Newars. For instance, the fact that a god is carnivorous does not render it automatically impure. Newar Brahmins have to eat meat and drink alcohol on certain ritual occasions: this does not modify their ritual purity.

Buddhism is yet another distinctive feature of Newar ethnic identity when it is compared to Indo-Nepalese society: oral tradition which maintains that originally all Newars were Buddhists is in contradiction with the inscriptions and historical documents.[15]

The study of Buddhism was not my main preoccupation. But as Buddhists, for instance artisans such as painters, were part of the population I was curious to visit the Buddhist monasteries at Bhaktapur than those at Patan. My first visit to Bhaktapur occurred during the rainy season when I watched and was astonished by the festival and the procession of Buddha Dīpaṅkara. In Indo-Tibetan Buddhism the historical Buddha, Śakyamuni, is no longer the only focus of worship. In Bhaktapur I saw that the so-called mythical Buddha of the past could be as important as the historical Buddha. The Dīpaṅkara Buddha is the only Buddha whose effigy is taken out in procession and these processions are one of the main social events among the Buddhist community in all the localities of the Valley.[16]

I was particularly interested in the social aspects of Buddhism and puzzled about the status of Buddhists in the local hierarchies which differed from one locality to another. Thanks to Bhadri Guruju's help I was able to understand certain rituals, addressed to Avalokiteśvara, such as Aṣṭamī vrata, etc. He is a Buddhist priest, a *vajrācārya,* who is much concerned with the task of preserving and conserving Newar Buddhism. He has very considerable knowledge of the rituals employed and writes and edits pamphlets and books on the deities of the Buddhist pantheon. He has opened a school for the sons of *vajrācārya* who are to be initiated into Mahāyāna Buddhism. I am particularly grateful to him because he alone, among my informants, took care to forewarn me of the exact dates and times when rituals were due to take place, and his explanations of ceremonies were always very precise. Perhaps my relationship with him was made easier because he was Thakurlal Manandhar's family priest.

In my early days in Nepal, I had difficulty in understanding what people were saying: but I watched rituals, an essential part of their lives, particularly annual lineage rituals which took place in the months of April and May. To begin with this was difficult for me because Newar women did not participate in the rituals which were carried out at a sanctuary situated outside the town-limits. I was therefore restricted to male informants who were well informed about lineage histories and were also the organizers of, as well as the participants in, these annual celebrations. However I was in a somewhat ambiguous situation with regard to Newar women who were, frankly, suspicious about my interests. How could anyone come from so far, at so much expense, to watch such local happenings?

The climax of these rituals was often an animal sacrifice. As a European, although I had seen bull-fights, I was not accustomed to seeing animals being sacrificed violently with considerable bloodshed. It is one thing to read descriptions of sacrifice and quite another to experience the atmosphere in which this slaughter takes place. I was much impressed when I saw the sacrifices of the goats for the lineage deity (*Digu Dyo*) or of the pigs slaughtered at the Nava Durgā dances. It took me some time to get used to this blood-letting. Often I used to watch the first sacrifice and then move away, during the second one. I was, and I still am, very much impressed by the sudden changes in an individual's behaviour at the time when a sacrifice is carried out. The urgent need to sacrifice to the deity at a precise moment, which is clearly felt and manifested by the participants, communicates itself forcibly to the observer.

Clearly I cannot mention here the names of all those who helped me nor describe all my contacts. I was very conscious throughout of being not only "the participant observer" but also "the observer observed".[17] Often it was women who made personal remarks about the way I was dressed, the necklace, the bangles or the rings I was wearing. Their curiosity was constant— as was their encouragement.

I was, and I am, full of admiration for the artistic accomplishments of the Newars and much impressed by the quality of their sculptures and the sense of proportion evident in their temple architecture. The extraordinary cultural richness of Newar civilization in the Valley only became clear to me once I had gone outside the Valley and moved around a little in the hill areas where there was such an absence of memorable architecture and art. If an European comparison be allowed, when coming out of the hills into the Valley, I thought of Tuscany in Northern Italy where one gets the same impression of a concentration and continuity of artistic creation over many centuries. Perhaps contact with a culture so different from that of Europe, and in which there were few points in common with that I had known previously, changed my own outlook. Not only was the Newar language different from my own, but also Newar social and moral values were not those of French society. Previously I had read a lot about "cultural diversity" without experiencing what this expression really signifies. Today, after my experience in Nepal, it is easier for me to see my own culture from an outsider's viewpoint.

I should like to emphasize that, contrary to what is often imagined to be the case, a large part of anthropological research is not carried out in the field. Fieldwork experience alone does not suffice to make a man or woman an anthropologist. After participant observation in the activities of the inhabitants of his chosen field, and the collection of copious field-notes, the anthropologist returns home and begins to describe and analyse his field experience. Such analysis involves not only a reassessment of the information and theories provided by his informants. To compare and to contrast his own materials with those of others, the anthropologist must also consult the enormous data bank of ethnographic facts and theories collected throughout the world in the past centuries. For there is no description without theory: the author himself becomes an interpreter of social facts. The text he signs is the product not only of fieldwork and discussions in seminars with colleagues. It is also the result of many hours of reading in libraries. Indeed rather than operating alone the anthropologist makes use of a veritable network. The Centre National de la Recherche Scientifique (C.N.R.S.) in Paris and the Université de Paris X, Nanterre, the Collège de France and the Centre d'Études Indiennes et d'Asie du Sud (CEIAS) have provided the main constituents of my own network. To them I owe not only my intellectual training but also funds for fieldwork on frequent occasions, and the stimulus of constant criticism. Then, on the perimeter of the network, are the international contacts with foreign scholars, friends and enemies—not only with anthropologists but also with historians and Indologists: Nepalese, Indians, Americans, Germans for the most part. All these have contributed to widening what was, at the start, my somewhat parochial vision of Newar society.

At the end I would like to quote C. Geertz: "Being there authorially, palpably on the page, is in any case as difficult a trick to bring off as 'being there' personally, which after all demands at the minimum hardly more than a travel-booking and permission to land; a willingness to endure, a certain amount of loneliness, invasion of privacy, and physical discomfort; a relaxed way with odd growths and unexplained fevers; a capacity to stand still for artistic insults, and the sort of patience that can support an endless search for invisible needles in infinite haystacks".[18]

Themes

I began by describing the Newars, my relations with them and their society. I would now like to explain why I chose the themes of research which occupy the pages which follow. The themes of the articles grouped together here are the result both of circumstances and of choice. There is a large part of subjectivity in the formation of an anthropologist's interests and perspectives: one is influenced by one's personal experiences, professional training and by the people one meets in the course of fieldwork and their occupations, preoccupations, and perspectives and also by what C. Geertz calls "local knowledge".[19] The ethnography is essentially interpretative.[20]

I was influenced by the constant discussions and arguments I listened to about people's positions in the social hierarchy. Soon it became clear to me that the population of Bhaktapur formed on the ground a living map, the paradigm of a complex social hierarchy. A town like Bhaktapur is a much more difficult object of study than a village because it is inhabited by a whole range of castes whose activities are centred on ritual functions. The members of these castes do not worship just anywhere nor do they reside just anywhere. Caste associations are linked to territories. In Nepal, caste associations (*guthi*) are, in the first place, corporations having the same professions and with a common god who ensures their protection. They occupy areas of residence within the town-limits in function of their positions in the local social hierarchy. Each town, from an administrative point of view, is divided into quarters. In the article on religious associations (*guthi*) I have tried to show the relationship between quarters, castes and temples in Bhaktapur.

Royal Palaces in Nepal are relatively small when compared to those of North and Central India, for instance those in Rajasthan or in Madhya Pradesh. In Kathmandu Valley till the Rana period (nineteenth century) they remained integrated in local architectural styles: the Newar Royal Palace is not a fortress although access to its interior is screened by various caste prohibitions. Ideally the Palace is situated in the centre of the town.[21] Even today those who live close to the Royal Palace and thus close to the town's ideal centre are mainly Brahmins. This is also true of other royal towns in Northern India, such as Jodhpur. The position of an individual in the social hierarchy could be calculated in function of the relative distance at which he resided from the Palace. Today Untouchables, such as sweepers and fishermen, reside outside the town-limits, whereas low caste artisans who are not Untouchables dwell within the town-limits.

Twenty years ago, German teams, including those which were involved in the restoration of monuments, had already begun to draw and publish plans of Bhaktapur, first situating monuments within the town, and then including different types of houses which in themselves testified to social differences.[22] These plans were of considerable help towards my understanding of the lay-out of Bhaktapur; the itineraries followed by the processions of different divinities on festive occasions, once situated in the context of these plans, made apparent the Newar insistence on distinguishing what is "inside" the town from what is "outside" it. Ramapati Raj constantly employed the categories of "inside" and "outside" in his attempts to explain events to me. What was inside, he emphasized, was private, secret; what was outside was public, open. But now I began to grasp that these were also, to the Newars, spatial concepts. Within a house and within a town were comparable units of thought, in the same way as outside a house and outside a town.

During my first stay in Nepal the major theme, as I have mentioned earlier, was the study of lineage which resulted in my article "A Lineage Deity of the Newars: *Digu Dyo*". This seemed to me to be the most important social unit constituting, as it does, groups of worship. When people spoke to me about their lineage, they established a link between its members and the territory on which they lived. Before I started my research, the reading of Louis Dumont's study about the god Ayanar had already helped me to understand the relation between the god Ayanar and the lineage, between the social and religious in general. The difference between Newar and South Indian Hinduism such as the latter is presented by Dumont is the Tantric dimension. The vegetarian god Viṣṇu Nārāyaṇa is distinguished from the carnivorous goddess.[23] Among the Newars, the fact that a deity is carnivorous does not render it automatically impure.[24] Another anthropologist, A. Mayer, in *Caste and Kinship in Central India,* when analysing kinship links in Central India, had shown that kinship links are formed in function of a deity.[25] What seemed to me specific to the Newars both Hindus and Buddhists was the relation between a lineage deity and a particular territory. The divinity was situated obligatorily in the same area as that in which the ancestors and senior members of the lineage resided. Even if people are unable to explain in detail their own genealogies they always know where their lineage deity is situated. The remark of T.N. Madan concerning kinship among the Pandits of Kashmir seems relevant in the Newar context: "It became clear to me that, beyond certain limits, kinship is territorially validated. One might say that, what the Pandits do not store in memory, they mark on the ground. By compressing and coding a substantial part of knowledge about kinship ties in territorial terms, the Pandits have devised a cultural means of easy and efficient information management."[26] In comparison with other ethnic groups in Nepal the Newars have always marked their territory with sanctuaries and temples of a sophisticated architecture.

At the begining of my research on lineage, I had tried to record and even reconstitute genealogies. This proved to be very difficult because, even with "very good" informants, things were only clear up to the third generation. However informants always stressed that, in principle, genealogical enquiries were very important to them too, particularly when marriages were being envisaged. Ideally, it seemed, these enquiries had to be made. Yet, when I looked through the ethnographic works on the Newars, although hundreds of printed pages had been devoted to their society, no genealogies seemed ever to have been published. I then tried to see, on the occasion of the annual celebration for the dead—*śrāddha*—how many generations of ancestors did, in reality, receive homage. Unfortunately for the anthropologists, this *śrāddha* normally takes place among Newars in the Tantric sanctuary, and cannot be observed by outsiders. Recently, among Rajputs of West Rajasthan, where genealogies are also important, I asked the same questions: and I found that among the Rajputs, as among the Newars, offerings are rarely made to ancestors further back than the grandfather. It would seem then that, in both societies, the dead, after three generations, lose their social identity. The main preoccupation is to make the dead disappear or to shuffle them as rapidly as possible into a collective category.

To begin with, the performances of the annual festival of the lineage seemed to me very complicated. I did not understand what was going on. I knew little about Tantrism: I knew nothing of techniques of meditation, nor of the mental construction of *maṇḍala*, nor of the mental worship of gods. When I asked questions in Bhaktapur, the answers I received seemed strange to me. Doubtless my questions seemed strange to my teacher, Ramapati Raj. It was later, after working with André Padoux and other specialists in his team in Paris, that I began to understand the significance of what I had observed in the field as ritual sequences and fully realized the importance of the texts whether or not they were consulted or read during the ceremonies observed in the field ("The Image of the Lineage Deity").

The study of the organization of territory from a religious standpoint had been a central preoccupation of a number of scholars who worked in Nepal over the past twenty years. In comparison with India and its huge territory, populated in a very unequal manner, the Valley of Kathmandu presents the advantage for scholars of being a relatively small territory with a very high population density in which the interaction of people with monuments during festivals is easier to observe.

For an outsider, the notion of territory, in the sense of political or religious territory inside the locality, as it is experienced by the Newars of a given locality, is not easy to understand. When watching the itineraries followed each day by men and women going to make their devotions, it became clear to me that not only was the town divided into quarters (*tol*), it was also considered as a *maṇḍala*, divided into nine parts, each of which was watched over by a particular goddess. When someone lived, for instance, in the eastern part of the town, he or she carried out his or her devotions in that part of the town, and not in the west or the south. With regard to the Śaivaite temples in Bhaktapur, I showed some years ago how the *maṇḍala* functions; the *maṇḍala* is not just a static, mental representation of the town: it is lived, and it has a functional purpose with regard to monuments ("Śaivaite Temples in Bhaktapur"). The ordinary Newar man or woman often does not have precise notions concerning the whole of the *maṇḍala* but can clearly give in detail the list of the shrines in his or her quarter. It is during the great festivals, in particular the *Bisket Jātrā* in Bhaktapur, and Dasāī, which corresponds to the festival of Dasahra in India, that statues of gods and goddesses are taken out in processions. At that moment the links between the divinities, their hierarchization and their territory become visible. But, in this hierarchy, politics has precedence over religion. The centre of the *maṇḍala* of Bhaktapur is occupied by the goddess Tripurasundarī whose temple is also, ideally, in the centre of the town. However, the goddess to whom all divinities make homage in the course of these festivals is Taleju, tutelary goddess of the ancient Malla dynasty, who was adopted by the rulers of the Shah dynasty to legitimize their power at the end of the eighteenth century when they conquered the Valley ("Taleju, Sovereign Deity of Bhaktapur").

Tantrism had a considerable influence in the organization of territory. Oral traditions have established a link between the territory and the dismemberment of the body of Satī, locally the most significant of Tantric myths. A text such as the *Kālikāpurāṇa*, which tells the story of Satī, the daughter of Dakṣa Prajāpati, has been known in the Valley for centuries. The different parts of the body of the goddess after dismemberment are linked with territory and, in this particular case, with the sites of the eight *mātṛkā* temples surrounding the town of Bhaktapur. Certain Indian scholars, such as D.C. Sircar, have established links between texts and a certain geography of India.[27] A. Bharati, in his study on Hindu Tantrism, has established a link between Tantric texts and different pilgrimage sites in Northern India[28] In the case of the Kathmandu Valley, it is important to emphasize that such ideas are still held with conviction and are very much alive. The Indian myth of Prajāpati which explains the social organization of Indian society is not however vehicled by Newar oral tradition.

In this Tantric conception of territory, in the centre of each locality is a Tantric goddess. Later chronicles of the nineteenth century show that the religious organization was decided on and implemented by kings: it was not due to a god or a goddess. In all ceremonies it is the goddess Taleju, representing political power, whose temple is located next to the Royal Palace, whose power is superior to the religious power: and the centre of the *maṇḍala* is represented by the goddess Tripurasundarī.

When I asked questions about the neighbourhood, the people I spoke to could almost always give me lists of temples in it. The layout of monuments within the town had already been mapped out by some of my German predecessors in Bhaktapur. What interested me was to try to understand how the inhabitants themselves perceived the territory they lived in and how they represented it to themselves. It was clear to me that the local perception of space was quite different from that of Europeans. When situating themselves in territory, Europeans point first to the North and then usually to the South. The Newars, following the Indian usage, start with the East when, for instance, they enumerate the open sanctuaries of the eight goddesses which surround the town. Each cardinal point is auspicious or inauspicious in a given context.

Jean Filliozat wrote about Indian space: "There is one fact in particular which strikes a person who lives in India or in an Indianised country or a part of the world influenced by India: it is not only that, as is sometimes the case with us, peasants have more notions about the stars and the changes in the heavens than do the town-dwellers but also that people do not much like using the words right and left for situating positions relative to themselves: they always know where they are in space and will say that one must go west or east: they will not say that this door is on my right or on your left but will say that it is to the east. Thus man considers himself as englobed by nature and not as independent."[29]

The links which royal power established between the centre of a territory, its capital, and its boundaries are represented, to some extent, but not entirely, by the rituals. In studying rituals of the Nava Durgā dancers I came to understand the relations existing in former days between the Royal Palace and the divinity installed in it, the Goddess Taleju, and the localities of the surrounding areas. The Goddess Taleju is the lineage deity of the former Malla kings of Bhaktapur: her temple is in the Palace Complex. She is not only the king's ally but also the source of his military power. Each year she infuses with new power the masks of the dancers of Nava Durgā. In the article "Ritual Planning of Bhaktapur Kingdom" I tried to show how the dancers who wear or carry these masks start annually from the centre of the ancient kingdom and, through their dances, trace out the limits of the sovereign's power, the frontiers of his realm. Here, again, we are in the presence of a power which radiates from a centre, the Royal Palace, in all directions, up to a periphery.

I think it was my reading of the work on the Barabudur of the French orientalist Paul Mus which provided the main incentive to my study of spatial concepts in Bhaktapur. P. Mus conceptualized a religion of the cardinal points, the content of its framework being formulated differently by animism, Brahmanism and Buddhism. It seemed to me that it was Mus who had done most to clarify the concepts of central power and peripheral power when studying the territory, the group and its ruler.[30]

Recently the anthropological study of S.J. Tambiah has shown the interaction between centre and periphery in a Buddhist kingdom, that of Thailand, and drawn attention to the term "galactic polity" "The concentric system, representing the centre-periphery relations, was ordered thus: In the center was the king's capital and the region of its direct control, which was surrounded by a circle of provinces ruled by princes and governors appointed by the king, and these again were surrounded by three circles of earthen ramparts, with four gateways at the cardinal points.... If we keep in mind the expanding and shrinking character of the political constellations under scrutiny, a central, perhaps the central, feature to be grasped is that although the constituent political units differ in size, nevertheless each lesser unit is a reproduction and imitation of the larger. Thus we have before us a galactic picture of a central planet surrounded by differentiated satellites which are more or less 'autonomous' entities held in orbit and within the sphere of influence of the center."[31]

A striking aspect of Newar society is the co-existence therein of Hinduism and Buddhism. Fascinated by this, I chose to study the celebration by Hindus and Buddhists of what was considered to be the same ceremony: and I observed as closely as I could the *ihi*, the joint simultaneous marriage of girls, before puberty, to a deity. ("The Social Consequences of Marrying Viṣṇu Nārāyaṇa. The Primary Marriage among the Newars of Kathmandu Valley"). My observations led me to understand that, in this case, if the rituals for Hindus and Buddhists were not identical—the priests and the gods invoked were not the same—from a social point of view the differences between the two celebrations were practically unimportant. Hindus and Buddhists do, of course, celebrate the ritual separately. However, both were right to tell me that this ritual was specific to Newar society as a whole, when compared to that of the Nepalese Parbatiya. This marriage can be considered as an initiation into womanhood: yet, at the same time, it is a "rite de passage". The initiation of a young Newar boy, on the other hand, is an individual ritual, which concerns primarily his membership of the lineage. From a social point of view, the Newars are constantly preoccupied by the necessity for carrying out correctly the *saṃskāra.*

What is noteworthy in the case of the Buddhism of the Valley of Kathmandu is its great capacity for adapting itself to Hindu ideology and practice. Buddhists, without losing their identity and abandoning their ideology, have accepted the Hindu caste system and the rules of ritual purity. More precisely the transformation of a previous monastic community into a caste played a major role in the survival of Buddhism. Despite appearances, ideological conflicts between Hindus and Buddhists have existed for a very long time in Nepal. For instance, the chronicles, *vaṃśāvalī*, are either Hindu or Buddhist in inspiration, and seek to demonstrate the superiority of one or the other religion. They are in no way impartial; and there has never been perfect harmony between the two systems of belief. Each community has retained its "gods", its "pantheon", its rituals and practices. Certain rituals such as *Aṣṭamī vrata* in honour of Amoghapāśa Lokeśvara, or festivals such as that of Buddha Dīpaṅkara, are Buddhist; and Hindus do not participate in them to any extent. The participation in certain festivals reveals a certain religious identification. D. Gellner, in a recent study on Newar Buddhism, has demonstrated that rituals were more important than ideology.[32]

In the annual cycle of festivals celebrated in the Valley, the royal festivals of the three ancient Newar kingdoms, those of Matsyendranāth at Patan, the Indra Jātrā at Kathmandu, and the *Bisket Jātrā* at Bhaktapur, occupy a special place. In them, the entire population participates with few caste constraints and little religious exclusivity. In addition to these three great festivals, the festivals of Dasai—in India it is called *Dasahra*—has, over the past two hundred years, assumed much greater importance in Nepal as part of the process of Hinduization of the entire country, consequent on the conquest of the Valley, in 1768, by king Prithivi Narayan Shah. There is indeed a schema common to these great festivals of the Valley which, today, are much better known than they were only a few years ago, thanks to many ethnographic descriptions.[33] It is at present indeed possible to discover in them certain common features which were not highlighted in previous studies.

From a structural perspective all three Newar festivals of the Valley aim at ensuring the prosperity of the kingdom. All take place over a period of nine days as does the greatest festival of North India. The similarity in the conception of time which they manifest is important. All include processions of divinities taking place inside town-limits, displaying in this manner the hierarchy of the gods among themselves and also the relationship between the gods and the inhabitants of the territory. These processions celebrate the foundation of the king's capital and the regeneration of the social and religious order ("The Killing of the Serpents or the Foundation of the Town of Bhaktapur"). The analysis of the royal festival of the ancient kingdom of Patan, the only such festival which celebrates a Buddhist deity—Rato Lokeśvara, a form of Avalokiteśvara—will begin by the examination of a narrative painting (*vilampu*) which depicts the festival ('The King as Rain maker'). In order to understand this painting I made use of my own field notes and the ethnographic descriptions of the festival, in particular those to be found in J.K. Locke's book. I considered the painting primarily as a historical document. It is well known that all the major festivals of the Valley have suffered changes in the course of time. For instance, the name of Matsyendranāth does not figure in the painting which only bears the names of Bunga dyo and Lokeśvara. This fact reinforces the argument advanced by J.K. Locke that the designation of Avalokiteśvara by Matsyendranāth must be recent and date from the nineteenth century. While ritual details and the names of deities change, the structural framework of the festival does however remain unaltered: the king, in person, is present at the festival; the deity is honoured by being taken out in procession on a chariot, the deity's image is bathed by priests and finally takes place the procession to the temple of the village of Bungamati where the statue resides for six months. This article links anthropology to art in a tangible manner. As C. Geertz wrote: "A theory of art is thus at the same time a theory of culture, and not an autonomous enterprise. And if it is a semiotic theory of art it must trace the life of signs in society, not in an invented world of dualities, transformations, parallels and equivalences."[34]

What is common to all the articles included in this book? Three elements emerge constantly in the course of my research: gods, men and territory. Different anthropological studies on India have shown the relationship between the world of the gods and the world of men in mythology, in rituals and in festivals.[35] In the case of the Newars who live in the Valley of Kathmandu, not only do gods and men come together to meet one another within that territory: the gods have also precise "sites" in sanctuaries and temples in the Valley. It seems to me impossible to analyse the Newar notion of territory in its social and political aspects without taking into account these temples and sanctuaries: this seems valid for both Hindus and Buddhists. Today, after the expansion of anthropological and historical research throughout Nepal, we are much better informed than twenty years ago about the different ethnic groups who live outside the Valley of Kathmandu. It has become evident that one of the basic differences between Newar social organization of territory and that of other populations is the quantity and the variety of the religious edifices in the areas inhabited by the Newars. In the Newar case all these buildings are not just decorative but are also functional. Each and every festival in the Valley takes place around a temple. The territory which the Newars inhabit is marked out by its temples. The site of the god who presides over a festival is fixed. With the exception of the royal god Avalokiteśvara-Matsyendranāth, gods and goddesses do not leave the ritual limits of their particular localities at festival times when they are led out in procession.

The distinction made by J.P. Vernant for the Greeks and then by Ch. Malamoud for the Indian world between inhabited "domestic space" and "non-domestic space",[36] the forest, seems highly relevant in this context. In the Newar world what is inside (*dune*) the locality is within the ritual limits of the town, what is outside (*pine*) is space which has not been put in order. Often the dangerous forms of the deities are situated outside the ritual limits. If we take into consideration Durkheim's opposition of sacred and profane, within a Newar locality is manifested a certain polarity between these two extremes: some sites are constantly sacred, for instance an important temple, others are constantly profane, for instance a market square. But between the two a whole range of possibilities opens up: a place can become much more sacred at certain times than at others. For instance, at Bhaktapur, Taumadhi square, which is, at ordinary times, a market place, and where the temple of Ākāśa Bhairava, the main god of the festival, is situated, becomes a sacred place during the nine days of the annual festival of *Bisket Jātrā*.

At festivals in the Valley when the processions of deities take place, a hierarchy is established among them. The Newars manifest forcefully the need to establish a religious and a political centre. At Bhaktapur, such a centre is represented by two goddesses: the royal goddess, Taleju, is the political centre and the goddess Tripurasundarī is the religious centre of the *maṇḍala* of the town. If one takes into consideration the rituals executed throughout the year there is no doubt that the royal goddess Taleju is the sovereign deity of the town, so it is clear that the political centre of the town has primacy over the religious centre. The seats of the deities within a territory are situated in concentric circles: the best example of this is the representation of the town of Bhaktapur in the form of a *maṇḍala*.[37] The whole Valley of Kathmandu is also represented as a *maṇḍala* and, again, the divinities are located within concentric circles.

A distinctive feature of the territories of the Newar kingdoms of the Malla period and of Newar built-up localities today lies in the manner of organizing territory, first inside the locality, and then, inside the territory of the kingdom, the king establishing the relation between the centre, the capital and the periphery, in this instance the different localities of the kingdom. As in North India, the king is not only the organizer of space but also the founder of the kingdom and the capital.

Throughout my research I have tried to show the relationship between gods as members of divine groups and men as members of social groups—the lineage, the caste association *guthi*, castes— rather than the relationship between gods and individuals. Gods are never posited in isolation but always as being in a certain hierarchical relationship to other gods. They have kin links, positional relationships, an entourage. For instance, one of the nine goddesses surrounding the town of Bhaktapur can exist only in relationship to the eight others. Gods and goddesses are never taken out in procession as solitary figures: a festival is never dedicated to one lone deity: they are accompanied either by a "wife" (or a *parèdre*) or a brother as it is the case for Avalokiteśvara Matsyendranāth.

During Buddhist festivals what is important is that the gods meet one another; and this is perhaps one of the most significant traits in the festival of Buddha Dīpaṅkara. In Bhaktapur at the end of the celebrations, the five statues, coming from five different monasteries, are brought together. During the celebration once every twelve years of the Buddha Dīpaṅkara (*samyak*), all the statues representing the Buddha Dīpaṅkara of the Valley are brought together near Svayambhunāth. In the iconography of Buddhist monuments in Nepal one does not find the five "transcendent" Buddha represented as individuals but as members of a group of five. Like a human being, a god is never alone: he is always conceptualized as a member of a larger group outside of which he has no social reality.

Notes

1. T.N. Madan, For a Sociology of India, *Contributions to Indian Sociology*, IX, 9-16; *Sociology in India. Retrospect and Prospect*, ed. by P.K.B. Nayar. Delhi, B.R. Publishing Corporation, 1982.
2. S. Lévi, *Le Népal*, Paris, E. Leroux, 1905, vol. I., pp. 248-249. See also G. Toffin, La notion de ville dans une société asiatique traditionnelle: 1, exemple des Néwar de la vallée de Kathmandou, *L'Homme*, vol. XXII, no. 4 (1982), pp. 101-111.
3. T.L. Manandhar is the author of the Newari-English Dictionary. *Modern Language of Kathmandu Valley*. Ed. by A. Vergati. Agam Kala Prakashan, New Delhi, 1986.
4. S. Joshi and B. Josh, *Struggle for Hegemony in India*, Vol. III: *Culture, Community and Power*. Delhi, Sage, 1994, pp. 63-65, "The cow as a cultural symbol".
5. A.W. Macdonald and A. Vergati, *Newar Art. Nepalese Art during the Malla Period*. Warminster, Aris and Phillips, 1979.
6. I published a study about a sketch book which was used by Vishnu Bahadur Citrakar, *A Sketch Book of Newar Iconography*, Delhi, International Academy of Indian Culture, 1982, p. 59.
7. These comments recall the injunctions combined in certain Sanskrit texts, for instance B. Dagens, *Mayamata, Traité Sanskrit d'Architecture*, IFI Pondichéry, 1976, p. 360, "Rénovation des images".
8. M. Allen, *The Cult of Kumari. Virgin Worship in Nepal*. INAS, Tribhuvan University, Nepal, 1975, p. 55: "Group membership is commonly defined by ritual initiation and social boundaries are maintained by secrecy and closure".
9. Locke, J.K. *Buddhist Monasteries of Nepal*. Kathmandu, Sahayogi Press, 1985, pp. 13-14; D.N. Gellner. *Monk, Householder and Tantric Priest. Newar Buddhism and its Hierarchy of Ritual*. Cambridge University Press, 1992.
10. C. Geertz, *Works and Lives. The Anthropologist as Author*, Stanford, Stanford University Press, 1988, p. 14.
11. L. Dumont, *Homo Hierarchicus*, Paris, Gallimard, 1968, p. 178: "Among Brahmins, a man who eats must be in a state of purity (he has taken a bath and his torso is naked) and shelter himself from any impure

contact. He eats alone or in a small group in a pure square (*cauka*) in the kitchen, or in a part of the house close to it, which is carefully protected from incursions. Any unexpected contact not only with a man of low caste sometimes even with his very shadow or an animal, but even with a member of the household (wife, child or man not purified for the meal), would make the food unfit for consumption" (my translation).

12. D.N. Gellner, Language, Caste, Religion and Territory. Newar Identity: Ancient and Modern. *Archives Européennes de Sociologie*, XXVII (1986), 102-148, p. 138: "Nonetheless, Newars feel that they have a special claim to Nepal (i.e. the Kathmandu Valley) and that all others (Parbatiyas, Muslims, Indians, Tibetans) who now live there are interlopers. Paradoxically at the same time, within Newar society different castes claim status by tracing their descent from outside, to the 'Aryan' south (e.g; the Rajkarnikars, sweetmakers, claim to be descended from Indian Brahmans; the Sakyas claim descent from the tribe of the Buddha). Each caste has its own sense of identity, an amalgam derived from a particular profession, its own myth of origin, certain forms of worship and deities peculiar to it, and the practice of endogamy. Theories which define ethnic groups purely in terms of a subjective sense of difference would make an ethnic group of each caste."
13. L. Petech, *Medieval History of Nepal.* Second edition, Roma, ISMEO, 1984, p.116: "The Harisimha episode played no role in Nepalese history of the 14th century. But it assumed a posthumous relevance in the 17th century when rulers such as Pratapamalla and Siddhinarasimhamalla, being proud of their Karnata (i.e. Maithili) lineage, chose to ignore their ancestor, the great Jayasthitimalla, and traced their descent from Nanyadeva to Harisimha and then straight on to Jayayaksamalla (1428-1482)."
14. A. Höfer, *The Caste Hierarchy and the State in Nepal. A Study of the Muluki Ain of 1854.* Universitatsverlag Wagner, Innsbruck, 1979.
15. D. Gellner, *op. cit.*, 1986, pp. 134-138: "The relationship between Buddhism and Newar ethnic identity".
16. D. Gellner, (*Monk, Householder and Tantric Priest. Newar Buddhism and its Hierarchy of Ritual.* Cambridge University Press, 1992) described the ceremony of Buddha Dīpaṅkara in Patan.
17. See A.C. Mayer, "On Becoming a Participant Observer" in *Encounter and Experience. Personal Accounts of Fieldwork.* Ed. by A. Béteille and T.N. Madan, Vikas, Delhi, 1975, pp. 27-42. See also P. Bourdieu, *Théorie de la pratique.* Geneva, Librairie Droz, 1972. chap. "L'observateur observé", pp. 157-162.
18. C. Geertz, *op. cit.*, 1988, p. 23.
19. C. Geertz, *Local Knowledge, Further Essays in Interpretative Anthropology.* Basic Books, New York, 1983. See chap.3: "From the native's point of

view: on the nature of anthropological understanding", pp. 55-70. "The ethnographer does not, and largely cannot, perceive what his informants perceive. What he perceives, and that uncertainly enough, is what they perceive 'with' or 'by means of' or 'through'...or whatever the word would be. In the country of the blind, who are not as observant as they look, the one-eyed is not king, he is spectator", p. 58.

20. D. Sperber, "Interpretation and description in the study of culture", 1980 (mss). See also *Anthropological Knowledge,* Cambridge University Press, 1982.
21. M. Shepherd Slusser, *Nepal Mandala. A Cultural Study of the Kathmandu Valley.* Princeton University Press, 1982, pp. 188-213; G. Toffin, Les aspects religieux de la royauté néwar au Népal. *Archives des Sciences Sociales des religions,* No. 48 (1), 1979, pp. 53-82.
22. N. Gutschow and B. Kölver, *Ordered Space Concepts and Functions in a Town in Nepal,* Wiesbaden, F. Steiner Verlag, 1975.
23. L. Dumont, Définition structurale d'un dieu populaire tamoul: Aiya Nar, le Maître, *Journal Asiatique,* 1953, pp. 255-270.
24. A. Sanderson, "Purity and power among the Brahmans of Kashmir" in *The Category of the Person,* ed. by M. Carrithers, S.Collins, S. Lukes, Cambridge University Press, 1985, pp. 190-217.
25. A. Mayer, *Caste and Kinship in Central India. A Village in its Region.* London, Routledge and Kegan Paul, 1960, pp. 184-188 "Clan Goddess Worship".
26. T.N. Madan, "On living intimately with strangers" in *Encounter and Experience. Personal Accounts of Fieldwork.* Ed. by A. Béteille and T.N. Madan, Vikas, 1975, pp. 131-157.
27. D. C. Sircar, *The Sakta Pithas,* Delhi, Motilal Banarsidass, 1973.
28. A. Bharati, *The Tantric Tradition,* London, Rider Company, 1975.
29. J. Filliozat, Le temps et l'espace dans les conceptions du monde indien, in *Revue de synthèse,* XC, July-Dec. 1969, pp. 281-95 and in English in *Religion, Philosophy, Yoga, A Selection of Articles by J. Filliozat,* Delhi, Motilal Banarsidass, 1991.
30. P. Mus, *Barabuḍur, Esquisse d'une histoire du Bouddhisme fondée sur la critique archéologique des textes.* Hanoi, Ecole Francaise d'Extrême Orient, 1935.
31. C. Geertz, *op. cit.,* chap. 6: "Centers, Kings and Charisma: Reflections on the Symbolics of Power", pp. 121-147; S. Tambiah, *World Conqueror and World Renouncer. A Study of Buddhism and Polity in Thailand against a Historical Background.* Cambridge University Press, 1976. Chap. Galactic Polity, pp. 102-132; H. Kulke, "Fragmentation and Segmentation versus Integration? Reflections on the Concept of Indian Feudalism and the Segmentary State in Indian History", *Studies in History,* New Delhi, vol. 4, 1982, pp. 237-63.
32. D. Gellner, *op. cit.,* 1992, p. 105: "Worship is perhaps the religious act

par excellence, and pervades Newar society, both within and outside the organized frame of the scriptural religions....Worship is in fact fundamental to each of the Three Ways of Traditional Newar Buddhism."

33. Description of the Buddhist festivals of Red Avalokiteśvara in Patan by J. Locke, *Karunamaya. The Cult of Avalokiteśvara- Matsyendranath in the Valley of Nepal*, Kathmandu, Sahayogi Press, 1980.
    See also N. Gutschow, *Stadtraum und Ritual der newarischen Städte im Kathmandu-Tal*, Kolhammer, Stuttgart, 1982.
    G. Toffin, L'indra jatra à Pyangaon: essai sur une fête néwar de la Vallée de Kathmandu. *L'Ethnographie*, No. 76, pp. 109-137.
34. C. Geertz, *op. cit.*, 1983, p. 109.
35. G.S. Ghurye, *Gods and Men*, Bombay, Popular Book Depot, 1962; M. L. Reiniche, *Les Dieux et les hommes. Etude des cultes d'un village du Tirunvelveli, Inde du Sud.* 1979. Paris/La Haye, Mouton, Cahiers de l'homme XVIII.
36. J.P. Vernant, *Mythe et Pensée chez les Grecs*, Paris, Maspero, 1971. chap. "Organisation de l'espace", pp. 124-207; Ch. Malamoud, Village et forêt dans l'idéologie brahmanique, *Archives Européennes de Sociologie*, 17 (1976), pp. 3-20.
37. B. Kölver, "A Ritual Map from Nepal", *Folia Rara*, 1976, pp. 65-80.

Digu Dyo: A Lineage Deity of the Newars*

Bhaktapur, one of the three principal towns of the Valley of Kathmandu, has an ethnically homogeneous community in the sense that the majority of the population is Newar. According to the population census of 1971, it has roughly 40,000 inhabitants. The locality, an ancient royal town, has remained relatively isolated and little marked by the social changes which have affected the population of Kathmandu and of Patan since 1953, the year in which Nepal was opened to the outside world. This is partly the consequence of the policy of the "Gorkha"[1] government which, since 1768, has tried to keep the Newars out of political life and to impose one legal code throughout the whole country.

The principal activity of the inhabitants of Bhaktapur who nevertheless consider themselves to be townsmen is still farming. The Jyāpū, who compose the caste of farmers, represent 80 per cent of the population: some of them work on handicrafts as a secondary activity.[2] At Bhaktapur Newar society is hierarchized: it is divided into several castes, each one having its own name and a traditional and hereditary occupation, although nowadays this is no longer a specific feature of a caste. The influence of India, in the build-up of this hierarchy, has been predominant: even today the position of each caste in the hierarchy is expressed in the language of ritual purity.

According to oral tradition, it was during the reign of

Jayasthiti Malla, that is to say at the end of the 14th century, that a legal code established the hierarchy of the castes. Society would then have been divided into sixty-four castes, sixty-four being a number frequently employed in Indian classifications. Whatever may be the truth of this tradition, today castes are separated hierarchically according to three criteria: first, by marriage rules; second, by prohibitions concerning death, and birth; and third, by the fact that a caste member does or does not accept water or boiled rice from a member of another caste. Social status (I mean by this the position of the individual in the caste hierarchy) is not necessarily related to his economic condition. For instance, certain Rājopādhyāya Brahmins, who are in the leading position in the local hierarchy of castes at Bhaktapur, are poorer than individuals who themselves belong to low castes such as the Kasai (butchers) or the Manandhar (oil pressers)

At Bhaktapur, Hinduism is the religion which dominates. Roughly 90 per cent of the population is Hindu (*śivamārgī*), the rest being Buddhist (*buddhamārgī*). Rituals and religious ceremonies, both Hindu and Buddhist, are executed according to Tantric practice. Buddhist Newars are integrated into the caste system and observe the same rules concerning impurity as do the Hindus. This fact always surprised foreign travellers and researchers of the 18th and 19th centuries for Buddhism had then the reputation of being outside the caste system or opposed to it.

Let us emphasize to begin with that within the Newar community of the Valley of Kathmandu (there are approximately 500,000 Newars in the Valley) one and the same caste can have a different status according to the locality it occupies: the *Manandhars* who are traditionally oil-pressers, have a higher status in the caste hierarchy at Kathmandu than at Bhaktapur. On the other hand, certain castes can be completely absent from a locality: the Udas, well-known for their commercial activity at Lhasa, are absent from Bhaktapur and the Manandhars are almost absent from Patan.[3] It is impossible to establish for all Newar localities one single list of the hierarchy of castes: yet many researchers up to now have tried to do this. In my opinion, in order to analyse Newar society more thoroughly, one would have to establish at least three separate lists for the three main towns of the Valley: Patan, Kathmandu and Bhaktapur, and perhaps even a fourth list for the town of Kirtipur.

The social hierarchy is linked to the principal divinity in a locality. At Bhaktapur she is the goddess Taleju, a divinity brought from India by king Harisimha Deva around 1324 C. E.[4] When the Hindu inhabitants of Bhaktapur define their position in the hierarchy, they always draw attention to their ritual function in the cult of the goddess Taleju. And if the *vajrācārya*, Buddhist priests, are situated very low in the local hierarchy at Bhaktapur, it is because they do not have the right to enter the temple of Taleju.[5] However, things are quite different for the *vajrācārya* of Patan, a Buddhist town whose principal divinity is Matsyendranātha: they are considered as equals to the Rājopādhyāya Brahmins.[6]

It is important to stress the link between social organization and territorial organization. In former times, it seems that each caste constituted not only a professional group but also a residential group and the settlement pattern of caste within a town was a function of its position in the social hierarchy.[7] Even at the present day the Untouchables (Pores, Kasais, Kulus, etc.) stay outside the town limits at Patan as well as at Bhaktapur and Kathmandu: not integrated into the local system of castes they were not therefore full members of society. The members of the high castes (Brahmins, Chathariya and Panchthariya) reside around the Royal Palace. A path of ritual circumambulaion (*pradakṣinapatha*) goes around the centre of Bhaktapur: it is followed at the annual festival *Bisket Jātrā* while keeping the centre of the town on one's right. Many of the Hindu Kasais (butchers, Untouchables) have houses on this path: but they are always situated on the left side of the path. If, in former times butchers were integrated into the town their residences were therefore situated outside the zone demarcated by the *pradakṣinapatha.* The only Untouchables allowed to live in the central zone were the Kusles, previously *Jogis,* worshippers of Gorakhnātha, the patron saint of the Gorkhas who had named their chief town after him.[8] Each town quarter had to have its Kusles whose responsibility was to carry out certain funerary rites.[9]

We pointed out earlier that the caste to which one belongs is of vital importance for marriages but castes and hierarchy vary according to the locality and also according to the local viewpoint of the informants. As a general rule, one must get married in one's locality, and so in Bhaktapur itself. It is exceptional for the Jyāpū of Bhaktapur to marry Jyāpū women from Kathmandu: one can therefore speak of a very marked territorial endogamy.[10] One can also affirm that there are more marriages between people of Kathmandu and of Patan than between people of Kathmandu and of Bhaktapur. This is doubtless due to the geographical isolation of Bhaktapur which is at the Eastern end of the Valley. Several informants from Kathmandu were of the view that it was not considered "good form" to marry women of Bhaktapur.

Inside Newar society in Bhaktapur several endogamous groups have been constituted: each group is composed of several castes which have the same ritual status and can intermarry. After the Brahmins, the highest group in the caste hierarchy is that of the Chathariya, the second that of the Panchthariya.[11] The *Jyāpūs,* the farmer caste, which comprises 80 per cent of the population, is divided into thirty-two groups: some of these groups are endogamous, others can intermarry on the condition that they respect the internal hierarchy of the Jyāpū caste. Next come the castes of handicraft workers, which according to the Nepalese code *Mulukī Ain,* are called "the seven *jati*"; these castes have the same ritual and hierarchical status but cannot intermarry, each one practising a preferential endogamy: Gatha, Bha, Nau, Kau, Kusah, Musa, Chipa, Pum (or Citrakar), Manandhar (or Syami).[12] The group of

Untouchables includes two subgroups: (a) those contact with whom does not make a purification obligatory: the Jogis (or Kusles), the Dhobis, the Kasais (or Nay) and (b) those contact with whom necessitates a purification: the Pores, the Ḥalahulus.[13]

Marriages with members of a higher caste are always allowed: the children who are the issue of a marriage with a woman of a lower caste do not retain the status of their father: they will have a lower status and will be put out of the paternal lineage. In the opposite case, when a man marries a woman of superior status the children will have a status higher perhaps than that of their father but less high than that of their mother. To understand thoroughly the system of matrimonial alliances it would be necessary to study it within each caste, and this work has not yet been undertaken. As an example, I shall take the Karmācārya who are situated among the Chathariya and the Panchthariya. They are also called Ācārya (Ācāju) and they carry out rituals for Hindu Newars.[14] Within this caste there are several sub-groups: the Taleju Karmācārya, the Mahākāli, the Mahālakṣmi, the Bhairav (the four leading sub-groups have taken the names of Tantric divinities), the Kinchẽ and the Jyāpū Karmācārya; the latter carry out rituals and ceremonies for the farmers (Jyāpū) only. The Kinchẽ Karmācārya are supposed to be the most ancient group, and they consider themselves higher than or equal to the Taleju Karmācārya: the power of the latter dates from the 14th century when the goddess Taleju became the tutelary divinity of the Malla dynasty: they cannot contract marriages with the other Karmācārya. The three sub-groups mentioned above, Kinchẽ, Mahākāli, Mahālakṣmi, can take their meals together and intermarry: the Bhairav Karmācārya constitute another endogamous group.

Marriages are not therefore decided at caste level: there exists an internal hierarchy. In reality marriages are decided at the level of the lineage (*phuki*) where the rule of exogamy is applied. A caste member refers to a common ancestor whose name is a matter of mythology : but the ancestor of a lineage is a human being whose name and identity can be verified.

The Newar define the lineage (*phuki*) in the following manner: (a) The members of a lineage must belong to the same caste, that is to say, they have the same status in the caste hierarchy. (b) As the members of a lineage must respect the same periods of impurity, after the death of a member, they must be cremated in the same area. (c) They cannot marry among themselves: the group is exogamous. (d) The children cannot marry members of the maternal lineage throughout seven generations (in reality the period varies from three to five generations). (e) The members of a lineage have the same lineage divinity, *Digu Dyo,* and must celebrate on the same day the annual festival of the lineage deity.

It is surprising that the Newars of Bhaktapur in arranging marriage take into consideration a genealogical depth of three or five generations as the other populations of Hindu religion in the Valley of Kathmandu (Brahmins, Chetris) respect the prohibition up to seven generations and sometimes even eleven. For instance, one of my high caste informants, a Chathariya, Munankarmi, confirmed that, for the marriage of his sons genealogical enquiries had been made only up to three generations. Although the inhabitants of Bhaktapur (especially high-caste members) affirm that the prohibition must be respected up to seven generations, when the time for marriage arrives, account is taken of only three or five generations in the case of both low and high castes.[15] When the Newars talk of the lineage, *phuki,* they always stress that to belong to the same lineage means that one has the same sanctuary and the same deity, *Digu Dyo.* The expression *Digu Dyo* refers to a category of gods and goddesses and is not the proper name of a deity. Moreover, it should be emphasized that residence is not an obligation for those belonging to the same lineage. Filiation is counted exclusively in the paternal line. A girl who marries leaves her family to go and live with the family of the husband. Henceforth she will no longer belong to her original lineage and will have to submit to the obligations imposed on her husband's lineage: in this respect, a woman marries not only an individual but also a lineage.

If lineage is defined by the Newars as the group of patrilineal descendants who pay homage to the same divinity and who celebrate its annual worship at the same date and in the same sanctuary, the household or domestic family is defined in the following terms "those who share the same kitchen": I will add that the members of a same lineage consider that they are blood relatives.

When deciding to study the annual worship of the lineage deity, I set out to analyse its social implications, its role in the system of matrimonial alliances and the content of the lineage; the ritual and the sacrifice which are part of the ceremony will be described later.

The sanctuaries where the annual ceremony for the deity of the lineage occurs are situated outside the limits of the town of Bhaktapur, "outside the walls" [16] These sanctuaries are open and are made of small-sized bricks which are not decorated with any image. They are situated close to cremation sites and to open sanctuaries (*pīṭh*) of the eight *devī*, the eight incarnations of Durgā and heiresses of the *aṣṭamātṛkā* of India[17] who are called by the high castes the eight mother goddesses, *aṣṭamātṛkā*, but in everyday speech are called 'goddesses'. The town of Bhaktapur is divided into nine parts, each one having as principal divinity one of the goddesses: Brahmāyanī (East), Maheśvarī (South-East), Kaumārī (South), Vaiṣṇavī (South-West), Vārāhī (West), Indrāyanī (North-West) Mahākālī (North), Mahālakṣmī (North-East); in the centre of the eight goddesses we find the goddess Tripurasundarī, the site of her temple is considered as the centre of the town. Seemingly there is no connection between the goddess Taleju and the nine goddesses. In addition to the open sanctuary, *piṭh*, outside the limits of the town, each mother goddess has, inside the town, a sanctuary called in Newari *dyo-chẽ*, which means the house of the deity, where the statue of the goddess is kept. Its worship is secret; the statue is taken out and homage is paid to it once a year during the festival of *Bisket Jātrā.* The open sanctuary of Tripurasundarī is situated close to her *dyo chẽ* and is called *madhya piṭh.* There is also a social difference between this open sanctuary and the others which are situated "outside the walls"; the officiants in charge of the *piṭh* of the eight goddesses are Pores, who, in the Newar caste system, are Untouchables; the officiant in charge of the open sanctuary of Tripurasundarī is a Kusle, who belongs to a caste of Untouchables which is of a higher status than that of the Pores; the Kusles are entitled to live inside the town.

The resemblance between the *piṭh* and the sanctuaries of the *Digu Dyo* is striking: both are established outside the town and are built with stones of the same shape and with the same decoration: in both places blood sacrifices must be made. Is there a difference between the Buddhist sanctuaries and Hindu sanctuaries? One would expect to be able to recognize them through the presence, for instance, of a *caitya* in the Buddhist sanctuaries or of a *yoni* in the Hindu sanctuaries. In reality the differences are not obvious: Hindus can worship a Buddhist deity and Buddhists a Hindu deity; this is the case of the Udas, their *Digu Dyo* is Viṣṇugupta in the form of Rāma; other Buddhist lineages have a Śiva Liṅga as *Digu Dyo.*[18]

What are the social implications of this worship? In the event of a marriage between people from different castes, if, for instance, the woman is of lower caste, the children issued from the marriage will not be able to celebrate the annual festival with their father's lineage: they are then excluded from their original lineage for their status ranks them lower in the social hierarchy. They will go to carry out the ceremony of the *Digu Dyo* at the same place as the others but at a different date. The last date for this ceremony of the *Digu Dyo* is the sixth day of the bright clear fortnight of the month of May: this day is called in Newari *sithinakha.* The date at which the ceremony is celebrated has social significance. One can be certain that those who celebrate it on the day of *sithinakha* are, in some way or another, excluded from their original lineage. Others celebrate it at a different date during the stipulated period between *Akṣaya tṛtīya*, the third day of the month of *Baisakh* (April-May) and *sithinakha*, the sixth day of month of *Jeth* (May-June). After a split within a lineage, the members who have separated celebrate the festival in the same sanctuary or at the same site but at different dates.

In the case of lineages where several brothers separate, each of the brothers will give his personal name to a new lineage. In the *thar* of Munankarmi there are thus four lineages which necessarily celebrate the festival at the same sanctuary but not together. These four lineages have in common lands given by an ancestor: the revenue from these lands is employed each year in turn by one of the lineages to pay for the expenses of the festival of *Digu Dyo*. Several lineages of the same caste can unite to celebrate together the annual festival: such associations are called *digu pūjā guthi*.[19] This is the case of the caste of potters (Prājapatī or Kuma) of Bhaktapur.[20] If an association (*guthi*) is constituted, its members will be able to pay a priest and spend less on ceremonies which are very costly.

The high castes (Brahmins, Chathariya, Panchthariya) have not only sanctuaries outside the town, *Digu Dyo*, for lineage deities but also temples "within the walls" *āgama chẽ*. What is noteworthy in the case of the Newars is the association of the word *āgama* with the word *chẽ* which signifies a house. In Newari the word *āgama* is not used as in Sanskrit to designate the tradition or the texts of a religious tradition but the edifice where worship is offered to a deity (*āga-dyo*) in a traditional manner. *Āga-dyo* like *Digu-Dyo* is not the proper name of the deity but of its category. At present I will not analyse the proper names of the divinities honoured in the *āgama chẽ*: these are often those of great figures in the Tantric pantheon: Cakrasaṃvara, Vajravārāhī, Hevajra, etc. In the inventory of the monuments of the Valley of Kathmandu the *āgama chẽ* are defined as follows: "Similar to the *dyo-chẽns* but are generally more enclosed. They contain shrines of the *Kuldevatas*,

Istadevata and *Ogamdevata* (family, patron or secret deities) No one is permitted to enter for worship without prior initiation. The enshrined images are never taken out of the building".[21] The temple "within the walls" can be situated as a free-standing building or in house of a lineage member: it is here that ritual objects are kept as well as the image of the divinity of a lineage, *āga dyo*, for the *āgama-chẽ* is considered a pure place, sheltered from impurity. The *āgama-chẽ* (or *āgama*) is always situated in the upper part of the building.[22] However this may be, the divinity is hidden and the worship is secret and reserved to initiates. Among the Buddhists, the *āgama* can be situated in a monastery (*baha* or *vihara*) Describing the characteristic aspects of a Buddhist monastery at Patan, M. Allen writes: "The *āgama*, which is generally located over the main non-Tantric shrine, is the centre of Vajrayāna ritual. It consists of two rooms, a larger outer one which is used for both feasts and various rituals, and an inner and much more sacred chamber which contains images of Vajrayāna divinities—frequently Chakrasambar, Yogambar and Hevajra."[23]

If in the sanctuary extra-muros, *digu dyo*, the worship of the lineage deity takes place once a year, in the *āgama-chẽ*, worship takes place daily (*nitya-pūjā*): the cult can be celebrated by a male member of the lineage or by an officiant, generally a Karmācārya, who is employed by the lineage and paid for his services. Certain high-caste lineages do not have sanctuaries, *digu dyo*, outside the walls, they only have temples "inside the walls", *āgama-chẽ*: this is the case of the Taleju Karmācāryas. According to my informants, this is due to the fact that the group is of Indian origin; this argument does not seem to me convincing for other castes also, according to oral tradition, came from India with Harisimha Deva in the 14th century.

We find lineage temples within the walls, *āgama-chẽ*, among Buddhists as well as among Hindus: what is pertinent in this case is the difference between high and low castes. Differences are not due to the fact that one belongs to one religion or another, they are social distinctions: the Jyāpūs and the low castes do not have *āgama-chẽ* and do not practice the ritual of initiation, the *dīkṣā*.[24] There is one exception to this rule: two castes of artisans, the painters (Citrakars) and the brick-makers and masons (Avas), are initiated through the *dīkṣā* and have temples within the walls, *āgama-chẽ*. This exception is the consequence of the professions exercised by these two castes: the painters execute religious paintings inside temples and sanctuaries which are built by masons.

Among the members of a lineage those who have gone through the *dīkṣā*—defined by the Newars as an initiation to the secret things of Tantrism—are considered otherwise than those who have not done so. As a general rule, the ritual is only for boys and takes place after the ceremony of *vratabandha*. The rite of initiation *dīkṣā* is secret and is always held in the *āgama*. The *dīkṣā* is, above all, a teaching of secret formula (*mantra śāstra*) transmitted from master to disciple. Informants emphasize that the modalities of initiation vary according to individual customs. The divinity in the *āgama* is veiled: it can only be seen by initiates. Illegitimate male children do not have the right to enter the sanctuary nor to be initiated. At the death of a lineage member, no male member has the right to enter the *āgama* for a period of thirteen days and daily worship may have to be stopped temporarily if the lineage does not have in its service an officiant (*Karmācārya*). In exceptional circumstances the *dīkṣā* can be given to a girl in her lineage of origin before her marriage, or to a woman married with a member of the lineage who has never had a male child so as to ensure the continuation of daily worship during the period of impurity following a death. In all cases, the initiation of women is less strict than that of boys: even if they have the right to enter the *āgama-chẽ* women have not the right to see the image of the divinity which is veiled.

It is important to specify that it is the same divinity who is in the *āgama-chẽ* and in the outer sanctuary *digu dyo*. During the annual ceremony of the *digu dyo* the officiant begins by invoking the name of the divinity who is in the *āgama-chẽ* (the rite of *āvāhana*).[25] The participants must render homage while meditating on the image of the divinity. It is a divinity which receives blood sacrifices which is invoked: during the *digu dyo* ceremony, he-goats are sacrificed.

The *dīkṣā* ritual of initiation is not obligatory: more and more young boys refuse to be initiated because those who have been initiated must respect the very strict dietary prohibitions and worship the deity every day. Nowadays only the eldest son is initiated so as to be able to ensure that worship continues. In so far as the *vajrācārya* (Buddhist priests) of Kathmandu are concerned, things are more complicated: if they are not initiated at the *dīkṣā*, they do not have the right to celebrate the Tantric rituals in the *āgama* and become Śakya, and so lower in the social hierarchy.[26] The god or goddess which is situated in the *āgama-chẽ* can be the deity of a lineage or the protective deity of a whole caste in a particular locality. In the latter case, the deity is considered as having been established by the mythical ancestor of the group. This is the case of the *vajrācārya* of Kathmandu who claim to descend from a common ancestor, Śāntikar Ācārya, the first man who received the *dīkṣā* in the Valley of Kathmandu. Initiated in the cave at Svayambhunāth, he transformed the grotto into Vajrayāna temple[27] where he installed an image of Herukacakrasaṃvara and of Vajravārāhī. All the *vajrācārya* of Kathmandu are initiated in this temple called Śāntipur; and Herukacakrasaṃvara is the deity of all the *vajrācārya* of Kathmandu.

The Newars consider the existence of a temple "within the walls", and the rituals which takes place there as an integral part of their culture; the other populations of Hindu religion in the Valley of Kathmandu have no knowledge of this aspect of Tantrism. K.B. Bista, who describes in a detailed manner the ceremonial and the ritual of worship of the lineage divinity among the Chetri, a Hindu population of the Kathmandu Valley, does not mention a lineage deity having a temple in the village and to which daily worship is paid.[28] There are doubtless several features common to the worship of the lineage deity among the Chetris and that of the *digu dyo* among the Newar: in both cases the festival is annual; it takes place outside the village or town, includes a blood sacrifice and concerns only the patrilineal descendants.

Three other ceremonies are linked with the cult of the *Digu Dyo* deity: (1) *Vratabandha* (Skt.) or *Kayeta Pūjā* (New), the ceremony of putting-on the loin-cloth which is done for boys between three and nine years old; (2) *Ihi*, the marriage with Viṣṇu Nārāyaṇa, a ceremony carried out for young girls prior to puberty (between five and eleven years of age); (3) Introducing young women married into the lineage to the deity. I observed the first and second of these ceremonies when they were performed in the group of the pot-makers (Surge Mari Prajapatya).[29] These are rituals of transition or of initiation: it is only after these ceremonies that boys and girls become full members of the social group. The ceremony carried out for boys, *Kayeta pūjā*, concerns the lineage in as much as it must be celebrated by members of the lineage (*phuki*); one part of the ritual takes place at the open sanctuary (*piṭh*) and only men participate in this; and the other part takes place inside the house where women play an important role. The Newar Buddhist Banre (the caste is divided into two sub-castes: *Vajrācārya* and Śakya) have another ritual of initiation which is the substitute for the *Kayeta pūjā*. "The ceremony symbolically represents the assumption of ascetic life and preserves the old memories when the Vanras used to be initiated as ascetics. Generally, the *Bare chuyegu* is observed on a mass scale."[30]

The *ihi* ceremony (in Newari *ihi* means "marriage") is collective: not only do girls of different lineages take part but also girls of different castes: members of all pure castes can celebrate the ceremony together. The Untouchables (Nae, Kusle, Pore, Chyami, Halahulu) do not celebrate it. This ceremony does not include a lineage meal (*bhojya*) and, according to the Newar, this puts it apart, to some extent, from the *Kayeta pūjā*. Generally, the expenses of the *ihi* are not payable by the lineage but are debited to one person who may or may not have kinship links with the girls, being initiated: he is an individual who by financing the ritual, seeks to acquire merits (Sk. *puṇya*). The girls do not go to the open sanctuary: only the officiant will go to the main *piṭh* of each girl and will make a blood sacrifice there. Later the girl will receive a part of the animal sacrificed: the sacrifice at the *piṭh* is therefore separate from the ceremony. For *Kayeta pūjā* the sacrifice takes place before the attribution of the loin-cloth and the boys must be present. The marriage of young girls to a divinity is peculiar to the Newar: the other populations of Hindu religion (Chetris, Brahmins, Parbatiyas) do not celebrate it, considering it to be non-Hindu. The young girl is given in marriage by her father (or by an uncle or a paternal cousin) to Viṣṇu Nārāyaṇa with Śiva as witness: all informants claim that the *bel* fruit represents Śiva. It is not a case of marriage with a fruit but with a deity.[31] The marriage with Viṣṇu is for a lifetime: according to the Newar, a young girl who goes through this ceremony will never be a widow for she will continue to be the wife of Viṣṇu Nārāyaṇa. Newar women can divorce and, if they become widows can remarry, a fact which scandalizes orthodox Hindus, that is to say, the Brahmins and Chetris of the Valley of Kathmandu.

All married women are introduced to the lineage deity, *Digu Dyo,* so as to become full members of their husbands' lineages. Another ceremony takes place to admit married women into the *āgama-chẽ*: the rituals are more complex and, generally, women must have a child before entering the *āgama-chẽ*. For wives, mothers of a male child, the ritual of initiation (*dīkṣā*) can only take place after the birth of their first child: the twelfth day after the birth, an initiation ritual (*thategu*) is held for the children in the *āgama-chẽ*. The deity should then accept the child and give its blessing to it. During the first year of her marriage, a woman does not take part in the annual festival of the lineage of her husband as, during this first year of marriage, she still belongs to the lineage of her parents. However her husband's lineage will send offerings

(New. *kisli*) to the *Digu Dyo* on her behalf: an earthen pot, rice, betel nut or a few coins (*paisa*). The following year she will be able to accompany her husband's lineage but she will not take part in the religious ceremony nor in the sacrifice; she will, however, receive the blessings from the officiant after the sacrifice and will then become a full member of the husband's lineage.

Up until today, researchers and travellers have sought above all to distinguish in the rites what is Buddhist and what is Hindu. In my opinion that is not a very positive manner of trying to understand Newar society. What is important are the differences between the religious and social practices of the high and the low castes. We have seen that only the high Newar castes whether they be Hindu or Buddhist have a temple "inside the walls", *āgama-chẽ*. The role of the *āgama-chẽ* is certainly always linked to Tantric rituals. However we find the opposition interior exterior (or, if you like, complementarity) between the temples "inside the walls" and the sanctuaries "outside the walls" in the case of the eight mother-goddesses. For each goddess has a temple within the walls, *dyo chẽ*, where the statue of the divinity is kept and where worship is secret, and a *piṭh* outside the walls, situated close to a *ghat*, which is an open sanctuary to which everyone has access. The religious organization of the lineage sanctuaries of the high castes is therefore in conformity with that of the protective gods and goddesses of the town. The religious practices of the low castes do not conform to this model. The Newar, whether they be Buddhist or Hindu, emphasize the importance of the difference between what is *guhya* and what is *bahira*. *Guhya* refers to what is secret and closed (*āgama-chẽ*) while *bahira* refers to things which are outside, in open sanctuaries, like the sanctuaries for lineage deities *Digu Dyo*. This dichotomy is fundamental not only in categories of religious thought but in the whole social life of the Newar.

As a social unit, the lineage assumes great importance for marriages are decided at this level and not at the caste level:

when it is a question of arranging the marriage of a boy and a girl, genealogical enquiries are made by members of the lineage and not by all the members of a caste or of a sub-caste; and it is difficult to affirm the existence of an endogamy of caste for the Newar of Bhaktapur. The lineage does not only constitute a social unit but also a group of worship: its members do not only consider themselves to be blood relatives but also as the necessary co-worshippers in an annual ceremony and they must respect the same periods of impurity after death or at birth. The allies, on the other hand, do not join in the annual festival and impurity after death does not concern them directly. The annual ceremony of *Digu-Dyo* is at the same time a means of social control. Those who are excluded from the group must constitute another one and celebrate the festival at another date. Their place in the social hierarchy will be lower than that of their fathers. Those who do not have a lineage deity are in a certain manner excluded from their society: they cannot marry in their locality (no one will accept to marry them for fear of transgressing the incest-prohibition): and they are considered as without status.

Notes

* This article is based on fieldwork carried out from May to October 1975 and from February to July 1976, financed by the C.N.R.S. (U.M.R.116). In Nepal itself, I benefited from the help of Thakur Lal Manandhar, Rama Pati Raj Sharma and A.W. Macdonald; and, in Paris, from the advice of Professor R. Levy, when he passed through. I express my grateful thanks to them.

1. Gorkha is a little town situated 80 kilometres North West of Kathmandu, where the present reigning dynasty originated. It is from there that it set out to conquer the country in 1768.
2. In *Population Census of Nepal*, 1971 (Kathmandu, Central Bureau of Statistics, 1973), we find the following figures for Bhaktapur: "Total economically active populations: 14,528; 11573 (male) and 2955 (women). Agriculture: 9553; manufacturing: 1197; commerce: 1240; personal and community service: 2197."
3. A. Vergati Stahl, "Greenwold et les Newar. Doit-on vraiment recourir à deux modèles du système des castes au Népal?", in *Archives Européennes*

de Sociologie, Paris, 1975, XVI, p. 314.

4. S. Lévi, *Le Népal*, Paris, E. Leroux, 1905, Vol. I, p. 251 et p. 378.
5. Other explanations for the low status of the *vajrācārya* are also put forward by Hindu informants: the "mythical" ancestor of this caste is not known, or he was a thief: in both cases it is not possible to find an ancestor. See also the article by P.S. Filliozat, "The right to enter temples of Śiva in the eleventh century" in *Journal Asiatique*, t.CCLXIII (1975), fasc. 1-2, pp. 103-119.
6. One of the main Buddhist divinities of Nepal venerated by Hindus also. Cf J.K.Locke, *Rato Matsyendranath of Patan and Bungamati*, Kirtipur, University Press, 1973.
7. H.A. Oldfield, *Sketches from Nipal*, London, W.H. Allen, 1880,I,pp. 95-96: "The limits of each city are, however, still strictly marked along the line where the ancient walls stood and no Hindus but those of good castes are allowed to dwell within the precincts. This rule does not apply to Musulmans several of whom reside within the city of Kathmandu but it is strictly enforced against Hindu outcastes such as sweepers, butchers, executioners all of whom are obliged to live in the suburbs of the city."
8. See G.W. Briggs, *Gorakhnath and the Kanphata Yogis*. Calcutta, Y.M.C.A. Publishing House, 1938, reprinted by Motilal Banarsidass, Delhi, 1973.
9. For the religious and territorial organization of Bhaktapur see G. Auer and N. Gutschow, *Bhaktapur, Gestalt, Funktionen, und religiöse Symbolik einer nepalischen Stadt in vor industriellen Entwicklungsstadium*. Darmstadt, Technische Hochschule, 1974 and N. Gutschow and B. Kölver, *Ordered Space, Concepts and Functions in a Town in Nepal*. F. Steiner, Wiesbaden, 1975.
10. G.S. Nepali, *The Newars*, Bombay, United Asia Publications, 1965, p. 207: "This local preference for marriage has resulted in the concentration of Newar marriage ties over a limited area. For example there are more marriage ties between the localities of Kathmandu than between Kathmandu and its neighbourhood. Similarly, there are more marriage ties between Kathmandu town and its neighbouring regions than between Kathmandu town and Patan than between the former and Bhaktapur which is situated towards the eastern extremity of the Valley".
11. The Nepali terminology Chathariya and Panchthariya, adopted by the Newar, can be misunderstood, for nowadays each group counts more than six or five *thar*. In the first group we find, for instance, Malla Kayesta, Jonchẽ, Josi, Sayeju, Munakarmi, Phanju, Hoda, Padhananga, Khaiju, Bijukchẽ, Karmācārya; the second includes: Josi, Maske, Baidya, Kacipati, Phalikel, Bhandari, Madhikamri, Kiaju, Banepali, Bijukchẽ, Gonga, Karmācārya. *Thar* is a Nepali word and has been adopted recently by the Newars. Some anthropologists have

translated it by the word clan: "These clans are sometimes referred to by the Nepali term *thar*, but there seems to be no Newari word in current use for such agnatic, maximal lineages, though some of these were described to me as consisting of a single *phuki*" in Ch. von Fürer Haimendorf, "Elements of Newar Social Structure", *Journal of the Royal Anthropological Institute*, London, 1956, No. 86, p. 26.

12. The designations in the *Mulukī Ain* no longer correspond at present to reality and it is not certain that they did so in the past.
13. A.W. Macdonald in *Essays on the Ethnology of Nepal and South Asia*, Kirtipur, University Press, 1975, p. 282 gives the list of the *jat* or Untouchables according to the *Mulukī Ain*.
14. N. Gutschow and B. Kölver, *op. cit.*, p. 56 call them "Tantric priests" but in my opinion they are officiants rather than priests.
15. See also G.Toffin "Newar kinship terminology. Descriptive and comparative analysis" in *L'Homme*, Paris, 1975, XV, No. 3-4, p. 134.
16. The expressions "outside the walls" and "within the walls" are used by L. Dumont in *Une sous-caste de l'Inde du Sud. Organisation sociale et religion des Pramalai Kallar.* Paris, Mouton, 1957.
17. On the *pīṭha* in India see D.C. Sircar, "The Sakta Pithas", *Journal of the Royal Asiatic Society of Bengal*, 14, No.1, Calcutta, 1948, pp. 1-108; A. Bharati, *The Tantric Tradition*, London, Rider and Company, 1965, pp. 86-92.
18. M. Shepherd Slusser and Gautama *Vajrācārya* "Some Nepalese Stone Sculptures: Further Notes" in *Artibus Asiae*, Ascona, 1973, XXV (3), p. 270.
19. For *digu pūjā guthi* cf. G.S. Nepali, *op. cit.*, pp. 333-334 et pp. 389-397. For *guthi* in general see M.C. Regmi, *Land Tenure and Taxation in Nepal*, Berkeley, Institute of International Studies, 1968, IV: *Religious and Charitable Land Endowments: Guthi Tenure.*
20. The sub-caste of potters (Prajapati or Kuma) belong to the Jyāpū caste; they are both farmers and potters. For a complete list of the castes at Bhaktapur see N. Gutschow and B. Kölver, *op. cit.*, pp. 56-58.
21. *Kathmandu Valley. The Preservation of Physical Environment and Cultural Heritage. A Protective Inventory.* Ed. by A Schroll, Vienne, 1975, Vol.I, p. 35.
22. M. Shepherd Slusser and Gautama *Vajrācārya*, "Two Medieval Nepalese Buildings: An Architectural and Cultural Study" in *Artibus Asiae*, Ascona, 1974, p.177: "A rather unusual feature of the upper storey is the presence of an *āgama*, or secret shrine, a masonry walled room in front of which is the screened sleeping area". See also S. Lévi, *op. cit.*, Vol. I, p. 383: "The sage Jayasthiti Malla, wishing to calm the rage of Sitala the goddess of small-pox, installed the Unmatta Bhairava but took care to set above the Bhairava an *āgama devata*, charged with controlling her lapses and keeping her within her role".
23. M. Allen, "Buddhism without Monks: The Vajrayana Religion of the

Newars of Kathmandu Valley", *Journal of South Asian Studies*, No. 3, 1973 (University of Western Australia Press).

24. L. Renou and J. Filliozat, *L'Inde Classique. Manuel des Etudes Indiennes*, Paris, Payot, 1947, vol. I, p. 597: "The basic act of initiation which, on the whole is inspired by the Vedic *dīkṣā*, is the giving of the *mantra* to the pupil by his spiritual master, the guru, who can be his father or even a woman, for instance his mother". See also S. Lévi, *La doctrine du sacrifice dans les Brahmana*. Paris, E. Leroux, 1898, pp. 102 and 104-106.
25. For the notion of *āvāhana* see L. Renou and J. Filliozat, *op. cit.*, p. 574 and also G. Tucci, *Théorie et pratique du mandala*, Paris, Fayard, 1974, pp. 89-94.
26. J.K. Locke, "Newar Buddhist Initiation Rites", *Contributions to Nepalese Studies*, Vol. 2 (1975), pp. 1-23.
27. J.K. Locke, *ibid.*, p.14.
28. K.B. Bista, *Le culte de Kuldevata au Nepal*, Paris, Editions Nove, 1972.
29. They are at the same time *Śivamargi* and *Buddhamargi*; during the *ihi* ceremony I noticed that they had a Hindu officiant and a *vajrācārya*.
30. J.K. Locke, *ibid.*, p.5.
31. L. Dumont, *Homo Hierarchicus. Essai sur le système des castes.* Paris, Gallimard, 1966. See the chapter "The regulation of marriage: separation and hierarchy", pp. 143-167 and in particular, p. 155.

The Image of the Divinity in the Lineage Cult among the Newars*

By now we have to hand good descriptions of *pūjā* and of *sādhana* which are called Tantric. These are based on textual editions, or observations made in North India or in Tamilnadu.[1] In a similar way, Tibetan Tantric rituals, often of Indian origin,[2] have been subjected to detailed studies.[3] In Nepal, research has not made such progress, and this may seem something of a paradox when we realize the extent to which Tantric cults are still alive in that country. The main festivals of the Valley of Kathmandu have been fairly well described:[4] personal and domestic rituals (*ātma pūjā, saṃskāra,* etc) have, on the other hand, been mentioned only briefly.[5] With the exception of certain Buddhist rites such as *bare chuyegu* or *homa* etc. described by J. Locke[6] Newar rituals have never been described in a detailed manner, and there is nothing in the literature devoted to the religions of Nepal comparable to the study of Tantric *pūjā* given by S. Gupta.[7] The reason for this is probably that a large part of these rituals is kept secret even today. The non-initiated and, with greater reason, non-Hindus and non-Buddhists do not have access to the places where the rituals take place. Access to Hindu temples is strictly forbidden to non-Hindus: they are never allowed to see the image of the divinity which is worshipped in the cult. This is true of the temples of Paśupatināth and of Guheśvarī at Deopatan, of the temple of the Goddess Vajrayoginī at Sankhu, etc. and of the lineage sanctuaries (*āgam chẽ*) which are usually situated on the top floors of houses. The first storey of the Buddhist monasteries, where is to be found the sanctuary of the Tantric divinity, is not accessible either to non-Buddhists or to non-initiates. Pandits, whether Hindus or Buddhists, keep the secret from those who are not initiated. Even someone like J.K. Locke, who knows Newar Buddhism well, has not been able, after twenty years of residence in Nepal, to learn the names of the Tantric divinities honoured in the *āgam chẽ* of the monasteries he studied.[8] The rituals of initiation *dīkṣā* still practised in the Valley of Kathmandu, whether for the initiation of Buddhist priests (*vajrācārya*) or for high caste Hindu Newar castes, have not been open to investigation as they take place in the *āgam chẽ*. The descriptions of these rituals which do exist are based on information provided by informants. Brahmins and *Vajrācārya* become evasive whenever there is a question of going into the details of such rituals. For instance, they refuse even to give a hint which might lead to identifying the statue which is the object of the Tantric worship.

The description which follows concerns a ritual for which, to my knowledge, there exists no manual (*paddhati*) and about which the participants do not wish to speak. So the account which follows is based, in great part, on direct observation: the explanations I was able to collect were not always as detailed as I might have wished. However hasty they may appear to be, particularly if one compares them with the descriptions evoked earlier, the remarks which follow have at least the merit of describing habits of worship common to all layers of Newar society, to all castes, to Buddhists and to Śaivites. We know that every Newar lineage is either Buddhist or Hindu: the essential difference is that the former has as priest a *vajrācārya* and the latter a Brahmin or a *karmācārya*.[9]

Two series of deities occupy a special place in the Newar pantheon: the mother goddesses (Skt. *mātṛkā*, New. *ajimā*)[10] and the lineage deities (New. *digu dyo*).[11] The homology between these two series is not a matter of function: it pertains to worship. The mother goddess and the lineage deities are the only deities of the Newar pantheon to have two sanctuaries, one inside the locality and the other outside it. The mother goddesses have inside the locality a temple (New. *dyo chẽ*) where, usually, only the *karmācārya* responsible for the daily *pūjā* enters. The metal image of the goddess, kept on the first floor, is taken out in procession once a year during the main festival of the locality: at Bhaktapur, this is the festival of *Bisket yātrā*, at Panauti, *Indra yātrā*, etc.[12] The image of the goddess carved on the wooden tympanum (*toraṇa*) of the temple gives an approximate idea of her appearance. In addition, each of the mother goddesses has, outside the ritual limits of the locality, an open sanctuary (*pīṭh*) where, either three or five (or more) stones, oval in shape, are installed and where the worshippers, whatever be their caste, do *pūjā* throughout the year.

The lineage deities, in like manner, have a sanctuary inside the locality. It is a private temple situated in the upper part of the house of the head of the lineage, or, in the case of high castes, is a small, free standing, separate edifice. Only those who are initiated have the right to enter it. The metal image of the chosen deity of the lineage, called in this instance *iṣṭadevatā*, is kept here the year round and is never taken out. Once a year, the members of the lineage (*phuki*) worship the lineage deity outside the limits of the town. The deity, which is thought to be the same as that in the inner temple (*āgam chẽ*), is then called *digu dyo*, a generic term, and represented by one or several stones installed in the open fields. Outside this festival period, the stones are left neglected.

The mother goddesses and lineage goddesses are thus the only divinities of the Newar pantheon to be worshipped at the same time in the form of an icon (secret worship, inside the town) and in an aniconic form (public worship) outside the town. One can ask oneself what relationship exists for the worshipper between the image, which he has supposedly seen, and the stones to which he renders a solemn cult (in the exact sense of the term) once a year. The study of the ritual of the *pūjā* in the lineage cult allows a partial answer to be given to this question.

For the Hindu participants in these ceremonies which I observed at Bhaktapur, the answer is, in any case, not open to doubt. Everyone told me that the deity at present honoured in an aniconic form (rough stones) was exactly the same as that the image of which is kept in the inner sanctuary (*āgam chẽ*). Now they knew this image because they had seen it: for all those who are initiated can enter the *āgam chẽ* and almost all the members of the lineage, up to the present, were, at least theoretically, initiated.

The annual lineage cult outside the walls of the locality does not require the services of a ritual specialist, whether a *karmācārya* for the Hindus or a *vajrācārya* for the Buddhists. The high castes sometimes call on them but the farmers (*jyāpū*) more rarely. Whether worship is led by a professional or by the head of the lineage (New. *nayo*, Nep. *thakali*), in both cases, in contrast to other domestic rituals, such as the marriage to a divinity before puberty (New. *ihi*),[13] no written text is used and no text is recited. I do not know if manuals in Newari or Sanskrit exist. I have never seen any—neither during the ceremonies nor in the houses of my informants. However, ritual specialists and high caste men have sometimes considerable religious knowledge. Quite often they employ Sanskrit terms, which I, in turn, will copy.[14] One can then suppose that texts have had a certain influence: but as the ceremonies occur without any visible sign of manuals, they can be described only after directly observing concrete examples.

The annual ceremony always takes place according to the following schema: the *pūjā* begins with a meditation by all the members of the lineage who, in their minds, focus on the image of their chosen deity. The head of the lineage (or the ritual specialist) invites the deity to take its place in the stones.

An animal victim is then slaughtered, generally a black he-goat.[15] The animal is dismembered, and its intestines are wound around the stones, where they are placed like a garland. The rest of the carcass is shared out between the members of the lineage in the course of a ritual banquet which closes the ceremony. Only the first part of this *pūjā*, that which precedes the sacrifice, is the concern of this article, and it alone will be here subject to detailed analysis.

The *pūjā* of the lineage divinities outside the walls take place in the spring, between April-May (*baisākh*) and the sixth day of May-June (*jēṭh*) i.e. during the hot season. The first of these dates corresponds to Akṣaya tṛtīya, an auspicious day, and the latter day to *sithi nakha*, a small festival before the monsoon in the course of which wells are cleared and homage is paid to snakes so as to ensure abundant rains. An astrologer fixes the dates of the annual festival for each lineage. On the eve of the day chosen by him, the male members of the lineage prepare themselves for the ceremony by a ritual fast. On the day itself, they meet together in the morning in the house of the head of the lineage. The latter takes out from the *āgam chē̃* the ritual objects necessary for the *pūjā*: diadems (*mukuṭa*), various vases, knife, powder, etc. and puts them in order so as to transport them in a big, open bronze recipient, which is provided with a cover (New. *khota*). A procession then leaves carrying the recipient, flowers, lustral water, and dragging or carrying the animal to be sacrificed, preceded by musicians playing cymbals.

When they have reached the fields, they disengage the stones covered by grass but do not specially prepare the site. The stone which represents the lineage deity (*digu dyo*) can sometimes be recognized by the fact that it is marked by a hollowed-out triangle. Another stone, sometimes marked with an incised triangle with the point upwards, is thought to represent Viṣṇu and receives only vegetable offerings.[16]

With the exception of these signs, the stones are not in any way fashioned. In certain exceptional cases, they are enchased in a stone tympanum (*torāṇa*). The fact that one of these stones is Viṣṇu, even when the lineage is Śaivite, and that the *digu dyo* is marked as if feminine, indicates clearly that the lineage deity is a goddess. Her name is never revealed, for the worship is Tantric. One might suppose that the lineage deity is the paredra of Viṣṇu (Śrī, Lakṣmī, Vaiṣṇavī, etc.) but it seems that she may be a divinity classified as Śaivite (Kālī, Durgā, etc.).

Next, the members of the lineage purify themselves: they form up in a line facing the stones, sprinkle themselves with lustral water (New. *snān*, literally "bath" or *abhisek*: "to sprinkle") and put on some *pañcāmṛta*.[17] The priest or the head of the lineage lights a lamp, called in Newari *sukunda*, which is used in all *pūjā*. It is a standing lamp, made to be put on the ground: it is decorated on its outside and lower part with a Gaṇeśa who receives the first offering. Wicks are lit which are thought to represent Sūrya and Agni.[18] This is followed by homage to the *guru* (*guru namaskar*). In complete silence, the officiant and the initiated members of the lineage meditate on the image of the divinity. They place the divinities, the number of which varies according to the *guru*'s teaching, in different points of their body (*nyāsa*). The officiant then sprinkles lustral water on the ritual instruments while reciting a *mantra* in such a manner that one can neither see nor hear it. The *ātma pūjā* can now begin: the officiant makes a coloured mark (*tika*) on his forehead and on the *digu dyo* stone.[19] He sprinkles rice on the other stones and puts a coloured mark on the forehead of the other participants. The preliminaries to the *pūjā* are now finished.

Those who participate in the *pūjā* stand facing the stones. The officiant is in front of them, also facing the stones. All are bare-headed, with hands joined at chest level, fingers pointing to the ground. The participants attempt to visualize the image of the deity and to project it into the stone. Before this silent meditation (*āvāhana*) which lasts several minutes, the *digu dyo* stone is only a stone: afterwards, it is the seat of the divinity throughout the duration of the ceremony.[20]

It is impossible for an outside observer to know exactly what takes place in the course of this meditation. But all the participants, I questioned, said that they try to arouse in themselves, by building it up mentally, an image of the deity such as they have see in the *āgam chẽ.* It is clear that this meditation overlays previous meditations and it will not be the same in the case of a deeply religious individual (a mystic or a brahmin) and for a non-initiated person. At its most simple level, meditation on the divinity seems to be calling to mind the statue already seen. As soon as the goddess has been "brought into" her stone, Viṣṇu is automaticaaly "brought into" his, and Śiva is present.[21] My informant, Rama Pati Raj, explained to me that the evocation of the goddess entails *ipso facto* that of her entourage (*parivāra*) and that in consequence he did not have to meditate specially on Viṣṇu. After this meditation, the deities having taken their places in the stones, the *pūjā* can follow its course exactly as if there were images being worshipped in which the deity is present. The officiant sprinkles lustral water on the stone; he puts a second white and yellow mark (*tika*) on the stones, *digu dyo*: he scatters grains of rice mixed with curd (Nep. *akseta*), then he winds around the stone a string made of five threads of cotton of different colours, neither twisted, nor braided. He lays on the stone representing Viṣṇu a garland of flowers and scatters rice grains. He decorates the stone representing *digu dyo* with a diadem (*mukuṭa*) in metal, the copy of the one represented on the tympanum on which the *digu dyo* is often mounted. He places eyes made of paper on the stone and murmurs (*japa*) mantra. The blood sacrifice can then start. Generally a black he-goat (or a duck) is sacrificed: the throat of the animal is cut and the victim's blood must spurt onto the stones representing the goddess. The animal body is dismembered, its intestines wound round the stones like a necklace: the head is shared out between the members of the lineage in the course of a ritual meal.

Whatever may be the place of worship, the private sanctuary inside the town or the open sanctuary outside the limits of the town, the deity is present in its mental image. The support of this image is the statue kept inside the private sanctuary which can be seen only by the initiated. The aniconical representation is outside the town: in this case, worship is public and everything which is outside can be seen. The manner in which the lineage deity is represented materially depends, in the last resort, on the situation of the place of worship. But, for the pious, its mental image is the same. It will be noted that the public ritual includes parts which one can describe as secret although they take place in sight of everyone: homage to the deity, *nyāsa*, and especially *āvāhana*. The method of *āvāhana*, defined as visualization of the divinity in oneself and transfer of the latter into the stone, is a process which is in complete conformity with the individual or collective Tantric *sādhana*. This observation leads us to consider from another viewpoint the opposition between public worship and private worship: to an important extent, public worship itself remains individual and, in part, secret.

Notes

* L'Image Divine, ed. by A. Padoux. Paris. C.N.R.S. 1990.

1. Brunner-Lachaux, Hélène *Somaśambhupaddhati*. 3 vols. Pondicherry, 1963-1977. See also S. Gupta, Jan Hoens Dirk and T. Goudriaan, *Hindu Tantrism*, Leiden, 1979; K.R.Van Kooij, *Worship of the Goddesses according to the Kālikāpurāṇa*, part I, Leiden, E. Brill, 1972.
2. D. Snellgrove, *Indo-Tibetan Buddhism: Indian Buddhists and their Tibetan Successors*, London, Serindia Publications, 1987, Chap "Tantric Buddhism", pp. 117-294.
3. Among the numerous studies of Tibetan rituals published in recent years one can consult that by Per Kvaernne who describes the ritual of the "Lion of Speech" where the mental evocation of the divinity is the central part of the ritual. Per Kvaernne, *"Le rituel tibétain" illustré par l'évocation dans la religion Bonpo du "Lion de la parole" in Essais sur le rituel*, Bibliothèque de l'Ecole des Hautes Etudes, Sciences Religieuses, Vol.XCII, Louvain-Paris, Peters, 1988, pp. 147-159.
4. Lévi, S. *Le Népal. Etude historique d'un Royaume Hindou*. Paris, E. Leroux, 1908, Vol. II, pp. 1-60. See also Nepali G. Singh, *The Newars: An Ethno-Sociological Study of a Himalayan Community*, Bombay, United

Asia Publications, 1965, Chap. "Festivals- Communtiy Events", pp. 343-81. See also Toffin, G. *Société et Religion chez les Néwar du Népal.* Paris, C.N.R.S., 1984. Chap. "Calendrier des fêtes et Pèlerinages" and N. Gutschow, *Städtraum und Ritual der newarischen Städte in Kathmandu Tal.* Stuttgart, Verlag W. Kolhammer, 1982, pp.10-11.

5. G. Toffin, *op. cit.*, pp. 556-58 and J.K. Locke, *Karunamaya, The Cult of Avalokiteśvara Matsyendranātha in the Valley of Nepal,* Kathmandu, Sahayogi Prakashan, 1980. He gives a fuller description of the *dīkṣā* (New. *dekha*) of the Newar Buddhists, pp. 50-55.
6. J.K. Locke, *op. cit.*, Chap. II "The Principal Ritual of the *Vajrācārya*", pp. 67-121.
7. S. Gupta, *op. cit.*, "Modes of Worship and Meditation", pp. 121-183.
8. J.K. Locke, *Buddhist Monasteries of Nepal,* Kathmandu, Sahayogi Press, 1985, "Lineage Deity", pp. 13-14.
9. Fürer Haimendorf, C. von "Elements of Newar Social Structure", *The Journal of the Royal Anthropological Institute of Great Britain and Ireland,* Vol. LXXXXV, No. 2, pp. 15-35.
10. The town of Bhaktapur is conceived ideally as a *maṇḍala* in the form of a lotus: it is divided into nine parts, each part being designated by the name of a goddess. The open sanctuaries (Skt. *pīṭha,* New. *piṭh*) of the eight goddesses are situated around the town at the four cardinal points and at the four intermediary directions: Brahmāyanī is in the East, Maheśvarī in the South-East, Kaumārī in the South, Vaiṣṇavī (or Bhadrakālī) in the South-West, Vārāhī in the West, Indrāyanī in the North-West, Mahākālī (or Cāmuṇḍā) in the North, Mahālakṣmī in the North-East. In the middle of the eight goddesses is the goddess Tripurasundarī and in consequence her open sanctuary (*piṭh*) is the only one situated inside the town. See N. Gutschow, *op. cit.*, pp. 30-54 and A.W. Macdonald and A. Vergati Stahl, *Newar Art: Nepalese Art during the Malla Period,* Warminster, Aris and Phillips, 1979, pp. 83-105.
11. A. Vergati, "Une divinité lignagère des Néwar: *Digu Dyo*" in *Bulletin de l'Ecole Française d'Extrême Orient,* t. LXVI (1979), pp. 115-27: G. Toffin, *op. cit.*, pp. 488-95; Nepali G. Singh, *op. cit.*, pp. 383-96.
12. N. Gutschow, *op. cit.* and G. Toffin, *op. cit.*, pp. 501-45.
13. A. Vergati, "Social Consequences of Marrying Viṣṇu Nārāyaṇa: Primary Marriage among the Newar of Kathmandu Valley", *Contributions to Indian Sociology* (NS), Vol. 16, No 2 (1982), pp. 271-87.
14. I wish to thank particularly Ramapati Raj Sharma Rājopādhyāya and Kedar Rāj Rājopādhyāya, both Newar brahmins, and rāj *guru* of the ancient Malla royal family.
15. For sharing out of the animal sacrificed, see G. Singh Nepali, *op. cit.*, p. 395: "The cult of Shika Bhu is a unique feature among the Newars. It consists of the distribution of the various parts of the head of the sacrificed goat among the eight senior members of the group. The

head is first cooked and its various parts are distributed in the following order: priest-snout; Thakali-right eye; Nokuli-left eye; Sokuli right ear; Pekuli-left ear; Nyakuli-right side of lower jaw; Khakuli-left side of the lower jaw; Nheluli-tongue. They eat their respective share on the spot with profuse consumption of liquor and tho(n). This ritual eating is tabooed being seen by others". See G. Toffin, Festin de la tête chez les Néwar, *Kailash*, Vol. IV, (1976), No. 4, pp. 329-38.

16. L. Dumont, "Définition structurale d'un dieu populaire tamoul: Aiya Nar, le Maître", *Journal Asiatique*, 1953, pp. 255-70 stresses the difference between vegetarian and carnivorous gods in the lineage cults of South India.
17. The *pañcāmṛta*, a mixture of cow milk, curd, melted butter, honey and sugar is used to purify the participants in the ritual. It is used in the rituals both by Hindus and by Buddhists.
18. G. Singh Nepali, *op. cit.*, p. 392: "The worship of *Digu Dyo* is preceded by worship of the Sun, Guheswari, Jogini, Bhairava and Ganesha. Ganesha, Bhairava and Jogini are as usual represented, respectively, by the *sukunda* (ceremonial lamp), *anti* (a pot containing rice beer) and *khaye kuri* (a pot containing liquor)".
19. Each ritual has its particular *tika*. In the case of the lineage cult, the latter is composed of three items: a yellow powder (*sindhu*), grains of cooked rice and powder of red sandal wood.
20. G. Tucci, *Théorie et pratique du mandala*, Paris, Fayard, 1969, p. 31. Kooij Van K.R., *op. cit.*, p. 19: "Another method is to bring the deity into the air by blowing one's breath out and to lead her from there into the *maṇḍala* by means of a special position of the hands (*āvāhana mudra*) and a mantra (*āvāhana mantra*), both meant to invoke the deity in one's hand and to bring her down with one's hands closed"
21. The observer's perception of what happens when, in religious practice a divinity animates an anthropomorphic statue or an aniconic stone has been studied recently in the Japanese Buddhist tradition by B. Frank in his article "Vacuité et corps actualisé". The problem of the presence of "personages venerated" in their images according to Japanese Buddhist tradition. *Corps des dieux*, Paris, Gallimard, series "Le Temps de la Réflexion", 1986 (VII), pp. 141-71.

Social Consequences of Marrying Viṣṇu Nārāyaṇa: Primary Marriage among the Newars of Kathmandu Valley*

The Newars are the original inhabitants of the Kathmandu Valley in Nepal. Their present population is about 1,500,000. Until 1768 they held political power which they lost when the Malla kingdoms were conquered by the Shah dynasty of Gorkha. The principal occupation of the Newars has always been agriculture, but trade also has been important as the Valley is situated on a commercial route between India, Tibet and China. Hinduism and Buddhism have co-existed in the Valley for 2000 years but the former has always been the state religion.[1]

The status of Newar women differs from that of other Hindu women such as the Chetrinī or Brahmins.[2] Crucially, Newar widows may remarry and widowhood does not involve a loss of status in their society. Divorce too is allowed. A woman may have, successively, several husbands provided that they are of the same caste as her's. The status peculiar to Newar women as compared to women of other Nepalese ethnic groups[3] is said to be the consequence of their having passed through the initiation ceremony for girls who have not yet reached puberty. This ceremony is a ritual marriage to Viṣṇu Nārāyaṇa. In Nepal Viṣṇu is worshipped in the form of

Nārāyaṇa. In contrast to Śiva and different manifestations of the Devī, he never receives bloody sacrifices but only vegetable offerings. It is Viṣṇu who ensures order in the world: the kings of Nepal have always been considered as living symbols of Viṣṇu. In Newari the ceremony is called *ihi*: the literal meaning of this word is marriage and it is synonymous with the Sanskrit word *vivāha*.[4] The ritual marriage is celebrated both by Hindus and Buddhists. Today the majority, 80 per cent, of the Kathmandu Valley Newars are Hindus. The rest (20 per cent) are Buddhists, concentrated mainly in the town of Patan, and conform to the Vajrayāna form of Mahāyāna Buddhism. Both Hindu and Buddhist traditions are ancient in Nepal and it should not be supposed that Hinduization is of recent date. According to archaeological evidence, Hinduism has always been dominant in the Valley, for since the fourth century A.D., it has been the state religion. Since the fourteenth century, Buddhists have been integrated into the local Hindu context: in adopting the caste system, they have continued to observe its injunctions concerning ritual purity and are likewise respectful of relative status positions in the social hierarchy.

For Whom is Marriage to Viṣṇu Nārāyaṇa Performed?

It is their age which determines whether girls are to pass through the ritual marriage with Viṣṇu Nārāyaṇa: they must be between five and nine years of age. This ritual marriage is quite different from the *bahra tayegu* ceremony performed at the time of puberty. The latter must be performed by all castes. Ritual marriage (*ihi*) is, however, celebrated only by pure castes (*ju piṃ*). This statement must be qualified by drawing attention to the fact that the castes situated at the two poles of the social hierarchy, namely the Rajopādhyāya Brahmins or Deo Baju, at the summit, and the Untouchables, at the base, do not celebrate it.

The Rajopādhyāya Brahmins, domestic priests of the Hindu Newars, represent only approximately 1 per cent of total

Newar population of the Valley. According to oral tradition, they came into the Valley in the thirteenth century from the region of Mithila in north India. In former times they occupied the function of *rājguru* to the sovereigns of the Malla dynasty. Locally these Deo Baju, because of their consumption of meat and alcohol in the course of Tantric rituals, are not considered equal to Parbatiya Brahmins. On the other hand, their lower relative ranking in the nineteenth century Mulukī Ain is to be attributed to the fact that it was after the conquest of the Valley by the Gorkhas in the late eighteenth century that this legal code was promulgated. The Deo Baju, we must emphasize, consider themselves higher than the Parbatiya Brahmins. They constitute an endogamous group. In many respects they have remained different from the rest of Newar society. They themselves assert that their women are not entitled to remarry and that their men should not marry a widow as such—a man's social status would be lowered in consequence. However, it is these Deo Baju who officiate at *ihi*. Among the Hindu Newars, at a popular level, the Brahmin is regarded as Viṣṇu Nārāyaṇa: everyone touches his feet with his head. This may explain why the daughters of the Brahmins do not have to go through *ihi*.

The Untouchables (*ma ju piṃ*), butchers (*nāy* or *kasāi*), tailor- musicians (*kusle*, previously *yogi*), fishermen-sweepers (*poḍe*), tanners (*kulu*), sweepers (*cyāme or hālāhulu*) live above all on the slopes on the outskirts of towns. They represent approximately 8 per cent of the Newar population of the Valley. The reason for their not celebrating *ihi* is that this ceremony requires a priest to officiate at it, and no priest, whether Hindu or Buddhist, would consent to play this role for the Untouchables.[5]

Socially speaking, *ihi* is very significant.[6] It is the only Newar domestic ceremony of a collective nature: girls belonging to different castes, whose parents in normal circumstances do not have relations of commensality or intermarriage, celebrate the ritual together. Both Hindu and Buddhist informants emphasize the collective aspect of this ritual marriage. Its celebration usually involves between five and forty girls who are, in no way, linked by kinship. It is the domestic priest (*purohita*) who knows the local community very well, who draws up the lists of the girls of the right age to undergo the ceremony.

Ihi necessitates considerable expenditure and, according to my informants, that is one of the reasons for celebrating the ritual collectively. Generally, it is financed by a man who has no kinship links with the girls involved but who wishes to acquire merit (*puṇya*) — a preoccupation very widespread among the Hindus and the Buddhists alike. Frequently, an elderly person who goes through the ritual of *Jyā jhanko* (Sk. *bhima ratha*) pays also for the celebraton of *ihi*.[7] *Jyā jhanko* is a ritual of initiation carried out when a man or woman reaches the age of seven days, seven months or seventy-seven years: it ensures the passage of the individual in question from the world of men to that of the gods. For instance, a Buddhist woman of my acquaintance, Gyana Maya of the village of Thimi, now 80 years of age, at the time of celebrating her *jyā jhanko* paid for the *ihi* ceremony of five young girls. *Ihi* can also be celebrated at the same time as the inauguration ceremony for a *stūpa* or any other monument. It is staged between the months of *Māgh* (January-February) and *Baisākh* (April- May), a period of the year which is auspicious: pandits and *purohitas* celebrate at that time the marriage of Śiva and Pārvatī, and the *Svasthāni kathā* is read. The auspicious day (*bhingu khunu*) is fixed either by the astrologer or by a Buddhist priest (*vajrācārya*) who, among the Newars, often plays the role of astrologer. The ritual marriage, which usually lasts three days, can take place either in the house of the person who finances it (the Newari *koji che, koji* is synonymous with the Sanskrit word *yajamāna*; *che* means house) if the house is large enough or in the courtyard of a temple or a Buddhist monastery (*bāhā*, Sk. *vihāra*)

The Ritual Complex of "*Ihi*"

The first day of *ihi* is devoted to ritual purification of the bodies of the girls and those of their parents. This ritual is called *nīsī yaye* and takes place early in the morning at the girls' houses. The purification is performed on the ground floor of the house: in all Newar houses the top floor is reserved for the divinities. As in all Newar domestic ceremonies of purification the barber's wife (*nauni*) plays an important role, for it is she who is responsible for purifying the girls' bodies—a process which is always symbolized by the cutting of the toe nails. On this day, the girl to be married must not take any food except milk and curd (*dhau sagam*) which are considered pure foods. After ritual purification, the girls, accompanied by their mothers, visit their maternal uncles (*pāju*) who give them presents of new clothes.

It is the second day which marks the real beginning of the ceremony. It is called *doso khunu.* Purification rites may be performed on this day also early in the morning. For both the Hindus and the Buddhists alike, it is compulsory for the ceremony to be performed under the guidance of a domestic priest: for those who are *Śivamārgī* he will be a Rājopādhyāya Brahmin who is helped by a *karmācārya* and for the *Buddha mārgī* a Buddhist priest who is helped by a *śakya.* Important household ceremonies such as marriages and funerals can be celebrated only by Brahmins or by Buddhist priests. In the case of *ihi* the ceremony cannot be celebrated by a *karmācārya* or a *śakya* for the ritual of the sacrificial fire (*homa*) cannot be accomplished by them.[8] The ceremony starts very early in the morning. Before the sun rises the priest must arrange the *duso maṇḍala* and fix the seat (*svastika āsana*) of each girl.

It is not my purpose here to give the details of the entire ritual: it should be sufficient to emphasize that, on the whole, the important moments of the ritual are the same for the Buddhists, and the Hindus alike and that the social consequences also are identical. One difference must be noted, however, which differentiates Hindu from Buddhist practices.

Early on this day, for Hindus, but not for Buddhists, there is a *śrāddha* for the ancestors of the girls on both sides. As in the celebration of all Hindu marriages in Nepal there is a *śrāddha* which in this instance is officiated by a Deo Baju. In Hindu marriage, an auspicious *śrāddha* is a kind of insurance and protection against impurity (*sūtaka*) which might intervene in the case of the death of a member of the lineage.[9] Before the *śrāddha* starts, the *karmācārya*, who is in fact a *kulācārya*, goes to the open shrine of the goddess (*pīṭha*) in the locality where the girl in question resides and sacrifices a male goat (*dugu*). Informants maintain that in former days he had to go and render homage at all the eight open shrines of the goddess which encircle the town. When the *karmācārya* comes back from the shrine, the *śrāddha* for the dead is celebrated by the Deo Baju at the local Gaṇeśa temple.[10] I may quote the case of a Deo Baju from Bhaktapur, Ramapatiraj, one of my main informants, who in 1977, officiated as the priest at the *śrāddha* at the temple of Jyeṣṭha Gaṇeśa in the potters' quarters (*Kumale tol*). While the girls stay in the house, the *karmācārya* and the *koji che* (or the *thakuli*) go to the Gaṇeśa temple. The Deo Baju call this ceremony *Nandi mukh śrāddha* whereas the farmers (*jyapū*) call it *Yamalok śrāddha*. The divinity invoked is Mahadev. He is invoked in the form of Alin Dyo, represented by a clay pot made the previous day by the potters. The ancestors invoked at this moment are from both sides, maternal (*pāju*) and paternal (*phukī*). They are invoked up to three generations for each of the girls: *maṃ* (mother), *ajī* (grandmother), and *tāpa aji* (great grandmother); *bwā* (father), *ājā* (grandfather), and *tāpā ājā* (great grandfather). Beyond three generations the names of the ancestors are not mentioned: but the group is invoked together. This seems important as, for marriages, the middle caste Newars particularly take into account three generations. Distinctions concerning marriage prohibitions at Bhaktapur concern, in the first instance, high and low castes, the high castes respecting prohibitions concerning five generations while the low castes take account of only three generations.[11]

While the *śrāddha* is taking place, the girls who remain in the house of the *koji che* must take their places as indicated by the *thakuli nakinā*, who in the case of ritual celebrated by the Deo Baju Ramapatiraj was his wife, Durga Devi. In other cases, a senior woman, often called *gurumā* by the Buddhists, must watch over the correct conduct of the ceremony. The previous evening, a painter would have drawn on the ground the places where each girl should sit (*svastika āsana*) throughout the ritual marriage. For the Tantrics the intersecting lines of the *svastika* represent the union of the male and female principles. Generally speaking it is the mother who assists her daughter throughout the ceremony; in her absence, it is the maternal aunt. Five girls are chosen by the patron (*koji che*) according to his preferences and they are seated apart from the others. According to the Deo Baju Ramapatiraj, they symbolize five ideal "wives" (*pañca kanyā*) in Hindu mythology: Ahalyā, Draupadī, Tārā, Kuntī, and Mandodarī (see Stevenson 1971:62). The most important moment of the first day is called *sat brindika*. This is the moment when the measurement of each girl is taken by the *thakuli nakinā or the gurumā*. The measurement of each girl is taken with a yellow thread. She stands upright, arms stretched wide on either side at the level of her shoulders. The thread is passed upwards from under her feet, round the tip of her outstretched fingers of one hand, over her head and then downwards, over fingertips of the other hand, once more leading to the soles of her feet. The way of measurement is always the same but it can be done 21, 84 or 108 times. Afterwards, on the same day, yellow thread in the form of a necklace (*kumosoka*) will be placed in an unbaked clay dish (*solapan*) in front of each girl. In the Newar context the red colour symbolizes marriage and women, whereas yellow is appropriate to men. This yellow "necklace" will be given to the girl's human bridegroom on the occasion of her second marriage and will constitute the proof that the girl had already accomplished the *ihi* ceremony.

Next, the girls take their first meal of the day from a large copper platter (*thai bhu*) containing items of 84 different savours: flattened rice, meat from different parts of the animal, fish, eggs, five different varieties of sweetmeats, curd, different cooked vegetables, fruit, etc. Each girl must partake of this meal, *thai bhu,* in a ritualistic manner. She uses successively her thumb and each of the fingers of the right hand, then her thumb and each of the fingers of the left hand when taking mouthfuls. The eating of this food marks the end of the period of abstinence. This dish contains all the types of food the consumption of which is prohibited during the periods of impurity following the death of a relative. It is called *khaye sagaṃ* and, according to the pandits, corresponds to the *pañca makāra* of Tantrism. The latter, according to them, consists of cooked meat, a special kind of fish, fried bean-cake, alcohol and eggs. Offerings of *pañca makāra* are made only to the Tantric divinities. The *khaye sagaṃ* is to be distinguished from pure food, *pañcāmṛta* or *dhau sagaṃ* offered to all non-tantric divinities such as Nārāyaṇa or Kṛṣṇa. In Newari two other words are used: *ame* or "prohibited food" such as meat, fish, eggs, ground lentils, liquor; and *alaa* which means holy, sacred, unpolluted food usually prepared by Brahmins. What is called *pañcāmṛta* is consumed during periods of impurity and fasts. The platter called *thai bhu* is served on four occasions: (1) when a child takes its first solid food (the ceremony is called *jhanko*); (2) at the ritual marriage (*ihi*); (3) during the celebration of marriage to human bridegrooms; and (4) during the celebration of the ritual accomplished when an individual reaches the age of seventy-seven years, seven months, seven days (*jyā jhanko*).

The third day is the day of the ritual marriage. It is called *kanyādān khunu,* the day of the gift of a daughter. Early on that day, alongside the *duso maṇḍala,* the site for the sacrificial fire is made ready by the priest. The sacrificial fire (*yajña*) is lit on the altar constructed in theory of 108 unbaked bricks. The girls must remain seated in places allotted to them on the previous day; and, before the start of ceremony, they must again purify themselves. The senior woman (*thakuli nakinā*) makes a parting in the hair of each girl in turn. In this parting she puts vermilion (*sinco phāyegu*). This is the most notable sign of a married woman. Next she touches the head of each girl with a mirror (*jolaṃ*). The mother or maternal uncle then takes the yellow necklace, which is of the same length as the girl's body measurements, and puts it around her neck. Then a piece of paper on which is painted an image of Viṣṇu Nārāyaṇa is placed on each girl's forehead. If a girl's parents can afford it, a golden ornament may be used to represent Viṣṇu. Orthodox Buddhists, who wish to distinguish themselves from the Śivamārgī, will use instead a piece of paper on which an image of a holy vessel (*kalaśa*) is drawn. In the clay plate in front of each girl a *bel* fruit (*bya*, Sk. *bilva*), is deposited. The *purohita* then puts a red thread about 50 centimetres long, in each girl's plate. The father intervenes for the first time at this stage and ties this red thread round the chest of his daughter. He then takes the *bel* fruit and puts it in her hand along with flower petals, rice and betel-nuts. The girls remain seated in their fathers' laps, the father holding his daughter's hand in his. The symbolic gestures made by the girls' fathers clearly indicate that they are giving their daughters away to the divinity. If the father is absent, his role will be played by the girl's paternal uncle. All parents on the paternal side (*phuki*) must then sprinkle water, which has been brought from a *tirtha*, on to the girl's head. The moment in the ritual, well known in Hindu marriage as *kanyādān*, consists in the father giving his daughter away without receiving anything in exchange. It is the essential phase which sums up a Hindu ideology concerning marriage.

The next vital part of Hindu marriage ritual is the walk around the sacred fire. The *purohita* purifies the girls by sprinkling on them the "five products of the cow" (*pañca gavya*): milk, curd, ghee, cow-dung and urine. The fathers lift their daughters in their arms and carry them three times around the sacrificial fire in a clockwise direction. Once back in their places, the red threads tied around the girls' torsos are taken off by their fathers. The *bel* fruit is rolled in the palms of the fathers' hands, and then placed in the earthen platters in front of the daughters, along with the red threads.

The *vajrācārya* or the Deo Baju who conducts the ceremony, as well as the *karmācārya* who helps the Deo Baju, must remain seated in front of the sacrificial fire. The text read by the Deo Baju during the ceremony is the *Suvarṇa Kumāra vivāha.* I have seen several such manuscripts which often date from the seventeenth or eighteenth century and contain instructions for conducting the ritual. They are written in a mixture of Newari and Sanskrit and are illustrated with drawings of *maṇḍala* which serve as models for those erected on the first day next to the altar. During the ceremony, an image of gilt metal is placed close to the sacrificial fire. It is well known that in Hindu mythology Suvarṇa Kumāra is one of the bachelor sons of Śiva. However, participants, in *ihi,* as well as the *purohita,* always maintain that it is to Viṣṇu Nārāyaṇa that the girls are married and the *bel* fruit represents Śiva as witness to the marriage. According to certain Buddhist priests "the girl is considered to be united to a personification of *bodhicitta* represented by the *bel* fruit".[12] What seems particularly significant in the Buddhist rituals is the making of a new statue representing a Buddhist divinity of the Mahāyāna pantheon, such as Tārā, Avalokiteśvara or the Buddha, which is consecrated on the first day of *ihi.* This statue is called *numha dyo,* "new divinity": the divinity in question will henceforth be the protective deity of the girls who have been married ritually.

All around the *maṇḍala* are placed earthen pots, painted the previous day by a professional painter. Their number can vary from 12 to 32: each pot is the temporary seat of a divinity. On each pot there are different symbolic drawings made the previous day by a *citrakār,* which indicate the divinity it will shelter. Hindu Newars place in the centre of the other pots a large earthenware pot representing Brahmā. After the *kanyā dān*, the girls are sprinkled by the *purohita* with water from this pot. During the ceremony the *thakali nakinā* must prepare in the sacrificial fire ritual food consisting of rice cooked in milk and this is then consumed by all the participants.

During the annual celebration of the lineage festival (*digu dyo pūjā*) girls who have celebrated *ihi* in the course of the past year must offer the *bel* fruit to the lineage divinity. I saw this ceremony at Bhaktapur in 1975 when it was celebrated by the potters during their lineage festival. The girls, clad in red, and wearing traditional jewellery as during the ritual marriage to Viṣṇu, offered the *bel* fruit to the lineage divinity and they were accompanied by their fathers (see Vergati Stahl 1979: 125). It was interesting to note that the ceremony was supervised by a Brāhmin, a Deo Baju, and by a Buddhist priest and that it was to the latter that the girls gave the *bel* fruit. According to informants, the girls are then introduced to the divinity as their marriage and their new status must be made known to him. It is from this moment onwards that a girl becomes a full-fledged member of the father's lineage. At this lineage festival only those girls who belong to the patrilineage participate and not all the girls who had taken part in the *ihi*.

What distinguishes the ritual marriage to Viṣṇu Nārāyaṇa from the rituals carried out at puberty (*bahra tayegu*) is that the latter are accomplished individually.[13] A girl is at that time sequestered for 12 days in a dark room; during that time it is forbidden to her to see the light of the sun, Sūrya, who is of course a male god, as well as the men of her household. The latter are protected by the *bahra* ritual from the dangers of the girl's menstrual blood.[14] If other girls are present in the darkened room at that time, they are only to help her to dress, eat, etc. as she herself cannot leave the room. This ritual of puberty is considered by the Newars as a *saṃskāra* which all members of all castes, pure or impure, must perform. The ritual does not require the presence of a priest on the last day. Some Newar women told me that the human spouse is really the third husband, the second being, in their view, the god

Sūrya, to whom they are married on the twelfth day of the puberty celebration. The Pandits and *vajrācārya*, however, deny that there is a real marriage to Sūrya on that day.

The ritual marriage to Viṣṇu Nārāyaṇa is the only domestic ceremony in which members of different castes mingle. The initiation ritual carried out for boys between three and seven years of age (*Kayeta pūjā*) is done for each boy individually. Exceptionally, it may be done for two brothers at the same time, if there is no great difference in their ages. The *Kayeta pūjā* does not require the presence of a priest. The sacrifice, which takes place at the open shrine of the goddess of the town quarters, is carried out by the boy's father or by another member of his patrilineage. It is the lineage aspect of this initiation ritual which is the most important. This is in no way surprising in a patrilineal, and patrilocal society.

Comparison between Nayar and Newar Ritual Marriages

The Newar ritual marriage to Viṣṇu brings to mind the accounts of ritual marriage among the Nayars of Kerala, which has been studied by several authors.[15] Louis Dumont was the first to draw a parallel in 1961 between Nayar and Newar marriages and the social status of women.[16] At that time not much was known about the ritual marriage practised by the Newars. Dumont used the materials made available till then by Christoph von Fürer-Haimendorf, whose article (1964) was a general description of Newar social organization and the information on marriage which it contained was rather brief. On the other hand, the materials available on the Nayars were much more detailed. Nayar girls before puberty, aged from seven to eleven, are married ritually (*tali kettukalyanam*) to men of a linked lineage. Kathleen Gough tells us that "the ritual bridegrooms were selected in advance on the advice of the village astrologer: at a meeting of the neighbourhood assembly on the day fixed, they came in procession to the oldest ancestral house of the host lineage. There, after various ceremonies, each tied a gold ornament (*tali*) round the neck of his ritual bride. The girls had for the three days previously been secluded in an inner room of the house and caused to observe taboos as if they had menstruated. After the *tali* tying, each couple was secluded in private for three days. I was told that traditionally, if the girl was nearing puberty, sexual relations might take place" (1959:25).

As I have already stated, the only factor taken into account in the case of the Newar girls is their age. In the Indian context this is in no way surprising, for from the point of view of orthodox Hinduism, marriage, properly speaking, must precede any manifestation of sexuality in the girl concerned: this is one of the reasons often put forward to explain the custom of child marriage. In Brahmin ideology a girl is considered to be pure only before puberty—whence the necessity of celebrating the primary marriage before she reaches puberty.[17] There is however one difference between the Newar *ihi* and the Nayar ritual marriage which should be emphasized at the outset: in the case of the former there is no human, ritual, husband. According to customary law, Newar girls are not entitled to have sexual relations or to cohabit with a man before their second marriage, which is to a human being. When one thinks of the importance attached in general in primary Northern India marriages to establishing alliances, it is noteworthy that this aspect is totally absent in the Newar case. In both the Nayar and the Newar instances, we are dealing with a collective ceremony, the ritual marriage being celebrated for a group of girls and not for one individual. However, here again a distinction should be made: the Nayar girls involved all belong to the same caste whereas the Newar girls belong to pure but different castes which normally are not linked by commensality or marriage. It should be stressed that the differences between Nayar and Newar social organization are considerable. The former are matrilineal, practise matrilocal residence, and inheritance takes place along the maternal line: the latter practice Indian caste rules, patrilineal filiation, patrilocal residence and inheritance takes place along the paternal line.

In consequence of the ritual marriage the social status of the girls in both the cases changes: besides becoming full-fledged members of their caste, they acquire the social status of an adult woman. 'The *tali* rite marked various changes in the social position of a girl. First, it brought her to social maturity. She was now thought to be at least ritually endowed with sexual and procreative functions and was thenceforward accorded the status of a woman. After the rite the people addressed her in public by the respectful title *amma* meaning "mother"; and she might take part in the rites of adult women. Second, after the *tali* rite a girl must observe all the rules of etiquette associated with incest prohibitions in relations to men of her lineage. She might not touch them, might not sit in their presence; might not speak first to them and might not be alone in a room with one of them. Third, after the *tali* rite, as soon as she became old enough (i.e., shortly before or after puberty) a girl received as visiting husbands a number of men of her subcaste from outside her lineage, usually but not necessarily from her neighbourhood' (Gough 1959: 25). The Newar women emphasize that, prior to the celebration of *ihi,* a girl does not wear a woman's clothes and can play or eat with any other child of her locality, no account being taken of caste. After the *ihi,* in her general behaviour towards the men of her own lineage, she must, of course, observe the prohibitions inherent to the condition of a married woman.

Dumont has established for Hindu castes an important difference between primary and secondary marriages. This difference has multiple facets, which vary from one group to another, but "in all groups, an ideal type of marriage is recognised, the marriage par excellence, which is, in general, more rule bound, more solemn, more costly, and which enjoys the maximum possible prestige in the given group and constitutes most frequently the necessary preliminary to marriages or unions considered as inferior" (1961:11).

A detailed analysis of secondary marriage in Central India (the State of Gwalior) is to be found in Chambard (1961) Describing the primary marriages among the Kirar of Piparsod, he emphasizes that such marriages are celebrated when the future partners are between six and twelve years of age, usually at the age of seven or eight. Generally, however, the wife comes to live in her husband's house between three and six years after the marriage ceremony. He stresses that the secondary marriage of a woman is only possible on the condition that she has already been united with a partner in a primary marriage. However, for the woman concerned, it really is a secondary marriage whereas this is not the case for men who can contract secondary marriage without having earlier gone through a primary marriage.

It seems to me that the Newar ritual marriage to the God Viṣṇu Nārāyaṇa constitutes a perfect example of this type of primary marriage. From the point of view of Newar women, the only type of marriage which cannot be dissolved is that with Viṣṇu Nārāyaṇa: the latter is, according to the local expression, "an eternal husband". Newar women therefore never suffer from the stigma of widowhood in their society. The human spouse is only a second husband. Women attach less importance to this second marriage: it is less complex than the former; and the two most important rites in Hindu marriages—the *kanyādān* and the walk around the sacrificial fire—are absent in this case. The link between the primary marriage, *ihi*, and the secondary marrige with a human husband is, as reported earlier, the yellow necklace (*kumosoka*) which will be given to the human husband at the time of marriage.

In ideal terms, if a Newar woman leaves her mortal husband, she must take as second husband a man of her own caste, or of higher caste. Higher caste women affirm that divorce does not exist and that it is current only among women of the farmer (*jyāpū*) caste. They do, however, stress the necessity of accomplishing *ihi* which protects girls from becoming widows and assures the maintenance of their social status.

In the Indian tradition, marriage to Viṣṇu in order to avoid to widowhood is not unknown. Several authoritative texts mention it. Thus:

> Certain peculiar ceremonies relating to marriage may now be described very briefly. In order to avert early widowhood (which was judged from her horoscope) for the girl to be married a ceremony called *kumbha vivāha* was performed....On the day previous to marriage a jar of water, in which a golden image of Viṣṇu is dipped, is decked with flowers and the girl is surrounded in a network of threads. Varuṇa and Viṣṇu are worshipped and prayed to give long life to the intended bridegroom. Then the jar is taken out and broken in a pool of water and then sprinkled over the girl with five twigs and to the accompaniment of Ṛg Veda, VII, 49 and the brahmanas are fed (Kane 1974:546).

This text describes the marriage of an individual to Viṣṇu and not a collective ceremony. Another source mentions that a man must marry a fruit before marrying a third wife if he has already lost his two previous wives (Thurston 1970:41, 44).

For Nepal of the Indo-Nepalese castes, we note that the middle and lower castes have always allowed remarriage of widows: but with each successive marriage a woman's status tends to diminish. Sharma, citing the case of the Hill Chetris, writes:

> The common belief is that the full restoration to the Chetri caste of the offspring born of the Brahmin and the Chetri fathers from their hypergamous marriages is completed in three generations. Then an offspring is accepted as a full status caste member. This process puts faith in the process of gradual purification which results from a Hindu fathering of them. Despite this diversity of the origin of the Chetris it (sic!) has preserved an almost tribal feeling of

homogeneity and solidarity throughout Nepal (1977:288)

For marriages with human husbands Newar women strictly respect caste rules. The future bridegroom must be of the same caste but of different lineage. As a general rule, marriages are arranged by the respective parents of the prospective couple. Traditionally, the marriage age for girls is between 14 and 16.[18] The Newars practise a marked form of territorial endogamy. One marries someone from one's own locality. This may be due, in part, to status differences in the social hierarchy varying from one locality to another. Thus a Jyāpū (farmer) from Kathmandu will not marry a Jyāpū girl from Bhaktapur for in Kathmandu such girls are considered as inferior. We hasten to add that the caste of the farmers does not constitute a single endogamous group but is composed of several subcastes, each of these being an endogamous group and all being strictly hierarchized. For instance, let us quote the case of the Suwal Jyāpu who are at the top of the hierarchy and have the ritual role of cooking rice for the deity Taleju: they could never marry a girl of the potter subcaste.

If descent is traced formally through the paternal line, it is noteworthy that hierarchized status depends not only on paternal links but that account is also taken of the maternal side. Women of inferior status to that of their husbands will be excluded from the annual ritual celebration of the lineage divinity which is an instrument of social control. As a general rule a man will not eat rice cooked by his wife if she is of a status inferior to his. The status of Newar women, different from that of other Nepalese women, does not preclude polygamy. A man may frequently have two or three wives who cohabit with him, respecting at the same time the rules of ritual purity.

What is particular to Newar women of middle ranking castes is that a woman can raise the status of her husband, i.e. anagamy. The affirmation of Dumont (1964:96) that anagamy is confined to certain levels within a group is thus confirmed by the Newar case. Rosser (1966) gives a long description of how a Jyāpū can climb up into the position of a Shrestha, one of the necessary conditions being to marry a Shrestha woman. The Shrestha are particularly distrustful of the origins of each other's status: they do not practise commensality as other castes do. My personal observations suggest that if a man marries a woman of higher caste, he will have to change his residence if he also wants to change his status.

Concluding Remarks

One may well ask what is the main significance of this Newar form of primary marriage to Viṣṇu Nārāyaṇa. If age is taken into consideration and the fact that the marriage takes place prior to puberty, it is evident that the same rules are followed for child-marriages as in India. In north Indian child-marriages, the main aims are finding husbands and establishing allies. In the Newar case, the search for allies finds expression only in the secondary marriages with human husbands. In northern India, marriages of the *devadāsī* to Viṣṇu are, of course, known (see Marglin 1982): but in Nepal the *devadāsīs* are unknown. Theoretically, in India if a girl becomes a *devadāsī* and the wife of a god she can in no case take a human husband.[19] However, in the Newar case, marriage to Viṣṇu allows her to take a human husband. This is an inversion of the *devadāsī* case.

In my opinion, the main objectives in the Newar primary marriage are to maintain the hierarchical status of the woman and to confer on her the full status of a lineage and caste membership. This primary marriage ensures that she will never suffer a loss or a decline in status because of the death of her husband or following divorce from him. In Newar society, for both the Hindus and the Buddhists, the preoccupation with maintaining ritual purity is constant. Allen (1976:26) has rightly observed that the higher a group is placed in the caste hierarchy the greater is the concern of its members with maintaining the rules of ritual purity in general and with controlling female sexuality. Among the Nayars, girls who marry Nambudiri Brahmans as first ritual bridegrooms, before taking other husbands, likewise conserve thereby their status and their purity. In both cases, one might argue that we are in the presence of a form of hypergamy. However, *ihi* determines the purity and the status of the girl who goes through the ritual: it does not determine the purity or the impurity of her progeny. The purity and the social status acquired through *ihi* can be lost or squandered through a "bad" human marriage. With regard to the difference between women and men, the *ihi* "by linking women to the divinity frees them for life in this world whereas the male saṃskāras imprison men in the social life of this world with the promise of freedom in the next" (Macdonald and Vergati Stahl 1979:54).

Notes

* First published in *Contributions to Indian Sociology*, Vol. 16, No. 2, 1982.

1. My fieldwork was done in Bhaktapur (or Bhatgaon), one of the main towns of the Valley with about 40,000 inhabitants. It was financed by the C.N.R.S., Laboratoire d'Ethnologie, LA 140. I wish to thank in particular Rama Patiraj Sharma and his wife, Durga Devi. For all his help in the understanding of Buddhist rituals my thanks go to Bhadri Guruju of Kathmandu. I wish to thank T.N. Madan, A.W. Macdonald, M.L. Reiniche and Ph. Sagant for their helpful criticism of earlier drafts of this article.
2. I use "status" here to refer to the relative position in the local social hierarchy of a person, a group or a form of marriage.
3. Good descriptions of the social organization of the Indo-Nepalese castes are to be found in Gaborieau (1977) and von Fürer-Haimendorf (1957, 1959).
4. Unless otherwise stated, all the vernacular words or phrases in this article are from the Newari language as it is spoken today.
5. Toffin (1977: 38) writes that the inhabitants of the village of Pyangaon, who are considered true Newars and are low caste (*ko jat*), do not celebrate *ihi*.
6. C. von Fürer-Haimendorf (1956) had briefly drawn attention to this aspect of Newar social organization. A short description of the ritual marriage to Viṣṇu Nārāyaṇa as celebrated by Hindus has been given by Nepali (1965:106-12).

7. There is no ethnographic description of the *jhanko* (Sk. *bhīma ratha*) ritual. Nepali writes: A very notable feature in the ritual life-cycle of the Newars is the observance of the attainment of old age which is, however, not to be found among other ethnic groups of Nepal. They use the term *burha jhanko* to designate their observance which is held thrice in the life-time of an individual. The first *burha jhanko* takes place at the age of seventy-seven years, seven months, seven days, seven *ghadis* and seven *palas* according to the Hindu calendar. It is called *Bhīma Ratha Rohan.* On the completion of this ceremony a person is believed to enter upon the first stage of divinity and he gives up taking active interest in family affairs. It is commonly believed that if such an initiated one pronounces a curse upon someone, it is sure to be effective (1965:122).

8. Cf. Greenwold (1981:87): "The Vajracarya and the Brahman alone have access to the function associated with guardianship of the fire, and they alone are thereby empowered to serve as domestic priests (*purohita*)".

9. Cf. Stevenson (1971:62): The auspicious *śrāddha* (*vṛddhi śrāddha*) is a sort of insurance. The difficulty is that if some distant relative were to die, it would not only cause grief to his remote cousins, but also reduce their house to a state of such ceremonial impurity (*sūtaka*) that no one would be able to drink or eat in it. But if once this auspicious *śrāddha* has been performed, no *sūtaka* can attach itself to the house (unless the person so inconsiderably dying were a very relative indeed) and so without any harm people can feast there.

10. Cf. Pandey (1969:210): The ceremonies preceding the marriage day are the following: In the beginning the most auspicious god Gaṇeśa is worshipped and his symbol is installed in the nuptial canopy erected according to the rules laid down in the scriptures. The sacrificial altar for the *vaivāhika homa* is also built under the canopy. Then the father of the bride with his wife, in the first half of the day, having bathed, puts on an auspicious robe. Next having seated himself he sips water and restrains his breaths. After this he prays to place and time, and makes up his mind (*saṅkalpa*) to perform *Maṇḍapa pratiṣṭhā, Mātṛ pūjana, Vasudhārāpūjana, Āyuṣyajapa* and *Nāndi śrāddha* as ancillary to marriage.

11. Cf. Nepali (1971:205): "People have started marrying a woman from the third generation or the fourth generation if the relationship is traced through the female links only. Thus the Jyāpu of Panga say that they have started marrying into the families of father's sister's daughter; and mother's brother's daughter's daughter".

12. When reconsecrating a statue in the temple of Seto Avalokiteśvara (*Jana baha*) at Kathmandu, part of the ritual is devoted to *pānigraha* or the marriage rite:

After these preparatory rites, the priest places a flower on the *bel* fruit and meditates: "Consider this to be the form of *bodhicitta* in which there is no difference between the void and compassion. Consider that the seed letter residing in your own heart is flowering in the different *lokadhātus*; then it goes up to be in the *akaniṣṭha* heaven. From there attract it so that it disappears into the *bel* fruit". Then after performing a *pañcopacāra pūjā*, the priest wraps the *bel* fruit in a leaf and recites the following: "This (i.e., holding the *bel* in the hand-*pānigraha*) is the *mudrā* of the *tathāgatas*. It makes bright the light of the knowledge; it is the act of Buddha, Oh, Lord, you are a being who realizes the *maṇḍala* of *prajñā* and *upāya*: may you fulfil my wish". Then the *bel* fruit is placed in front of the deity and sprinkled with *pañcāmṛta* from the conch-shell and the "hands" of the *bel* and the deity are symbolically bound. This is the moment of the *pānigraha* (Locke 1979:216).

13. My findings do not concord with those of Nepali who writes: "It is generally held in groups in a dark room and several girls are huddled up together" (1971:112). All the women I questioned said that the *bahra tayegu* ritual must be done for one girl at a time.
14. Allen (1976 and MS) mentions the fact that the second husband is Sūrya.
15. For a good summary of the many descriptive and interpretative accounts of Nayars see Fuller (1976). I have used in particular Gough (1959).
16. Cf. Dumonṭ (1964), particularly the section "Nepal compared to India: The Newars and others", pp. 90-97.
17. While describing marriage among the Brahmins of Kashmir, Madan writes: "Only a virgin may be given in marriage because a woman who has had sexual intercourse with a man is unchaste and unworthy of being given as a ritual gift. The Pandits say that, in olden times, the bride used to be absolutely chaste because girls were married before menarche" (1965:120).
18. Cf. Bennett (1979:69): The National Code of 1963 came out against the custom of child marriage by stipulating that no girl could be married before the age of fourteen and no boy before the age of eighteen, even with the consent of their guardians. The sixth amendment, enacted during International Women's Year, raised the minimum age of marriage for a girl to sixteen with her guardian's consent and is now eighteen and twenty-one for a boy.
19. Cf. Marglin (1982:162): The *devadāsī* are locally referred to by other words also such as *veśya* and *dāri* which mean prostitute. They are also called the "auspicious women" (*maṅgala nārī*). One readily given explanation of their auspicious status is that they are married to the deity. They are always "women whose husband is alive" (*ahya* or *sudabhā*).

References

Allen, M., 1976, "Kumari or Virgin Worship in Kathmandu Valley", *Contributions to Indian Sociology*, 10, 2, pp. 293-317.

————, Girls' Pre-puberty Rites amongst the Newars of Kathmandu Valley, Unpublished Manuscript.

Bennett, L., 1979, *The Status of Women in Nepal*, Vol. I, Part 2, Kathmandu, Tribhuvan University.

Chambard, J.L., 1961, Marriages secondaires et foires aux femmes en Inde centrale. *L'Homme* 1,2, pp. 52-88.

Dumont, Louis, 1969. "Marriage in India: The Present State of the Question", *Contributions to Indian Sociology* 7,3, pp. 90-77.

Fuller, C.J., 1976, *The Nayars Today*, London, Cambridge University Press.

Gaborieau, M. 1977, "Les gens de caste ou l'Inde omniprésente", in *Le Népal et ses populations*. Bruxelles, Editions Complexe.

Gough, E.K., 1959, "The Nayars and the Definition of Marriage", *Journal of the Royal Anthropological Institute*, 89, pp. 23- 34.

Greenwold, S.M., 1981, "Caste: A Moral Structure and a Social System of Control" in A.C. Mayer, ed., *Culture and Morality: Essays in Honour of C. von Fürer-Haimendorf*, Delhi, Oxford Unversity Press, pp. 84-106.

Kane, P.V., 1974, *History of Dharmaśāstra*, Vol. II, Pt. I. Poona, Bhandarkar Oriental Research Institute.

Locke, J.K., 1979, *Karunamaya: The Cult of Avalokiteśvara Matsyendranāth in the Valley of Nepal*, Kathmandu, Sahayogi Prakashan.

Macdonald, A.W. and A. Vergati Stahl, 1979, *Newar Art: Nepalese Art during the Malla Period*, Warminister, Aris and Phillips.

Madan, T.N., 1965, *Family and Kinship: A Study of the Pandits of Rural Kashmir*, Bombay, Asia Publishing House.

Marglin, F.A. 1982, "Kings and Wives: The Separation of Status and Power", in T.N. Madan, ed., *Way of Life: King, Householder, Renouncer: Essays in Honour of Louis Dumont*, New Delhi, Vikas, pp. 155-81.

Nepali, G.S., 1965, *The Newars: An Ethno-sociological Study of a Himalayan Community*, Bombay, United Asia Publications.

Pandey, R.B., 1965, *Hindu Saṃskāras*, Delhi, Motilal Banarsidass.

Rosser, C., 1966, "Social Mobility in the Newar Caste System", in C. von Fürer-Haimendorf, ed., *Caste and Kin in Nepal, India and Ceylon*, London, Asia Publishing House, pp. 68-139.

Sharma, M., 1977, *Through the Valley of Gods*, New Delhi, Vision Books.

Sharma, P.R., 1977, "Caste, Social Mobility and Sanskritization: A Study of Nepal's Old Legal Code", *Kailash* 5,4.

Stevenson, S., 1971, *The Rites of the Twice Born*, New Delhi, Oriental Books, Reprint Corporation.

Thurston, E., 1907, *Ethnographic Notes*, Madras, Government Press.

Toffin, G., 1977, *Pyangaon, communauté néwar de la vallée de Kathmandu. La vie matérielle.* Paris, Editions C.N.R.S.

Vergati Stahl, A., 1979, Une divinité lignagère des Néwar, *Bulletin de l'Ecole Française d'Extrême Orient* 65: 125.

von Fürer-Haimendorf, Christoph, 1956, "Elements of Newar Social Structure", *Journal of the Royal Anthropological Institute,* 86.

————, 1957, "The Interrelations of Castes and Ethnic Groups in Nepal", *Bulletin of the School of Oriental and African Studies,* 20, pp. 245-53.

————, 1959, "Status Difference in a High Hindu Caste of Nepal", *Eastern Anthropologist,* 12, 4, pp. 223-33.

Taleju, Sovereign Deity of Bhaktapur*

Before 1768, the three towns of Kathmandu Valley had separate kings: each ruler had the same tutelary divinity: Taleju. It is only after the arrival of Taleju, in the fourteenth century, that a blueprint for the organization and hierarchization of the entire society of his kingdom— Buddhist as well as Hindu—was drawn up by Jayasthiti Malla. If Taleju occupies a position close to or within the Royal Palace in each of the three towns, the caste hierarchy is reflected in the settlement pattern which encircles the palace: the higher castes live closest to the palace, the others further away in roughly concentric circles. The divinity occupies, so to speak, the central position in a social *maṇḍala.*

Both anthropologists and historians tend to consider the Newars as the indigenous inhabitants of the Valley of Kathmandu. In reality, the Newars are a complex group. Elements from India are discernible in its present composition: and there is no means of determining whether the truly autochthonous component in their society is formed by the Jyapus which have not, as yet, been deeply studied. However some facts about Newars are certain. They still constitute more then 50 per cent of the population of the Valley: they are both Buddhamargi and Śivamargi, while at the same time respecting Viṣṇu; both Buddhist and Hindu Newar elements are integrated into a caste hierarchy which varies considerably from one locality to another within the 250 sq. miles of the Valley's surface. As the Valley was divided into three town-based kingships, the relationship between caste-hierarchy and royal power should not be analysed on an abstract plane. One must, whatever the difficulties involved, take into account the historical context in which Newar society evolved into its present form. Patan, Kathmandu, Bhaktapur (or Bhatgaon) did not have the same kings, but their kings had the same tutelary divinity: Taleju.

In the Newar pantheon, the only divinity constantly linked with royalty is Taleju. According to Newar oral tradition, this divinity came from India to Nepal in the middle of the fourteenth century with Harisiṃha Deva who was a king of the Karnatak dynasty, which originated from Ayodhya. He reigned in the Terai, at Simraongarh, not far from present-day Simra.[1] After a battle between Harisiṃha Deva and Ghiyas-ud din Tughlaq, the former had to flee into the mountains and entered Nepal. He brought with him a new form of Devī. "Her name, kept carefully secret, has come down to us in embarrassing variations: Tulasī, Tulajā, Taleju, Talagu. Among the titles usually accorded to the Devī, she was given by preference that of Bhavānī. Her true image, with which her person was identified, was said to have come from heaven. Carried off by Rāvaṇa, she had escaped from his clutches; Rāma had found her and installed her at Ayodhyā: she had then moved to Simraongarh, whence she had led Harisiṃha to the conquest of Nepal. Her prestige was so great that the Tibetans, impatient to procure the services of this powerful auxiliary, tried to kidnap her *manu militari*. Bequeathed by Harisiṃaha Deva's dynasty to the Mallas of Bhatgaon, she provoked the envy of the Mallas of Kathmandu until the day when Mahîndra Malla had the satisfaction of erecting in his own capital,in 1549, a temple to Tulajā Bhavānī."[2] Thus far Sylvain Lévi. K.B. Bista[3] quotes other traditions according to which, when Rāma was drowned in the Saryu river, the image of this protective divinity disappeared for several centuries. A prince of Simraongarh, who is identified as Nānya Deva, was advised by an astrologer to go to the bank of a river, at a certain place and time. There he would find something important: if he got hold of it, and carried it with him towards the north, he would be able to establish a kingdom. Nānya Deva followed the astrologer's advice, found the object, surrounded in the water by a swarm of bees, swam out to it, and took it with him towards the north. He reached the site of Bhatgaon, which at that time was covered with jungle, founded a kingdom, and raised there a temple for the object he had recuperated from the river. It is believed that this object was the secret divinity of Rāvaṇa, drowned by Rāma in the river Saryu. It is the temple built by Nānya Deva which is now known as that of Taleju.[4] Bista's account is noteworthy for drawing attention to the presence of Taleju at the foundation of the kingdom of Bhaktapur.

These are legends. The so-called conquest of the Valley of Nepal by Harisiṃha is not accepted by many historians. Some say that he never reached Bhaktapur but died on his way there from Dolakha; but the statue of Taleju was brought to Bhaktapur by his followers and made over to Jayarājadeva, king of Tripura (the ancient name of Bhaktapur) and Banepa (which the texts call Bhōta). Thakur Lal Manandhar told me that a manuscript *Gopālarajavamśāvali* states that "it was in Newar era 466, in the month of Māgh, on the third day of the bright fortnight, that the king of Tirhut called Harisiṃha was defeated and his kingdom taken over by Ghiyās-ud din Tughlaq Shah who came and destroyed Simraongarh. For this reason, the king of Tirhut and his ministers fled the country. Some of them afterwards entered our territory, and some went to Rājagāma on the way to Dolakhā. King Harisiṃha died at Tinpāta. His son and his minister were both taken prisoners and asked for refuge".[5]

Whatever the sources consulted, the history of Nepal, from the coming of Harisiṃha up to the begining of the reign of Jayasthitimalla in 1382, is an obscure period of dissensions and rivalries. Seventy years ago S. Lévi pointed out that the genealogy of Jayasthiti Malla has been deliberately falsified by his descendants so as to link it, by direct affiliation, to the family of the Siṃha.[6]

Jayasthiti Malla's reign (1382-95) and indeed the fourteenth century as a whole are very important for the understanding of the social history of the Newar kingdoms of the Valley. Not only was the political situation consolidated but several reforms were also undertaken, the most important of which was the codification of the caste system, a work undertaken with the help and advice of, among others, Rājopādhyāya Brahmins from Tirhut. The historicity of this reform has given rise to endless commentaries: the main problem is the absence of reliable contemporary sources and the consequent necessity of according a certain credence to the notoriously unreliable later chronicles.[7] Be this as it may, L. Petech has stressed that the advisory board of pandits "did not lay emphasis on the classical four *varṇas*, for which there was little justification in the reality of local conditions, but divided outright the people in a series of what in India would have been called subcastes."[8] The need for the codification may have been particularly pressing in view of the arrival in the Valley of immigrants from India, fleeing before the Muslim invasions. S. Lévi gave the names of Jayasthiti's advisory board and stressed "that Harisiṃha was reputed to have brought with him in his entourage seven castes: Brahmins, Bhadelas, Ācāryas, Jaisis, Vaidyas, Rajakas and Khadgis" "The list is significant" wrote S. Lévi: "Harisiṃha, driven out of the regions of the Terai where he was reigning by the Muslims, had taken care to bring with him, to the suspect place of refuge which was still open to him, those indispensable aids to pious life, to wit, the masters of sacred knowledge and the priests of the local divinities for the needs of the soul: and for the body's needs: doctors, laundrymen and butchers; the latter were no less necessary than the former. To confide one's limbs, one's underwear and one's meat to servants not authorized to play their roles, lays one open to risks which are not less than those to which one exposes oneself by neglecting one's most solemn duties. Harisiṃha was anxious to lose neither his soul nor his rank. His Hindu laundrymen and butchers, once introduced to Nepalese society, treated it with the same uncompromising haughtiness as did the Brahmins and Kṣatriyas: relegated by brahmanical law to an infamous rank, they relished nonetheless the honour conferred on them by their appointments: and their example influenced the lower strata in favour of the formation of castes, just as that of the Brahmin had been operative at the top rungs of the social ladder.[9] It is worthy of note that even today the members of the higher castes of Bhaktapur tell you that their ancestors are doubtless those to be found among the Rājopādhyāya Newar Brahmins who came from Mithila.[10]

And the lower castes also insist on their Indian origin. Let us cite the case of the Kasāī (or Nāy, Butchers). Oral tradition attributes to the goddess Taleju the fact that both Buddhist and Hindu Newars eat buffalo-meat. It is said that, when Harisiṃha Deva came up to Nepal in 1324, his army nearly died of hunger on the way: the king invoked Taleju, his protectress, who appeared to him in a vision and authorised him to eat whatever he might find the next morning. At dawn, Harisiṃha saw a wild buffalo, had it caught and brought before the goddess who gave detailed instructions as to how to choose a qualified slaughterer. Such a man was found, who was the ancestor of the Kasāī: he immolated the animal and the goddess allowed its flesh to be eaten.[11]

The originality of the codification attributed to Jayasthiti Malla is that it englobes for the first time all the society. It is certain that Jayasthiti Malla did not invent the caste system. Castes existed in Nepal hundreds of years before his time. Ṭh. Riccardi has recently summarized in an admirable manner the written proofs of their existence. "Several inscriptions" he writes in his analysis of the early medieval period, "use the term *aṣṭadaśaprakṛti* or '18 natures' in a context which is almost certainly relevant to caste. The term possibly refers to a division of peoples into eighteen sub-castes within the *varṇa* structure of four major caste divisions. The divisions are comparable to those of a much later tradition which divides the people of Nepal into four *varṇas* and thirty-six subcastes or *jats.* Unfortunately, none of the eighteen subcastes is named, nor is there any mention of the most important people of later medieval times, the Newars. Elements of their society must have been present, however. The evidence for this is almost entirely linguistic, for while the inscriptions give little evidence that any Indo-Aryan language other than Sanskrit was in use, they contain considerable evidence, mainly place names but administrative terms as well, which indicates that Tibeto-Burman languages were present in the valley at an early date".[12]

It is against this background, and in the context of the recent shaking-up which Newar society had received with the arrival of numerous immigrants from India, fleeing before the Muslim invaders, then that of the Muslim army itself that one should situate Jayasthiti Malla's gesture. The manner in which according to the nineteenth century chronicles which are our main source, he went about codifiying the fluid, unsettled society of his times, is in many respects comparable to the manner in which proceed the authors of other Hindu social blueprints such as the *Puruṣa-sūkta, The Laws of Manu* and the Nepalese *Muluki Ain* of 1853.[13] Jayasthiti Malla began, that is to say, by englobing, in a sort of cultural *pradakṣinā,* not just individual elements in its composition but the whole of that society the existence of which he was prepared to recognize, Hindu as well as Buddhist. Once the circle had been traced around society, and those within it separated from the surrounding barbarian darkness, they themselves were divided up once more into sub-groups whose honour and glory derived, precisely, from their situation within the larger cultural circle. According to the logic on which this system is based, it is better by far to be the servant of someone than a lord among nobodies: and the system, it must be admitted, has a certain cohesive force since it has bound Nepalese society together for many generations. Jayasthiti's effort concentrated on totalizing, in all their variety, the inhabitants of the Valley before assigning to each not only his rank but also his duties and his rights within that society. Before his time, such an effort does not seem to have been made. Names of castes are to be found: but there is no attempt at structural unification. Perhaps the effort was forced on Jayasthiti by the need to bring into the ever-widening sphere of the society he ruled not only orthodox Hindus but also the married Buddhist clergy as well as the rapidly multiplying and self-differentiating artisan classes of the latter faith.

Taleju is not the only Newar divinity who in oral tradition came from India: Matsyendranāth, identified with Lokeśvara, traditionally came from India at the time of Narendra Deva (second half of the seventh century) and is today the Buddhist protective divinity of the Valley. The Buddhist as well as the Hindu *Vaṃśāvalīs* associate Narendra Deva with the introduction of this divinity and even agree as to the date of the occurrence: 523 A.D. S. Lévi has shown that this date is impossible and that it should be corrected to 657 A.D., which does, in fact, coincide with the time of Narendra Deva's reign.[14]

Throughout the Malla period, Taleju is and remains the *Kul devata* of the Malla kings; the king's greatness or his decline as well as the prosperity of his kingdom, depended on her. The original site of Taleju in the Valley is considered as Bhaktapur. In the sixteenth century, the successors of Jayasthiti Malla once more divided the Valley into three kingdoms or rather king's townships for which parallels could be found in northern India. The Taleju temple of Kathmandu was built at the northern end of the Royal Palace (Hunuman Dhoka) at the time of Mahendra Malla (1549) and that of Patan in 1666 by Śrinivas Malla. At Bhaktapur and Patan the Taleju temples form part of the Palace enclaves. The Taleju temple at Kathmandu is a separate building with a pyramidal base, similar to those of Śaivite temples. The temples of Patan and

Kathmandu can be considered as "dédoublements" of that of Bhaktapur.[15]

After the Gorkha conquest of 1768 and the destruction of the Malla kingdoms, the new Shah dynasty adopted as tutelary divinity—as though to legitimate its right to the throne—Taleju. During Dasaim festival, on the seventh day, the day of Phulpati, they have brought from Gorkha to the royal palace in Kathmandu, the *kalāsa* symbolizing Taleju, which is carried by Parbatiya Brahmins.[16]

Bhaktapur, which is a Hindu town, the great majority of its inhabitants being Śivamargi, is still, in spite of recent economic and social changes, a locality which has conserved its traditional religious organization. The town is divided into nine sections, each of these being under the aegis of and vowed to the service of a goddess. The eight mother-goddesses, *Aṣtamātṛkā*, encircle the town with their protection. In their midst, in the middle of other eight sections of the town, is to be found the goddess Tripurasundarī.[17] The side on which her temple (*dyo chẽ*) stands is considered as the religious centre of the town. Oral tradition attributes to Tripurasundarī a role in the foundation of Bhaktapur. It will be recalled that Taleju, in the legend quoted by K.B. Bista, was also instrumental in establishing the town. While Tripurasundrī's presence marks the religious centre of Bhaktapur, Taleju's temple today stands inside the walls of the Darbar Square Palace, and can be considered as the political centre of the town. Many important processions start from the Taleju temple.

It has been clearly shown that, at Bhaktapur, territorial settlement and organization are closely linked to the social hierarchy.[18] Untouchables such as Pode (sweepers and fishermen) dwell outside the town limits. Brahmins and other high-ranking elements live clustered close to the palace whereas the Jyāpus, the bulk of the farming population, occupy intermediary zones. This is undoubtedly true; but it must also be stressed that, in the principal Newar towns, the caste hierarchy is directly related to the presence of the town's main political divinity. For instance, at Patan, where the principal divinity is Matsyendranāth and which is a Buddhist town, the Vajrācāryas occupy a higher position than they do in the Hindu town of Bhaktapur. And the Banre (Sakya and Vajrācārya) occupy at Bhaktapur, according to some Hindu informants, a low rank, and according to others, should even be considered as outside the caste system. The low rank of the Banre is justified by differing arguments: (a) They work with and thus destroy gold. Gold is identified with Viṣṇu. As the Banre are constantly dividing and breaking up Viṣṇu their rank is inevitably low. (b) The ancestor of the Banre is not known. (c) Their low status is evident because they are only allowed into certain courtyards of the Taleju temple at certain dates in the year. Whatever the respective value of such arguments, we must emphasize that even within castes the hierarchy is established in function of the role played in the service of Taleju. For instance, the Suvāl Jyāpus, who are responsible for boiling rice-cakes (*putumi*) for Taleju, rank higher at Bhaktapur than other Jyāpus. The local hierarchy is not linked to the worship of Tripurasundarī: the latter was not the personal protective divinity of those who wielded political power: the Malla kings.

The cult of Taleju remains secret. Even today we have no precise plan of the different courtyards within the palace.[19] These were reputed to be 99 in number: and this sounds like a ritual rather than an actual number. The use that is made of these courtyards in the worship of Taleju cannot be established by direct observation: and one is forced to rely on verbal accounts of Brahmins and members of other castes. What becomes clear from such accounts is that entrance to different parts of the temple-complex, at precise moments in the ritual year, is a carefully regulated right. All the citizens of Bhaktapur, even if they are Hindus, are not free to enter all parts of the temple at any moment. Restrictions on entrance to temples are, of course, known elsewhere. *Pierre Filliozat* has recently edited and translated an interesting eleventh century Śaivite text which clearly illustrates the restrictions imposed on those seeking a *darśana* of the deity within a temple: moreover the upkeep of the temple and the various tasks necessary for the gods' service are often linked, in India, to the individual's position in the caste hierarchy.[20] The same situation is to be found at Bhaktapur and is particularly noteworthy at the time of certain festivals. Access to the various inner-courtyards: Bekochok, Mulchok, Kumarichok, Bhairavachok, Jharunchok, Duimajuchok and Sada śiva chok (which is said to form the *garbhagṛha* of the temple) is restricted on a caste basis. The only day in the year on which the untouchables can enter the temple is Dasaim festival, on the ninth day, when twenty-one buffaloes are slaughtered inside the Taleju temple. All castes, including Untouchables, can then enter the Mulchok courtyard where the sacrifice takes place. This is moreover the only courtyard to which all have access at this time. Access to the *garbhagṛha* is said to be limited to Rājopādhyāya Brahmins, to Taleju Karmācārya and to Taleju Jośi. In former times, the Malla kings who were entiled to a *darśana* of the divinity had an initiation, *dīkśa*, which validated this privilege: none of the so-called descendants of the Malla has the right today to such an initiation. The sword of the Malla kings is, however, still kept alongside the statue of the goddess Taleju. It is their sceptre, symbolizing royal power. On the seventh day of Dasaim, which the Khas call Phulpati day, when the statue of Taleju is brought down from the upper storey, the sword is carried by a Taleju Jośi. The *Bisket Jātrā* festival, which concerns the whole township and which takes place every year in April, is a kind of New Year festival and starts with a procession from Taleju temple, leaving the royal palace. On that occasion the Malla kings used to leave their palace in the procession, carrying the sword. Nowadays it is a Brahmin who, in this instance, carries it.

Normally the sweepers inside the temple are Kusle, the *jāt* of former Jogis who are low in caste but not Untouchables and who, at other moments, make music for the goddess. However, on the ninth day, after the buffalo sacrifice at Dasaim, the Mulchok will be swept and cleaned by Pode, who are, exceptionally, as we have already noted, allowed there at that time.

While it may be true that, in former times, distinctions between castes were more firmly rooted in the occupations they practised than is the case today, one should not always equate occupations with social and ritual roles. The Gāthā, the caste of gardeners, brought and still bring the flowers for Taleju's cult; but, on other occasions, their role in society is to supply earthen pots to other castes; they have moreover other ritual religious duties and dance with the Nava Durgā masks. Quite distinct from its duties at Taleju's temple, a caste may have precise ritual roles to play in Newar society—at marriages, cremations and initiation ceremonies. One might remark that a caste's ritual function in the service of Taleju seems often to have been conserved even when no significance is attached today to its occupational role in society. Generally, in the course of conversation, the occupation of a higher caste person is seldom, if ever, mentioned—whereas that of a lower caste person may, if the circumstances call for it, be recalled contemptuously.

It is perhaps no accident that the codification of the caste system undertaken by Jayasthiti Malla took place after the arrival of Taleju at Bhaktapur, along with the numerous elements, of Indian origin, of the population. During the Malla epoch, the kings of all three towns were in need of Taleju in order to legitimate their authority. And when the Shah dynasty came into the Valley from Gorkha in 1768, they too felt obliged to improvise a ritual worship of Taleju at which, even today, are present not only the Nepalese Administrative Establishment but also the foreign Diplomatic Corps. Nowadays when by its silence, the latest edition of the *Muluki Ain* implies that caste has disappeared from the Nepalese social scene, the social hierarchy in Jayasthiti Malla's former capital Bhaktapur is still, it seems to me, determined, to no little degree, by men's previous roles in the service and worship of Taleju.

Notes

* First published in *Colloques Internationaux des C.N.R.S.* No 582.

1. Th. O. Ballinger, "Simraongarh Revisited: A Report on Some Observations made at the Ruins of the Former Capital of Mithila in the Terai of Nepal", *Kailash* (Kathmandu), Vol. I, No. 3, 1973, pp. 180-85.
2. S. Lévi, *Le Népal, Etude historique d'un royaume hindou.* Paris E. Leroux, 1905, Vol. I, pp. 378-79. M. Allen, *The Cult of Kumari*, Tribhuvan University, Kathmandu, 1975, pp. 48-49: Taleju herself is commonly equated with Durga in her role as protectress of the state, initially of Ram Chandra's kingdom of Ayodhya then of the Karnatic princess of Simraongadh, and finally of the Mallas and Shahas of Nepal.
3. K.B. Bista, *Le culte du Kuldevata au Népal en particulier chez certains Kṣatri de la vallée de Kathmandu,* Paris, Ed. Nove, 1972, Coll. Cahiers Nepalais, p. 59.
4. G. Singh Nepali, *The Newars,* Bombay, United Asia Publications, 1965. The author quotes a similar tradition, in which the principle protagonist is not Nanya Deva but Harisimha (p. 308).
5. The Ms. is that mentioned in Thakur Lal Manandhar "Nepal in its Early Medieval Period: Gleanings from the Bendall Vaṃśavali", *Journal of the Nepal Research Centre* (Kathmandu), Vol. I, 1977, p. 83. I myself have not had access to this manuscript.
6. S.Lévi, *op. cit.,* Vol. II, p. 232. D.R. Regmi, *Medieval Nepal,* Part I, Calcutta, K.L. Mukhopadhyay, 1965, pp. 346-52.
7. D.R. Regmi, *op. cit.*, Part I, pp. 352-60 for the list of documents of Jayasthiti Malla's reign and L. Petech, *Medieval History of Nepal* (750-1480), Roma, 1958, Serie Orientale Roma X. p. 181.
8. L. Petech, *op. cit.*, p. 180.
9. S. Lévi, *op.cit.*, Vol. I, p. 229.
10. M. Witzel, Zur Geschichte der Rajopadhyaya von Bhaktapur, *Folia Rara,* Wolfgang Vogt LXV Diem Natalem Celebranti, Wiesbaden, F. Steiner, 1976, pp. 159-79.
11. G. Singh Nepali, *op. cit.*, p. 176.
12. Th. Riccardi, Buddhism in Ancient and Early Medieval Nepal, Ms. pp. 3-4.
13. A.W. Macdonald, *Essays on the Ethnology of Nepal and South Asia,* Kathmandu, Ratna Pustak Bhandar, 1975, pp. 74-75 and 288, note 7
14. S. Lévi, *op.cit.*, Vol II, p. 163. S. Dasgupta, *Obscure Religious Cults,* Calcutta, F.L. Mukhopadhyay, 1969, pp. 382-91.
15. L. Dumont, *Une sous-caste de l'Inde du Sud*, Paris, Mouton, 1957. Chap. "Le culte des dieux" pp. 316-72.
16. Mary M. Anderson, *The Festivals of Nepal,* London, G. Allen and Unwin, 1971, p. 147.
17. G. Auer and N. Gutschow, *Bhaktapur, Gestalt, Funktionen und religiöse*

Symbolik einer nepalischen Stadt in vor-industriellen Entwicklungstadium, Darmstadt, Technische Hochschule, 1974.

18. N. Gutschow and B. Kölver, *Ordered Space, Concepts and Functions in a Town in Nepal*, Wiesbaden, Franz Steiner Verlag, 1975.
19. W. Korn, *The Traditional Architecture of the Kathmandu Valley*, Kathmandu, Ratna Pustak Bhandar, 1976, p. 59.
20. P.S. Filliozat, Le droit d'entrer dans les temples de Śiva au XIe siècle in *Journal Asiatique*, tome CCLXIII (1975), fasc. 1 et 2, pp. 103-19.

The Religious Associations (*Guṭhi*) of Kathmandu Valley Temples*

General Features of "*Guṭhi*"

One of the characteristic features of Newar social organization in the Kathmandu Valley is its corporate life. The visitor is immediately struck by the great diversity of religious associations (*guṭhi*), of which some work to organize various festivals, others to maintain the worship of a given lineage or regional god, and still others to take charge of funerals. Lastly, there are those whose task it is to protect, at a regional or caste level, the professional integrity of the caste as a corporate group. Each of these associations is attached to a temple or shrine,[1] which is at once a meeting place for and a common link between the members of the association. Three types of associations emerge out of the various kinds of organizations in this context. These are (a) lineage associations (*digu pūjā guṭhi*) connected with lineage temples, which are nearly always private associations; (b) those linked to a caste, such as the association serving to take charge of funeral rites, the *guṭhi* of the dead (Newari: *śii guṭhi*); and (c) those in which residence is the prime criterion for membership: this is the case with neighbourhood or regional temples, in which the *guṭhi* thus bears the name of the god with which it is connected.

The Newari word *guṭhi* corresponds to the Sanskrit *goṣthi*, and means "assembly, association".[2] In Nepal, the term has the technical sense of "religious association". Such are mentioned as far back as the Licchavi period (fifth to eighth centuries).[3] Documentary evidence indicates that these religious associations were not only a feature of Hindu temples and *māth*, but also of the Buddhist monasteries of this period. The desire to accumulate spiritual merit by performing charitable acts was the original reason for the creation of the *guṭhi*. At the time of a temple or monastery's foundation, donations of land were made to finance the celebration of specific rites or for building maintenance. People from every walk of life made such donations, at times very generous donations, to the temples of their choice. In ancient and medieval Nepal—that is, in the Valley—as in India, the term *guṭhi* appears to have been employed to designate an administrative council whose task it was to manage donations made to religious or philanthropic ends: it did not designate the donations themselves (Bose 1942:82). These donations to the *guṭhi* generally took the form of parcels of land, since land ensured permanent revenues and rural wealth and products.

Even today, the wealthiest of these associations are found in the Valley and, in the southern Terai country, in the Bara, Parsa, Rautahat, Sarlahi, Mahottari, Saptari and Morang districts. In Mahottari district, Janakpur, the mythical birthplace of Sītā, is one of the wealthiest of Nepal's temples. There is no proof that the system of religious associations came into being, outside the Valley, prior to 1768, the year in which the Gorkhas conquered the Valley (Regmi 1967: 4:3). Originally, the term *guṭhi* was not employed outside the Valley: it was during the nineteenth century that the institution gradually proliferated to cover the entire country.

After 1768, those Valley *guṭhi* able to retain their lands became few and far between: a large portion of the landed wealth of the Newars was confiscated at the end of the eighteenth century by the new Shah dynasty. In the nineteenth century, the Rāṇa families, who ruled the country for a century, also expropriated a great number of *guṭhi* landholders to finance the construction of palaces. At present, donations for temple maintenance and reconstruction take the form of gifts of land, as well as currency and religious objects. During the Malla period (1200-1786), every house was required to provide a fixed quantity of grain, levied by the king in order to pay for carrying out a ceremony in a certain neighbourhood. Legislation dating from 1953 defined the *guṭhi* as associations for the administration of real and personal estates, or of money used to finance religious or philanthropic undertakings. It is thus the donor's intentions that determine whether his donation does or does not fall under the *guṭhi* system. *Guṭhi* revenues are moreover not subject to taxation.

Every religious association has its own principal divinity and is attached to a temple or shrine, which is the place where its members come together. The *guṭhi* are also financial corporations which possess wealth and to which members pay annual dues in order to cover the association's costs, their priest's salary, temple upkeep, and the annual banquet which falls at the time of the divinity's festival. Whenever the inhabitants of the Valley speak of a *guṭhi*, the implication is that its association owns lands which it farms out for cultivation to tenants, who are generally members of the Jyāpū, or agricultural caste.

Each *guṭhi*, whether it be a lineage-, caste-, or temple-based association, is possessed of a highly developed hierarchical organization. In the lineage- and caste-based *guṭhi*, kinship rules predominate. The head of the association is the oldest lineage or caste member: he is called the *nayo* (Newari) or *thakali* (Nepali), which means "leader". He is assisted in his functions by three, five or seven subordinates, who are respectively designated, according to their age, by the titles of *noku* (the second), *soku* (third), *pyeuku* (fourth), *nyaku* (fifth), *khuku* (sixth) and *nheku* (seventh). The case is different in temple associations: the principle of seniority is not operative here, and functions are hereditary. The seniority principle comes into play at such times as members of a given lineage come to inherit various functions. In the case of a temple, it is a member of the priest's lineage, generally his eldest son, who is expected to succeed him. In the case of a Hindu monastery, a *māṭh,* the succession is effected from master to disciple. The hierarchy of a lineage- or caste-based *guṭhi* plays an important role at the time of annual feasts in which all the association members come together, and in which the ritual distribution of the sacrificial animal occurs.[4] Either the *nayo* or the *thakali* receives the right eye of the sacrificed animal: this signifies that they or he alone have the power of decision. In the lineage-based *guṭhi,* if the *nayo* dies, it is the *nokuli,* second in the association hierarchy, who succeeds him: the other members are not considered.

Internal discipline is maintained by means of a system of fines paid into the *guṭhi* coffers. These fines are levied if a member fails to pay his annual fees, if he does not attend the association's feasts and festivals, and if he fails to fulfil his functions. The ultimate penalty is exclusion from the *guṭhi*: at present, this especially occurs when a *guṭhi* member marries or cohabits with an untouchable woman, or if he becomes afflicted with a serious disease, such as leprosy.

Caste or lineage-based *guṭhi* constitute a means for social control. Thus a painter is obliged to belong to the painters' caste association, and a farmer to the association of agriculturalists. As for the Untouchables, they too have numerous associations which vary according to their place in the local hierarchy. Membership in funerary or neighbourhood temple associations is hereditary; it thus appears to be theoretically impossible for a person to change *guṭhi.* In practice, however, this obstacle may be overcome in one of two ways: one may either change one's address and become accepted into a new caste or neighbourhood association by paying higher than normal fees; or one may take a wife from a higher caste. It is thus easier to be accepted into a new *guṭhi* than it is to marry a woman from a caste higher than one's own (Rosser 1966:97). We should add that in practice, a person who enters into a hypergamic marriage is often required to change addresses, since his in-laws will not accept him into their lineage-based *guṭhi*.

Survey of Works on "*Guṭhi*"

A historical and economic study of the system of religious association has been undertaken by M.C. Regmi. He analyses religious donations made to temples on the basis of documents from the nineteenth and twentieth centuries. However, a history of Malla age (1200-1768) *guṭhi* systems remains to be written. Regmi sets up a primary distinction between public and private donations. Traditionally, gifts of land to the *guṭhi* are classified according to their donors: if the donor was a king, this was a *rāj guṭhi*; if he was a private individual, this was a private association, a *dunya guṭhi*. This distinction has lost its former significance, since the term *rāj guṭhi* today designates all donations of lands controlled by the state. Moreover, the distinction between private associations and public associations under state control is one that is constantly drawn by inhabitants of the Valley.

Donations of land made to the *guṭhi* are theoretically irrevocable and permanent. In the eighteenth and nineteenth centuries however, several parcels of land belonging to *guṭhi* were confiscated by the state and converted into *rāj guṭhi*. From an administrative standpoint, donations to the *rāj guṭhi* may be classified under two headings: *amanat* include *guṭhi* under the direct control of the government, and *chut* include lands set apart for temporary use by an individual. This distinction goes back to the nineteenth century. According to Regmi, the creation of the *chut guṭhi* was made necessary by a clause, stipulated in the certificate of donation, that attributed to its beneficiary the right to administer the *guṭhi* while alive, and to pass that right on to his descendants. Sometimes, a *rāj guṭhi* could be administered as a *chut guṭhi*, in cases in which the individual who took it over incurred personal expenses for

Plate 1. A general view of the town of Bhaktapur from roof tops of the house.

Plate 2. Thakur Lal Manandhar at Bhaktapur, 1981.

Plate 3. Ramapatiraj Rajopadhyaya at Bhaktapur during the festival of Nag Panchami.

Plate 4. The King Bhupatindra Malla (1699-1722) facing the temple of the royal goddess Taleju at Bhaktapur

Plate 8. A girl decked with ornaments during the ritual marriage (*ihi*) at Thimi.

Plate 9. The construction of the *maṇḍala* by the Bhuddhist priest (*vajrācārya*) Bhadri Guruji at Thĩmi.

Plate 10. A father with his daughters in his lap during the ritual marriage (*ihi*).

Plate 11. The temple of Akāśa Bhairava, the main god during the festival of Bisket *jātrā* at Bhaktapur.

Plate 12. The main entrance of the temple of Akāśa Bhairava at Bhaktapur.

Plate 13. The main entrance of the royal temple Nyatapola at Bhaktapur.

Plate 14. Offerings made by a *karmācārya* at a sanctuary of the lineage, *digu dya* during the annual festival at Bhaktapur.

Plate 15. The ritual meal which concludes the annual festival of the lineage (*digu dya puja*), Bhaktapur.

Plate 16. Procession of the Rajopadhyaya Brahmins leaving the Taleju temple carrying the sword of the former Malla kings for the opening of the festival of Bisket *jātrā*, Bhaktapur.

Plate 17. The procession of the chariot of Akāśa Bhairava during the festival of Bisket *jātrā* at Bhaktapur.

Plate 18. The offerings made to Akāśa Bhairava during the festival of Bisket *jātrā*.

Plate 19. Animal sacrifices on the third day of Bisket *jātrā*.

Plate 20. The mast erected on fourth day of Bisket *jātrā*. The banners represent the two snakes killed by the prince who founded the town and the kingdom of Bhaktapur.

Plate 21. Worship of Akāśa Bhairava at Hanumante river, Cyasilm *maṇḍapa*, Bhaktapur.

Plate 22. The author with Bal Gopal Baidya and the Nava Durga dancers at Bhaktapur.

Plate 23. The chariot carried by the Nava Durga dancers at Bhaktapur.

Plate 24. Musicians playing during the festival of Buddha Dipaṇkara.

Plate 25. The procession of the effigy of Buddha Dipaṇkara carried by a *vajrācārya* during the festival of Buddha Dipaṇkara in the month of August.

Plate 26. The procession of five effigies of Buddha Dipaṇkara at Bhaktapur.

Plate 27. Narrative painting (vilampu) illustrating the festival of Red Avalokiteśvara (or Bunga Dyo) at Patan, dated AD 1721 (2,20 length. Private collection, Paris).

Plate 28. Details of the painted scrol (*vilampu*) illustrating the legend of the Red Avalokiteśvara; the top row shows the king of Patan, Mahendra Malla, and the priests worshopping Amoghapaśa in the ritual commonly known as *aṣṭamivrata*. The second row shows the celestial chariot (*vahana*) on the way to Amitabha heaven. The third row shows the chariot procession of Red Avalokiteśvara (or Bunga Dyo) at Patan.

Plate 29. The temple of Red Avalokiteśvara (or Bunga Dyo) at Patan.

repair of the temple. The *chut guṭhi* system is in fact a compromise between the individual management of *guṭhi* and their control by the state. It thus reconciles individual control with authoritarian state administration. Only those *guṭhi* enjoying a large surplus of funds may be called *amanat guṭhi.* No *rāj guṭhi* have been clssified as *amanat,* which is to say that none are placed under direct state control so long as their wealth is sufficient to produce a surplus.

In his work, Regmi especially analyses the composition and utilization of *guṭhi* income, as well as nineteenth century relations between the *guṭhi* and state policy. He emphasizes the important changes that occurred in the nineteenth century, and shows how state appropriation of *guṭhi* lands was effected throughout the Rāṇa régime, starting in 1806 and continuing in the decades that followed. The government policies of the Shah dynasty in the nineteenth and twentieth centuries attempted to limit the expenses of the *rāj guṭhi* and *guṭhi* attached to temples—which explains the diminution and impoverishment of festivals in the Valley. Often, temple treasures consisting of ornaments, jewellery, etc. were pillaged by the kings, who used monies gained from them for military expenses. At the time of the1964 agrarian reforms, a national corporation of *guṭhi* (Guṭhi Samsthān) was created. This new legalization, whose aim it was to better control *guṭhi* revenues on a local level, nevertheless left the traditional structures in place.[5] The 1972 legislation (Guṭhi Corporation Act) abolished the system of donations to the *chut guṭhi* and defined the powers and functions of the Guṭhi Samsthān (Regmi 1976:70).

The first ethnologist to draw attention to the importance of the *guṭhi* system in the Newar social system was C. von Fürer-Haimendorf (1956). He showed the importance of the lineage-based associations (*digu pūjā guṭhi*) and gave a detailed description of the Manandhar, the oil-presser caste association of the Valley. The Manandhar caste is divided into seven *sa,* with the word *sa* designating a social unit based on domicile. Each unit has a role to play in the preparation of the *shingu guṭhi* festival which brings together all members of the Manandhar caste. The first *sa* attends to the organization of the feast, the second to liquid refreshments, the third to the preparation of the food, the fourth to milk curd and to the serving of the food, the fifth to meat, the sixth to rice flakes, and the seventh to vegetables.

In his 1966 article on social mobility in Newar society, C. Rosser gave a long description of the *guṭhi* of Buddhist priests (*vajrācārya*) in Kathmandu. The association is directed by a council of eighteen leaders (*thakali*), each of whom represents a Buddhist monastery in Kathmandu. The exclusive loci for the initiation rites of these priests' sons (*ācārya luyegu*) are Kathmandu's eighteen principal monasteries. These celebrations effect the admission of these boys into the monastic community (*saṃgha*), and so allow them to take on priestly functions. This caste association—the *ācārya guṭhi*—is the principal means for social control among Kathmandu's Buddhist priests. Each priest has a given number of families as his *jajman*. A set of arrangements within the association bars all unfair competition between priests, and takes sanctions against members who fail to abide by the rules. Expulsion from the association not only means social humiliation for the expelled individual and a sudden drop in his family's social standing vis-a-vis the *vajrācārya*'s other families, but also the disappearance of a particular priestly lineage. C. Rosser emphasizes the fact that one of the conditions that had to be fulfilled in order to change one's status in the social hierarchy was acceptance into a new association.

A very general description of the *guṭhi* system is found in a monograph by G. Singh Nepali (1966: 191-97). The author underscores the fact that the *guṭhi* system is a feature peculiar to the Newars, a feature which differentiates them from the Indo-Nepalese ethnic groups. He provides a list of the Manandhars, the oil-pressing *guṭhi* of the Kathmandu Valley, but the order in which he presents these is arbitrary. Like C.

Rosser, G. Singh Nepali shows that the lineage-based *guṭhi* and the *guṭhi* of the dead are means to social control which simultaneously serve to perpetuate caste norms.

Even more recently, G. Toffin (1982) devoted a chapter of his *thèse d'État* to religious associations. This chapter is in two parts: first, there is a detailed description of the two *guṭhi* of the temples of Brahmāyāṇī and of Bal Kumārī in the village of Theco: then follows a description of the painter's caste *guṭhi* in Bhaktapur (Toffin 1975). The two Theco village temple *guṭhi*, of which the first is called the "Brahmāyaṇī *guṭhi*" and the second the "Bal Kumārī *guṭhi*", manage the religious monuments consecrated to the goddesses Brahmāyaṇī and Bal Kumārī respectively, and ensure their regular worship. Their members are all inhabitants of Theco village. "Each association is endowed with a highly developed hierarchical structure. Here, place of residence and locality are the dominant parameters. Kinship relations are thus reduced to territorial relationships. Membership in these *guṭhi* is founded on the basis of neighbourhoods, or more precisely, on the divisions of inhabited space" (Toffin 1982: 286).

As for the Bhaktapur painters' caste, G. Toffin distinguishes between two forms of *guṭhi*: the *guṭhi* of the dead and local *guṭhi*. The *guṭhi* of the dead are neither controlled by lineage nor clan. Members of the association are not bound together by patrilineal kinship ties, and may marry among themselves so long as they respect the matrimonial prohibitions observed by their castes. The local *guṭhi* (*deśla guṭhi*) is of lesser importance, but it is also a means for social control, since it is a corporate group. A suggested comparison between town and village *guṭhi* remains only minimally convincing because it compares a village temple association with a town painters' caste association, and only concerns a small part of the town. In the town of Bhaktapur, for example, membership in a lineage-based *guṭhi* is based on kinship, whereas membership in a temple *guṭhi* is based on place of residence, just as in Theco village. In order to make such a generalization an acceptable one, it would be necessary to draw a comparison between such temple religious associations as those of Brahmāyaṇī and Bal Kumārī, and that of the temple of a known locality, that of Akāśa Bhairava or of Taleju for example.

We will see later in this study that the temple *guṭhi* do not all carry the same political weight; and that it is essential to distinguish between neighbourhood or local temples on the one hand, and royal temples on the other. A few observations on the Newar kingship of the Malla and its relationships with temples may thus enable us to better understand the ethnographic analysis of a case which largely appertains to it. This is the case of the royal temple of the Hindu goddess Taleju at Bhaktapur.

Royal Temples

The majority of royal temples are found in the Valley's three main towns—Kathmandu (or Kāntipura), Patan (or Lalitpura) and Bhaktapur (or Bhatgaon)—which were former capitals of the three Malla kingdoms. The Malla kings were Hindus, Hinduism having been the state religion since the fourth century A.D., and Buddhism only coexisting alongside it. Ideally, the Royal Palace was located at the centre of every town. A large space was laid out in front of the palace for the observation of public ceremonies. Religious monuments, generally linked to royal foundations, were also erected on these sites.

Among the many temples of the Valley, there are two that have been especially attached to kingship and to the idea of royal power: these are the temple of Paśupatināth, a form of Śiva; and that of the goddess Taleju, the tutelary divinity of the old Malla dynasty and that of the contemporary Shah dynasty. Founded in the fourth century, the temple of Paśupatināth played a considerable role in the Valley's political and religious life. Towards the ninth century, Paśupati became the "state divinity" and the god's official functions are elucidated in numerous documents. However, if we look at archaeological vestiges from a time prior to the seventh century, we find that Vaiṣṇavism generally dominated the kingdoms of the Valley in this time. During the Malla period, all of the kings were identified, under the name of Nārāyaṇa, as individuals dedicated to Viṣṇu, whereas kingship, or more precisely the royal function, were under the patronage of Śiva, in his Paśupati form. "Paśupati is the political incarnation of Nepal just as Matsyendranāth is its popular incarnation. Every dynasty, down to the Gurkhas themselves, has treated him with equal respect and equal fervour" (Lévi 1905: 2:360). Several inscriptions and manuscripts designate the king of Nepal as one who is king by the grace of Paśupati:

> In the year NS 502 (1382 A. D.) Paśupati was addressed in an inscription as the sovereign lord of Nepal, "Nepalādhipati". Evidently, Paśupati's role has developed from that of the rulers' divine patron to that of a national god, a new function which is reflected in the historiography of the later chronicles. There, the national life is identified with the history of the Paśupatināth temple and with the deity. Indeed, the only fact worth recording about many of the obscurer rulers of early times was some donation they made to the temple (Weisner 1978: 10).

During the Malla age, Paśupatināth symbolized the state. When the Valley was split into the three kingdoms, at the end of the fifteenth century, the three kings felt the need for the construction of a temple dedicated to Paśupatināth, in each of their capitals, as a means to legitimating their power. In fact, the Paśupatināth temples that were built in the three capitals—Bhaktapur, Kathmandu and Patan—are replicas of the original Deopatan temple (Wiesner 1978: 12-18). The first of these was constructed at Bhaktapur by king Yakṣamalla in the fifteenth century. The second, that of Kathmandu, was begun by king Mahendreśvara and was completed in the middle of the eighteenth century by king Pratapa Malla. At Patan, the temple of Kumbheśvara was an older foundation than the Kathmandu temple, but it was not made into a royal temple and dedicated to Paśupatināth until the end of the fifteenth century. The names given to these temples are formed from the name of their royal builder, to which was appended the term *iśvara.* Adjacent to the Paśupatināth temple we find, as is frequently the case in Nepal, a temple of the goddess. This is the main shrine of the goddess Guhyeśvarī, situated on the bank of the Bagmati river. "For the common man, Guhyeśvarī was the manifestation of the saving mother, the deliverer" (Lienhard 1978:258). To all appearances, there exists no direct link between royal power and the shrine of the goddess Guhyeśvarī. The ritual relationship that is established between the two goddesses Guhyeśvarī and Taleju during festival times may, however, point us towards the goddess's relationships with kingship. Relations between the shrines of Guhyeśvarī and Taleju are poorly known, since Guhyeśvarī's festival involves rites which are tantric, and thus secret. This annual festival occurs on the tenth day of the bright half of the lunar month falling in November/December. At this time, devotees bear offerings to the goddess's temple at Deopatan. The *kalaśa* representing the goddess Guhyeśvarī never leaves her temple. According to certain informants, the *kalaśa* carried from the Kathmandu temple of Taleju to that of Guhyeśvarī in Deopatan represents the goddess Taleju herself. The *kalaśa* is transported , during the night, in great secrecy.[6] On no occasion is there any identification of Guhyeśvarī with Kulai or with Taleju: there are three different forms of the goddess (Lienhard 1978:259). I will return later to the hierarchical relations obtaining between various divinities during their festivals.

Today the wealthiest temple in the Valley is that of Paśupatināth at Deopatan. "The most influential functionary from the point of view of land assignment is the chief priest of Paśupatināth temple with approximately 285 *ropanis* and additional perquisites in various forms" (Regmi 1967: 4:182).[7] The *mahābrāhmaṇa*, the temple's head priest, has direct relations with the king of the present dynasty. The temple is not subject to the statutes of the Guṭhi Samsthān. The functioning of the Paśupatināth *guṭhi* is poorly known: nevertheless, I was not permitted to study it, and I was unable to come into direct contact with the temple priests, who are Bhaṭṭa brahmans.

The Religious Associations of the Bhaktapur Temples

The major portion of my fieldwork was carried out at Bhaktapur, a town which, located in the eastern part of the valley, has preserved its traditional religious and social structure.[8] The investigation I undertook at Bhaktapur enabled me to distinguish the features that set a royal temple association, notably that of Taleju, apart from other religious associations. I studied different categories of religious associations: these included that of a royal temple, that of Taleju, that of a neighbourhood temple (in the western part of the town dedicated to the goddess Indrāyaṇī), and that of a Hindu high-caste lineage. I was most interested by the social features of these associations. Who are the priests and other persons incharge? What are the relationships between them? What are the aims of the associations? In spite of the confiscation of their lands, the religious associations have in fact retained their traditional structures.

The town of Bhaktapur is ideally conceived as a *maṇḍala* in the form of a lotus: it is divided into nine parts, with each part being designated by the name of a goddess. The open shrines (Skt. *piṭha*: Newari *pith*) of the eight goddesses are placed around the city at its four cardinal and four intermediary points. To the east is Brahmāyaṇī, to the south-east Maheśvari, to the south Kaumārī, to the southwest Vaiṣṇavī (or Bhadrakalī), to the west Vārāhī, to the northwest Indrāyaṇī, to the north Mahākalī (or Cāmuṇḍa), and to the northeast is Mahālakṣmi. In the midst of these eight goddesses is the goddess

Tripurasundarī and so hers is the only open shrine (*pīṭh*) situated within the town limits. The inhabitants of the town are required to make daily offerings in the quarter in which they reside, i.e. persons living in the eastern part of the town do not go to the southern quarter in order to offer their devotion. As for the cremation of the dead and the burial of newborn children who have died, these rites must also take place in the shrine of one's own neighbourhood goddess.

The open shrines (*piṭha*) define the limits of the inhabited space, thus forming a symbolic enclosing wall around the town. Those shrines of the goddess (*dyo chẽ*) which are located within the town limits organize its inhabited space. Here, it is important to emphasise that this religious organization of the town is said to have been established, according to oral tradition, by the kings of the Malla dynasty.

The goddess Tripurasundarī, whose shrine is situated in the heart of the town, is the goddess whom legend credits with having founded the town, along with king Anandadeva, in the twelfth century.[9] The local legend relates that she is the oldest goddess in the town. Certain texts maintain that, until the sixteenth century, the town was called Tripura (Slusser 1978:124). The fact that the town was founded by a goddess with the help of a king is not a feature unique to Bhaktapur: we find the same legend at Patan and at Kathmandu, with only the names of the king and goddess being changed. We might suggest that this is a particular feature of Newar representations of society. While it is the religious centre of the town, the Tripurasundarī temple has but little importance for local religious life. If we look at the relationships that are established between the gods during the *Bisket Jātrā* or *Dasaim* festivals, we find Tripurasundarī subordinated to the goddess Taleju.

The distinction between private temple and public temple is one that is always noted by the inhabitants of the town. The public temples are controlled by the state, more exactly by the Guṭhi Samsthān, whose task it is to administer the temples and the cultural heritage of the country. The private temples are, as a general rule, lineage-based or neighbourhood temples having few lands or resources. A second distinction may be drawn between neighbourhood temples (*dyo-chẽ*)– which are generally dedicated to the goddess, to Gaṇeśa or to Nārāyaṇa and play an important role in the local religious life–and temples of a locality such as those of the goddess Taleju or Akāśa Bhairava. The former only concern the inhabitants of a neighbuorhood, as opposed to the latter, which are frequented by the entire populace. In order that it may function, each temple needs to have a religious association to organize its annual festival, maintain its buildings, and afford the costs of its daily *pūjā* (*nityā pūjā*).

If one asks the inhabitants for a complete list of the town's temples, they generally classify these according to the musical instrument played in them. So, the first category includes those temples in which the nine musical instruments are played (Newari: *naubhajan data*).[10] All of these temples–Taleju, Bhairav Nāth (or Akāśa Bhairava), Bhadrakālī, Yache Gaṇeśa, Dattatreya, Waku Pati Nārāyaṇa, and Gache Nārāyaṇa–are royal foundations. The next category includes temples in which a group of instruments called the *Dhalcha Bhajan* is played.[11] The third category, the *Dhalcha Bhajan*, are instruments that only Jyāpū can play. The members of a temple religious association join regularly to play or listen to music in the evening. The musicians of the royal temples are Kusle or Jogi, former ascetics who have today become tailor- musicians who play an important role in funerary rites.[12] They also play in other temples on the occasion of important festivals. They are paid with land revenues granted to them by the king. For example, the Kusle of the Suryavinayak temple in the Bhaktapur have five or six *ropani* per group of ten persons, plus 3.5 *ropani* given to the community as a whole, for the celebrations of community festivals (Regmi 1967: 4:83). The Kusle of certain temples have been accorded the additional social privilege of receiving food and contributions from people living around the temples in which they play their music. In a temple such as

Taleju, they have the status of royal functionaries.

All of the *guṭhi* lands of royal temples today belong to the state. The Guṭhi Samsthān organization at Bhaktapur controls the revenues of each royal *guṭhi* and has very detailed lists of the expenses required at the time of the great festivals: these are *Bisket Jātrā* (from early March to April) and the goddess's festival (October-November). They know the precise quantity of rice, lamp oil, clarified butter, etc. necessary for these festivals. The tenants of the Taleju temple *guṭhi*, who are generally farmers (Jyāpū), must pay the Guṭhi Samsthān approximately thirty-two measures of rice per *ropani* of land.

Two local temples are very active throughout the year: these are the temples of Taleju and of Bhairava Nātha (or Akāśa Bhairava). The Taleju temple *guṭhi* includes members of various castes, all of whom live in Bhaktapur. Persons living in Kathmandu or Patan may not take part. The members of the Taleju *guṭhi* are called *rakami* and not *guṭhiyar*, which is the term employed for lineage-based or funerary associations. The *rakami* are persons whose duty it is to accomplish a particular ritual task. The term, however, is not limited to the context of royal temples. The term *rakam* designates all of the services and unpaid labour the king may demand of his subjects for public ends (Regmi 1976:156-62). In the case of the caste-based *guṭhi*, as with that of the *guṭhi* of the dead, the members have obligations to one another. More than anything else, these are mutual support systems. Contrariwise, in the case of temple-based *guṭhi*, the primary obligation of the members is towards the divinity. Each member has specific duties, for which he receives payment in money or foodstuffs from the Guṭhi Samsthān. During the Malla period, brahmans and officiants received donations of land. A member of the Taleju temple *guṭhi* must resign if he marries or lives with an Untouchable woman, but marriage with a woman of lower status does not result in exclusion as it does in lineage-based *guṭhi* (*digu pūjā guṭhi*), in which marriage regulations are very strict. If a man suffers some sort of bodily deformity, or if he comes down with some contagious disease, leprosy in particular, he must leave the association.

Whenever the question of who it was who originally decided upon the distribution of duties within the temple is asked, the response is always the same: it was the Malla kings. If the names of these kings differ from one informant to another, all affirm that the king alone was capable of deciding on temple organization and distribution of temple duties. On every major festival, the temple *guṭhi*'s tenants were required to provided rice, oil, fruits, flowers, and wood. The quantities to be supplied for each *pūjā* were formerly determined by the Malla kings, and they remain the same down to the present day. It appears that in the Malla period, the king supplemented these donations of money and food, at the time of the major festivals, in order to insure that these were carried out smoothly. The money was used to renovate the costumes for example those of the Nava Durga dancers, and to pay for the feast and carry out temple restorations. Often the town dwellers, especially those concerned with the organization of the *Bisket Jātrā* festival, complain that the current dynasty does not give enough money for the festivals. One is struck by the similarities between the activities ordered by the Malla kings of Nepal and those described by H.L. Seneviratne, at Kandy, for the Buddhist Daladā Māligāva temple: here he speaks of the temple functionaries and describes the role they play in the rituals:

> There is a second type of worship, which offers a contrast to the first (worship of the pious). The people who engage in this are appointed for the purpose: they are "officials" and not "worshippers". It follows that this second type of worship has been instituted by a higher authority at some stage in the history of the Temple: and we know that this authority was the king. The offerings of this category of worshippers–whether it be food or flowers or incense or light–are not provided by them, but by others who are

> themselves officials in the system of Temple ritual. The act of offering itself and the preparations immediately preceding it are the only acts performed by this category of worshippers. These acts are also subject to an elaborate division of labor. These functionaries are "paid worshippers" paid to perform ritual. Some of them are nowadays paid in cash, but in Kandyan times they were all paid in land, and some still are. The "worship" of these people is referred to as "work" (väda) or "duty to the king" (*rājakariva*) (Seneviratne 1978:26).

The situation at Bhaktapur is an analogous one because the functions are not only hereditary for the priests, but also for all those who have duties to fulfil. Such is the case, for example, for the farmers (Suwal Jyāpū) who are cooks and who prepare the rice offered to the god, for the butchers (Nay or Kasai) who sacrifice the animal victims during the ceremonies, for the musicians (Kusle), for the gardeners (Gāthā) who cultivate the flowers offered to the divinity, and so on (Vergati Stahl (1978):166-67). If an association member does not have a son capable of succeeding him, the task falls to his older brother, his younger brother (Newari: *deju kija*) or to a member of his lineage. The principle of seniority comes into play at the level of lineage, but not for the association as a whole.

The Taleju temple *guṭhi* is endowed with a highly developed hierarchical structure. Only the Jośi (astrologers), the *karmācārya* and the Rajopadhyāyā brahmans who have taken initiation (*dīkṣā*) have the right to see the goddess's statue. The presence of these three categories is required for the major *pūjā*, whereas for daily *pūjā* (*nitya pūjā*), the *karmācārya* alone is present. These three categories constitute that group which has access to the *garbhagṛha*, and are the "inner group" (New.: *dune*) in contrast to an "outer" group (New.: *pīne*), which is composed of all the other ritual participants. At the time of my investigations, in 1981, the Taleju temple *guṭhi* head was Jośi Prasad, who had inherited his function from his father. The *guṭhi* head's primary role is an administrative one, his task consisting of overseeing that the oil, clarified butter and rice necessary to the *pūjā* be supplied at the proper times by the Guṭhi Samsthān. He never takes an important decision without consulting with the temple's head brahman, who is considered to be the main priest. What is the relationship of the priest to the *jośi* who is the *guṭhi* head? At the time of such major festivals as Dasāī, the festival of the goddess, a buffalo is sacrificed, following which its bodily parts are distributed according to the local caste hierarchy (Toffin 1981:72), with the animal's head being consumed by the association leaders. As is the case at every Newar feast, the sacrificial victim's right eye is to be given to the leader, to the person who makes all the important decisions, who has authority. In this particular case, it is the priest, the brahman and not the *guṭhi* head–who eats the right eye. This fact is significant inasmuch as it clearly demonstrates that the *nayo* of a *raj guṭhi* is no more than an administrator: therefore, it is the priest who has the authority.

What is particular about the Taleju temple is that, in addition to the great festivals, major *pūjā* (New.: *tha*[13] *pūjā*) are celebrated there twice each month. These *pūjā* are unusual in many respects. First of all, their dates were not established for religious reasons: according to the temple priests, they were fixed by the Malla kings. Such and such a king, for example, on the occasion of his birthday, made a donation of land to the temple: the revenues from this were then used to cover the costs of one of these *tha pūjā*, to promote the prosperity of the king and the kingdom. Even today, the Guṭhi Samsthān maintains a detailed list of the number of *ropani* of the lands donated by each king, and of the place in which they are located. A second particularity of these *tha pūjā* is that the blood sacrifice (of a water buffalo, six black male goats and a duck) that is its pivotal moment takes place before an aniconic substitute for the goddess–rather than before the statue of Taleju herself–which is located on the second storey of the temple. This substitute is a black stone bearing the name

Duimaju. She is carried in procession at the time of *Bisket Jātrā*, remaining at all other times beneath a shelter in the temple's main courtyard. As for the statue of Taleju, it is never carried in procession outside of the temple. In her aniconic form, the goddess Duimaju is not located on the town limits but in the courtyard of the temple itself, in spite of the general rule by which goddesses' aniconic forms are to be situated in open shrines outside the city limits. In spite of the dynastic change that occurred in 1768, the celebration of these *tha pūjā* is still considered to be a commemoration of the Malla kings who founded them. This shows that the Taleju temple is first and foremost a lineage temple of the Malla dynasty. It functions as a tantric lineage temple (*āgam chẽ*). At the same time however, it is the temple of locality: as a royal temple, it is the temple at which every religious festival observed in common by the entire Bhaktapur populace begins. In this sense, we might consider it to be the town's political centre. Two examples will suffice to bear this out: the *Bisket Jātrā* festival which is the great local festival of Bhaktapur, only begins after the Taleju temple priest, wearing his traditional white robes and carrying the Malla sword in his hand, has gone out of the temple and seated himself in the chariot of the festival's main divinity, Akāśa Bhairava. During the procession that takes place a few days later, when goddess's statues from each of the town's neighbourhood temples are brought out and carried on a circuit around the town, they all make a required stop before the Taleju temple, to pay her their respects. Another example is the consecration of the Nāvā Durgā masks, which is not carried out by the priest of the temple in which they are kept (the Nāvā Durgā is located in the eastern part of the town), but by the Taleju temple priest.[14]

The sword symbolizes royal power. Formerly the king himself was expected to participate in the festival: it could not begin until he had sat down beside the brahman in the god's chariot. At Bhaktapur today, only the Rājopadhyāya priests of the Taleju temple have the right to bear the royal Malla sword.

This fact is not only characteristic of the town of Bhaktapur: in two other towns in the Valley, it is necessary that a brahman appear with the royal sword in hand, before the Avalokiteśvara-Matsyendranāth festivals of Patan, or the Indra Jātrā festival of Kathmandu are allowed to commence.

Are there any differences between the Buddhist temple *guṭhi* and those of the Hindu temples? John Locke, in his book *Karunamaya*, provides useful descriptions of the White Avalokiteśvara temple *guṭhi* in Kathmandu (the temple is located in the Jana Bāhā monastery), and of the Red Avalokiteśvara (or Rāto Matsyendranāth) temple at Bungamati and at Patan. The Avalokiteśvara-Matsyendranāth temples of Patan and the goddess Taleju's temple share many points in common. Both are at once royal temples and temples of localities. Both are royal gods, the chosen gods (*iṣṭadevata*) of the Malla kings.[15] It thus follows that the members of the *guṭhi* of the two Buddhist temples in question all belong to the Banra caste, which may be divided into two parts: (a) Buddhist priests (*vajrācārya*) and (b) its former monks, the *sakyas,* who are today goldsmiths. All of the members of the Ta bāhā temple community (*saṃgha*) are members of the *guṭhi,* whose duty it is to keep the temple functioning smoothly. In this particular case of a local temple, the essential difference between a Buddhist temple association and that of a Hindu temple is that the latter is an intercaste association, whereas the former is not. In the case of the Ta bāhā temple, its temple *guṭhi* members are simultaneously members of a *guṭhi* of the dead; by virtue of the fact that they all belong to the same caste, all of the officiating priests' functions are hereditary.

Categories of Hindu Temple Officiating Priests

A distinction must be drawn between the domestic priests (*purohita*) whose task it is to assist in and conduct rites of passage—the *saṃskāra*—and temple priests. At present, whether they be Buddhist (*vajrācārya*) or brahman priests, the functions of the domestic priests are hereditary. Throughout the entire Valley, there are ten times as many Buddhist priests as there are Rājopādhyāya brahmans. Only those *vajrācāryas'* sons who have received the *ācārya luyegu* initiation have the right to celebrate the fire oblation (*homa*) (Locke 1980:49).

There are three categories of brahmans in the Valley—the Rājopādhyāya, the Bhaṭṭa and the Jha—who form three distinct endogamous groups. The first of these, the Rājopādhyāya, were the *rāj guru* and domestic priests of the Malla dynasty kings. In contemporary Newar society, they alone officiate at rites of passage and the domestic ceremonies of *śivamargī* Hindu Newars. In the nineteenth century law code, the *Muluki Ain,* the Rājopādhyāya were considered to be inferior to the Indo-Nepalese brahmans who were the *rāj guru* of the Shah dynasty at that time. This classification may be explained in part by the fact that the Rājopādhyāya consume meat and alcohol in the course of tantric ceremonies. Yet, the Rājopādhyāya (or Deo Baju) consider themselves to be superior or equal to the Indo-Nepalese brahmans. Marriage between these two brahman groups is prohibited.[16] We should add that the Rājopādhyāya brahmans are the *pujāri* in the major temples of Viṣṇu Nārāyaṇa, of Wakupati Nārāyaṇa, and outside of the town of Bhaktapur, at Cangu Nārāyaṇa. They are also *pujārī* in the various Hindu monasteries (*māṭh*) of Bhaktapur: thus Rāma Pati Rāj is the *pujārī* of the *māṭh* located in the eastern part of the town, in the neighbourhood known as Kwatandau. The primary function of the Rājopādhyāya brahman however remains that of *guru* (New.: *bhaka khanegu*) to the high Hindu castes. The sons of brahmans who become priests must first go through the initiation ceremony of *dīkṣā,* which is a secret ceremony that I was never able to witness. According to oral descriptions, this consists of the transmission of a *mantra* from a master to his disciple, in a ceremony that must take place in the lineage's tantric temple (*āgam chẽ*).

According to the chronicles, the Bhaṭṭa brahmans came

from south India in the fifteenth century, in the time of king Jayayakṣa Malla (1428-1482), as *pujārī* to the Paśupatināth temple (Petech 1958:167). According to the oral tradition, the coming of brahmans from south India would have occurred prior to this date: Śaṅkarācārya, when he came to Nepal, is said to have driven the Buddhist monks out of Paśupatināth and installed Deccan brahmans in their place. Several Bhaṭṭa brahman families live in Bhaktapur today, and are the *pujārī* of various temples dedicated to Mahādeva (Mahādeo), as well as of certain Hindu monasteries (*māṭh*).[17]

The third category of brahmans, the Jha, are both the *pujārī* of various temples, and storytellers (New.: *khata khanegu*). They are said to have come from Mithila, and are considered to be inferior to the other categories of brahmans in the local social hierarchy. The *pujārī* of the Bhaktapur Paśupatināth temple is a Jha brahman.

In Nepal, we find that the hypothesis, according to which brahmans are never to be found inside the temples dedicated to the various forms of the goddess, is fully proven: in the numerous goddess-temples, the officiants are *karmācārya*. These also officiate in Gaṇeśa and Bhairava temples. There is but a single exception to this general rule: in the royal temples dedicated to the goddess Taleju—the tutelary divinity of the Malla kings and of the current Shah dynasty—the priests are Rājopādhyāya brahmans. It would appear that the situation in Kathmandu is different from that of Bhaktapur (Toffin (1981):74). At festival times, during which they play a considerable role, the *karmācārya*, who are often called "tantric priests" in the specialized literature, are found in greater numbers than are brahmans. Like brahmans, they are associated with a certain number of families, as their *kulācārya*. What is the difference between a Rājopādhyāya brahman and a *karmācārya*? According to brahmans, the *karmācārya* have no access to the Vedic texts and in the course of the ceremonies celebrated by them, they may not perform the fire oblation (*homa*), nor do they make use of texts. According to my direct observations, a *karmācārya* does not have the right to celebrate the *śrāddha* or the marriage rites. He assists the brahman, and often sacrifices animals in the householder's place in the course of certain ceremonies, such as the annual festival of the lineage god (*digu dyo pūjā*).

The goddess's temple officiants, which constitute several endogamous groups at Bhaktapur, reflect the hierarchy that is established between different forms of the goddess within the local pantheon.

The Bhaktapur *karmācārya* (or *ācāju*) are not a homogeneous group. They are divided into several sub-groups, including the Taleju *karmācārya,* the Mahākāli, the Mahālakṣmī, the Bhairava, Kinchẽ and the Jyāpūs: the last of these perform rites and ceremonies for farmers (Jyāpū) exclusively. The Taleju *karmācārya* consider themselves to be superior to all others, and may not intermarry with the other *karmācārya*; thus they constitute an endogamous group.

Neighbourhood and Lineage-Based Associations: Associations of the Dead

A few remarks on the neighbourhood, lineage-based and funerary associations will suffice to point out the complexity of these associations, which are at once linked to residence, kinship, profession, and caste. This will allow us to highlight the differences between these associations and those of a royal temple. So it is, for example, that the obligations owed to a divinity are levied and controlled by the king in a royal temple, whereas such is not the case in a lineage-based temple. In lineage-based associations, or associations of the dead, concerns for mutual support dominate the relations between their members.

Who makes up the membership in a neighbourhood goddess temple's association? The town of Bhaktapur is divided into twenty-four neighbourhoods (Nepali: *tol*; New.:

twah). At the centre of each neighborhood is a central square, used for either threshing and winnowing grain, or for public meetings. In each neighbourhood, there is a temple or shrine to Gaṇeśa and a small shrine to Nasadyo, a local form of Śiva Naṭarāja. A division of the town into nine parts is superimposed upon this division into twenty-four neighbourhoods. So it is that the residents of several neighbourhoods belong to the temple of a single goddess. Membership is exclusively determined by residency: members are thus people living in the neighbourhood. Although this is theoretically an intercaste association, it is only members of the pure castes who are allowed to take part in them. Thus the temple of the goddess Indrāyaṇī, that one of the eight goddesses who surround the town whose temple is situated in the western part of the town, only accepts into its *guṭhi* members of those castes residing in the neighbourhood of Khauma *tol.* Since the residences of the impure castes are pushed outside the town limits, the question of their induction is never addressed. In principle, the impure castes are to have their own *guṭhi.* The members of the neighbourhood temple association come together once a year, at the time of the annual festival in September, when the divinity is brought out in procession on the occasion of the Indra Jātrā festival. Each member contributes by paying a fixed sum of money to finance the festival, since land revenues are no longer sufficient to offset expenses. The right of membership into the Indrāyaṇī *guṭhi* is hereditary. A member may be expelled if he fails to fulfil his obligations, if he does not pay his dues, or if he does not participate in the annual festival. The leader (*nayo*) of this *guṭhi* belongs to the Chathariya caste, a high Hindu caste: his name is Nirjan Lal Gonga and he has inherited his position from his father. The seniority principle is no longer operative here, as it was in the case of lineage-based *guṭhi.*

The *guṭhi* of the dead (*Śii guṭhi*) appear at first to be cooperative or mutual associations in which the members lend assistance to another for the cremations of *guṭhi* members. The *guṭhi* of the dead, which are peculiar to the Newars, bring together persons belonging to the same caste or to castes having the same degree of purity in the local social hierarchy. As with every Newar association, the *guṭhi* of the dead assemble once a year for a feast, which falls on the day of the festival of the *guṭhi*'s chosen god. The association often bears the name of this chosen god: Bhairava or Mahākalī, for example. But in contrast to temple associations, the members are here bound to one another more through the spirit of mutual engagement they have accepted with regard to one another, than by worship they offer to a chosen god. On the other hand, and after the example of every other sort of *guṭhi*, the funerary associations often have at their disposal certain parcels of land, given to them by some ancestor. Revenues from these lands defray the cost of the wood necessary to their cremations. Just as the cremations *ghaṭ* are reserved for certain town neighbourhoods, so membership in a *guṭhi* of the dead is based on residence, in the broad sense of the word: members of a single *guṭhi* of the dead, while they may not live in the same neighbourhood (*tol*), must live in the same part of the town. This may be explained by the strict rules, observed in Newar society, for conducting the body from the home to the cremation ground. The routes traced by the 'paths of the dead' are not to be found within a single neighbourhood, but often cross three or four adjacent neighbourhoods (Kölver 1980:168).

As a general rule, the members of a single lineage, with the exception of sons, belong to different *sii guṭhi*. Membership is hereditary: often changes in residence make it the case today that sons belong to some other *guṭhi* than that of their fathers. The *guṭhi* leader is theoretically the oldest member in the association. The *guṭhi* of the dead thus appear to be those associations which are the least dependant upon place of residence, since they are not attached to any particular (lineage-based or other sort of) temple.

Place of residence is not a consideration in the case of lineage-based associations (*digu pūjā guṭhi*); here, kinship ties between members are all that matter. According to the Newars, the principal aim of the lineage-based association is to organize and finance its annual festival. In this way, members of the lineage (*phuki*) who have not lived in the town for several years come once a year for the lineage god's (*digu dyo*) festival: what is of greatest importance is the lineage god's shrine. Changes in the lineage god's shrine take place in extremely exceptional cases, and necessitate highly complex rituals.

If the lineage association possesses lands, the revenues from these lands are used to defray the costs of the annual festival. This festival is also a means for checking that caste rules are being respected, since it is at this time that new wives are presented to the divinity: all persons who have taken a wife whose social status is not equal to their own are excluded from the festival, and obliged to observe it on another date. In the case of the Munākarmi lineage, which was comprised of five members in 1980, members take turns cultivating the *guṭhi* lands, with revenues being used for the purchase of male goats, alcohol and rice for the festival. When the harvest is insufficient, each member is required to bring a sum of money in contribution. During the annual festival, it is the lineage leader (*nayo*) who performs the *pūjā* and sacrifices the animal.

All the tantric initiates in a lineage-based *guṭhi* celebrate a major *pūjā* (*thā pūjā*), on fixed dates, in their tantric temple (*āgam chẽ*). This temple, located in the town is dedicated to their lineage god (*āgã dyo*). The ceremonies here are less elaborate than those performed in a royal lineage temple such as that of the goddess Taleju, but the goal is an identical one: by the commemoration of an ancestor's birthday, one may insure the prosperity of the entire lineage. The worship offered to the gods in the *āgam chẽ* is secret, daily, and reserved for lineage members who have received initiation (*dīkṣā*). In an open shrine outside the town limits, the lineage members (*phuki*) come together once each year to celebrate the lineage god's (*digu dyo*) festival. The term *digu dyo,* like *āgã dyo,* is not the proper name of any god, but rather that of a category. It is important to specify here that it is same divinity who is worshipped in the *āgam chẽ* and in the open shrine (Vergati Stahl 1979:119). In both cases, these are tantric forms of the goddess, forms that are capable of receiving blood sacrifices. The *āgamic* divinity is thought to protect the members of the lineages with which it is associated. When the Newar speak of lineage, they emphasize the fact that belonging to a lineage means that members have the same shrine and divinity in common.

Conclusion

The *guṭhi* constitute a network undergirding the whole of Newar social and religious life. Every resident of the Valley belongs, of necessity, to several *guṭhi*, by virtue of which he or she is incorporated into the social fabric. These include *guṭhi* of caste: of the professional associations to which one belongs hereditarily; lineage-based *guṭhi*, in which membership is based on both birth and initiation, but in which kinship remains the determinant element; *guṭhi* of the dead, mutual-support groups in which membership is apparently voluntary; and temple *guṭhi*, in which membership depends upon place of domicile.

These temple associations play an essential role in Newar social life: they are intercaste associations, networks in which a resident is defined not only in terms of lineage and caste, but also by his or her appurtenance to a neighbourhood or locale. In truth, the word *guṭhi*, when it is applied to a royal temple, does not stand for an association so much as it does for various obligations imposed by the king upon a collective group (the residents of a village, an urban neighbourhood, or members of several castes), which is obliged to provide a quantity of goods or services in order to ensure the smooth functioning of a temple. The members of this sort of *guṭhi* have no obligations towards one another, but are rather engaged vis-vis the temple divinity, with these engagements becoming duties owed to the king. It is the divinity who establishes the bond between the members of this association. In comparison to a caste-oriented or neighbourhood temple association, the organization of a royal temple association is more elaborate: nearly every caste is represented here, and one finds in it a mirror of nearly the whole of the urban hierarchy.

The temple of the goddess Taleju, the lineage temple of the Malla kings, is at the same time a neighbourhood temple bearing hierarchical relations with the other temples in her neighbourhood. The goddesses of the neighbourhood temples are ritually subordinated to Taleju, with their neighbourhood temple associations being subordinated to the Taleju temple *guṭhi* as well. Here, however, this is an instance of a ritual dependence, which does not directly translate into changes of any kind in the internal administration of the respective *guṭhi*.

The temple of the goddess Taleju, the lineage-based temple of the Malla kings, is integrated into the Royal Palace complex, such that we here find an identification of the Palace with the temple. It is at the same time a neighbourhood temple, and maintains hierarchical relationships with all of the town's gods, both Buddhist (such as the Dīpaṅkara Buddha) and Hindu: every god in the town must pay homage to her during festival times and when they are brought out in procession. From this standpoint, the Malla kings governed the religious hierarchy of Bhaktapur through their lineage temple. In this regard, they wielded their political and religious mastery over society as a whole. We can conceive of the sovereigns of the Valley as attempting to strengthen their grip on society through a reinforcement of the Taleju temple *guṭhi*, an end which was realized by expanding land donations. The elaborate organization of this lineage temple allowed the king to maintain his control over the other divine temples and shrines of the town, and to control its festivals. Contrariwise, the Bhaktapur temple of Paśupatināth bears practically no ritual relationship to the other divinities of the town.

The case of the Deo Patan temple of Paśupatināth is quite

different: this concerns the space of the kingdom as a whole, in contrast to the Paśupatināth temples of the three ancient royal capitals, which are neighbourhood temples. In fact, the Malla kings were at once trustees of Śiva Paśupatināth, incarnations of Viṣṇu Nārāyaṇa, and husbands of the goddess Taleju. According to Newar thought, they were responsible not only for the founding of towns (with the goddess's help), but also for that of the religious space of the kingdom. Thus their temples were not only sites at which the relationships obtaining between king and divinity were established, but also means for insuring their control over territory and society. The Malla kings, who were only able to conquer lands outside the Valley with great difficulty, thus attached a great importance to the organization of the religious space of their kingdom.

Notes

* First published in *Puruṣārtha*, Vol. 10, 1986.

1. Out of a concern for simplicity, I designate as temple a closed construction inside of which the statue of a god is kept, by virtue of which fact it may be considered as the divinity's dwelling. I use the term "shrine" to designate what ought to be called an "open shrine" in which the god is often represented in the form of an unhewn stone or group of stones. On a lingustic level, the distinction between categories of temples is a clear one: a *dyo-chẽ* is a "house of the gods" and an *āgam chẽ*a "house of divinities receiving tantric worship". The terms *dega* (Newari) or *mandir* (Nepali) are also used to designate the temple. The open "shrines" are normally designated by the Sanskrit term *pīṭha* (Newari *pīṭh*).
2. Cf. Turner, (1965: 143): "*guṭhi*: land given to a temple, for which the original owner pays a nominal rent; *guṭhiyar*, the occupier of the *guṭhi* land".
3. Cf. Jha (1970: 222-23). For the Middle Ages, see also Regmi (1966: 735-39).
4. On the division of the sacrificial animal, see Nepali (1966: 395): "The cult of Sika Bhu is a unique feature among the Newars. It consists of the distribution of the various parts of the head of the sacrificed goat among the eight senior members of the group. The head is first cooked and its various parts are distributed in the following order: Priest–snout; Thakali–right eye; Nokuli–left eye; Sokuli–right ear;

Pekuli–left ear; Nyakuli– right side of the lower jaw; Khakuli–left side of the lower jaw; Nhekuli–tongue." See also Toffin (1975: 329-38).

5. Weisner (1978:11): "Just how important it was to legitimate royal power by providing a literal direct link between royal seat and Paśupati in order to satisfy popular feeling is shown by an incident that occurred in the kingdom of Kathmandu. We are told by a legend in Hasrat's chronicle that queen Ganga Rani had a subterranean passage laid to connect the temple at Deopatan with her residence at Kathmandu. Wright's history gives a different version of the story... Ganga Rani offered a flag to Paśupatinātha, one end of which was tied to the top of his temple and the other to the top of the durbar in Kāntipur (a distance of nearly three miles). This demonstration of the unity of palace and temple recurs in Pratapamalla's reign (1641-1674). This time Hasrat's account records how the king built a road from Kathmandu to Paśupati which he lined with temples, obviously a pilgrim's route. He, too, is said to have laid a subterranean passage between temple and palace."
6. Anderson (1971: 193) gives another version of the events proper to the festival to Guhyeśvarī: "Another (*kalaś*) which represents Guhyeśvarī is kept through the year at the temple of the goddess Taleju in Kathmandu and is carried to Guhyeśvarī on the previous evening, where it remains throughout the eve and the day of their festival, worshipped as the goddess herself. That evening the duplicate *kalash* of Guhyeśvarī is placed in a temple-like palanquin and carried on the shoulders of a group of men around and about the locality of Paśupatināth and eventually back into Taleju temple, accompanied all the while by musicians and a worshipping crowd of devotees." I myself was unable to observe this festival, and there are many contradictions in the information I received from my informants. The rites that take place in the night are secret and those who know them are not permitted to reveal them.
7. Regmi (1976: 235): *pathi*, "a volumetric unit equivalent to 2.34 kg. of paddy, 3.4 kg. of wheat or maize or 3.28 kg. of millet; one *pathi* consists of 8 *manas*'; *ropani*: "a unit of land measurement in the hill district, including Kathmandu Valley, comprising an area of 5,476 square feet or 0.05 hectares; one *ropani* is equal to 4 *muris* of land."
8. The town of Bhaktapur (or Bhatgaon) had approximately 40,000 inhabitants in 1975, of which 80 per cent were Śaivites (*śivamargī*) and 20 per cent Buddhists (*buddhamargī*). I gathered my data on religious associations in the course of two C.N.R.S. field-trips financed by L.A. 140 in 1975 and 1981. I am particularly grateful for the assistance I received from Rama Pati Raj Rājopādhyāya and Kedar Raj Rājopādhyāya, Taleju temple priests.
9. Other versions of Bhaktapur town's foundation legend give the

founding goddess other names: "Ananda Malla...being generous and wise, gave the sovereignty over the two cities (Kāntipur and Lalit Patan) and having invoked Annapurana Devī from Kasi, founded a city of 12,000 houses, which he named Bhaktapur (Bhatgaon) and included sixty small villages in his territory".

10. The *nau bhaja* are the nine musical instruments, which are different kinds of drums: the *lala khim, dyo khim, nay khim,* dah or *dam* (Nepali: *damphu*), *dhimay, nagara, pachima, dholak,* and *damaru*. To these are sometimes added an oboe (*mvahli*) and cymbals (*bhusyah*). The number of instruments may vary according to the locale in which a festival is celebrated: the number nine is a symbolic one. The *nagara* drum is a symbol of royal power. A complete list of Newar musical instruments is found in Wiehler (1980: 67-133).
11. T.L. Manandhar and A. Hale, *Newari-English Dictionary,* Delhi, 1986, s.v. *dapha*: "a type of music which is played with a certain set of musical instruments including a large drum, a large pipe and large cymbals."
12. The *Kusle* perform the *Nhaye-nhuma* ritual on the seventh day after death. After the seventh day the spirit of the deceased is supposed to leave the house (Nepali 1966: 135).
13. The word *thā* has no special meaning of its own in the Newari language: it is a grammatical element placed before or after a word, and used exclusively for *pūjā*.
14. Teilhet (1978: 93): "Ceremonially dressed the *gatha* proceed to the main temple Taleju with the Nava Durga masks. The masks are taken to Taleju to give them life-force independent of the *gatha* who wear them. 'The Nava Durga masks are given life by the priest of Taleju, by the Nava Durga gods and goddess, and by tantras and mantras.' This life-giving ritual occurs late at night or early in morning."
15. The king of Patan, Śrīnivāsa Malla (1661-84) adopted Śri Lokanātha (Rato Avalokiteśvara or Bunga Dyo) as his chosen god (*iṣṭadevata*). Cf. Locke 1980: 340. The Hindu goddess Taleju became the chosen god of the Malla kings at the end of the fourteenth century (Slusser 1982: 317).
16. Cf. Höfer (1979: 137): "The discrepancy between the status position as accorded by the law and by self-assessment remains, however, to be emphasized. It is significant that, among the Newars, the Deo Bhaju also go by the name Upadhyaya or Rajopadhyaya although the MA (Muluki Ain) reserves this name to the Parbatiya Upadhyaya and according to Nepali they do not intermarry with the latter".
17. Names of temples in which neighbourhoods (*tol*) the pujāri are Bhatta :

Yath Māhādeo	Chochẽ
Hathu Māṭh	Tibukchẽ
Nani Māhādeo	Taumadhi
Salan Gaṇeśa Māhādeo	Nasmana

References

Anderson, M. A., 1971, *The Festivals of Nepal*, London, George Allen and Unwin.

Auer, G. and Gutschow, N., 1974, *Gestalt, Funktionen und religiöse Symbolik einer nepalischen Stadt im vorindustriellen Entwicklungs Stadium*, Darmstadt.

Bose, A., 1942, *Social and Rural Economy of Northern India*, Calcutta, University of Calcutta.

Dumont, Louis, 1975, *Une sous-caste de l'Inde du Sud. Organization Sociale et Religion des Pramalai Kallar*, Paris, Mouton.

Fürer-Haimendorf, Chr. von 1956, "Elements of Newar Social Structure", *The Journal of the Royal Anthropological Institute of Great Britain and Ireland*, 86:2, pp. 15-38.

Gutschow, N. and Kölver, B. 1975, *Ordered Space, Concepts and Functions in a Town of Nepal*, Wiesbaden, Verlag F. Steiner.

Gutschow, N., 1982, *Stadtraum und Ritual der newarischen Stadte im Kathmandu-Tal. Eine architekturanthropologische Untersuchung*, Stuttgart, Verlag W. Kohlhammer.

Höfer, A., 1979, *The Caste Hierarchy and the State in Nepal. A Study of the Muluki Ain of 1854*, Innsbruck, Universitatsverlag Wagner.

Jha, N. H., 1970, *The Licchavis*, Varanasi, Chowkhamba Sanskrit Studies, Vol. 75.

Kölver, B., 1978, "Aspects of Nepalese Culture: Ancient Inscriptions and Modern Yatras" in *Proceedings of the First Symposium of Nepali and German Sanskritists*, Dang/Kathmandu, Institute of Sanskrit Studies, pp. 157-72.

Levi, S., 1905, *Le Népal: étude historique d'un royaume hindou*, Paris, E. Leroux, 3 vols.

Lienhard, S., 1978, "Problèmes de syncrétisme religieux au Nepal", *Bulletin de l'École Française d'Extrême-Orient* 65, pp. 239-70.

Locke, John K., 1980, *Karunamaya: The Cult of Avalokiteśvaramatsyendranāth in the Valley of Nepal*, Kathmandu, Tribhuvan University, Sahayogi Prakashan for Research Centre for Nepal and Asian Studies.

Nepali, G. S., *The Newars, An Ethno-Sociological Study of a Himalayan Community*, Bombay, United Asia Publications.

Parry, J. P., 1979, *Caste and Kinship in Kangra*, London, Routledge and Kegan Paul.

Petech, L., 1958, *Medieval History of Nepal*, Rome, Instituto Italiano per Medio ed Estremo Oriente.

Ray, A., 1968, "The Paśupatinātha Temple: Nepal," *Man in India*, 49, pp. 10-23.

Regmi, D.R., 1965, *Medieval Nepal*, Calcutta, Firma K. L. Mukhopadhyaya, 2 vols.

Regmi, M. Land, 1968, *Tenure and Taxation in Nepal. Religious and Charitable*

Land Endowments, Guṭhi Tenure, Vol. 4., Berklcley, University of California.

Regmi, M., 1976, *Landownership in Nepal*, Berkeley, University of California.

Rosser, C., 1966, "Social Mobility in the Newar Caste System" in *Caste and Kin in Nepal, India and Ceylon*, edited by Chr. von Fürer-Haimendorf, London, Asia Publishing House, pp. 68-140.

Seneviratne, H. L., 1978, *Rituals of the Kandyan State*, Cambridge, Cambridge University Press.

Slusser Shepherd, M., 1982, *Nepal Mandala. A Cultural Study of the Kathmandu Valley*, Princeton, Princeton University Press.

Teilhet, J. H., 1978, "The Tradition of the Nava Durga in Bhaktapur", Nepal, *Kailash*, 6:2, pp. 81-98.

Toffin, G. (1975), "Etudes sur les Néwar de la vallée de Kathmandu: *Guṭhi*, Funérailles et Castes", *L'Ethnographie*, 70, pp. 205-25.

Toffin, G., 1981, "Culte des déesses et fête du Dasāī chez les Néwar (Népal)", *Puruṣārtha*, 5, pp. 58-81.

Toffin G., 1982, *Société et Religion chez les Néwar du Népal* Thèse d'Etat en ethnologie, ms. Ecole des Hautes Etudes en Sciences Sociales.

Vergati-Stahl, A., 1979, "Taleju, Sovereign Deity of Bhaktapur" in *Asie du Sud. Traditions et Changements*, Paris, Editions de C.N.R.S., pp.163-67.

Vergati-Stahl, A., 1979, "Une divinité lignagére des Néwar: Digu Dyo" *Bulletin de l'École Française d'Extrême-Orient*, 66'. pp. 115-27.

Wiehler, S. and H. (1980), "Nevar Musical Instruments", *Journal of the Nepal Research Center*, 4, pp. 67-133.

Wiesner, U., 1978, *Nepalese Temple Architecture: Its Characteristics and its Relations to Indian Developments*, Leiden, E.J. Brill.

Śaivite Temples in Bhaktapur*

When the traveller who enters Bhaktapur[1] from the West, by the road from Kathmandu, arrives at the first big square, he is surprised to notice that the monuments situated in the centre of the town, in front of the ancient royal palace, are not frequented by the inhabitants. The sole exception to this first impression is constituted by the temple of Taleju. It is this temple which is the site of the divinity who protected the Malla kings and who is also the main divinity of the town.[2] At Taumadhi, the other important square in the town, are to be found two temples: Nyātapola and that of Ākāś Bhairav, each being very important in local religious life. All the religious processions which take place in Bhaktapur must pass through Taumadhi and part of the *Bisket Jātrā*, the town's most important festival, takes places in front of the temple of Ākāś Bhairav. When one moves further on towards the *ghāṭ*, the cremation-places which surround the town, one sees many women carrying trays of offerings who are on their way to make their *pūjā* in the open sanctuaries which are known as *pīṭh* in Newari[3] and *pīṭha* in Sanskrit, and which are situated outside the town and close to the *ghāṭ*.

The House-temples of the *Mātṛkā* (mother-goddesses)

Present-day religious life in Bhaktapur is dominated on the one hand by the cult of the *Aṣṭamātṛkā* and, on the other, by the cult rendered in the *Āgama chẽ*, which is an institution peculiar to the Newars of the Kathmandu Valley.[4] The temples of the *mātṛkā* are "town-quarter temples" for the cult of each *mātṛkā* is linked to a clearly-defined sector of the town, as we will see later.

Inside the town each of the *mātṛkā* has a temple which is called in Newari *dyo chẽ*, meaning "house of the divinity" and outside the town, an open sanctuary known as *pīṭh*. The temples of the *mātṛkā* and their *pīṭh* are situated as follows: in the East, Brahmāyanī; to the South-East, Māheśvarī; to the South, Kaumārī; to the South-West Vaiṣṇavī alias Bhadrakālī; to the West, Vārāhī; to the North-West, Indrāyanī; to the North, Māhākālī; and to the North-East, Mahālakṣmī. In the midst, in the centre of these eight mother-goddesses, is to be found the goddess Tripurasundarī. The place where the temple of Tripurasundarī is situated is considered as the religious centre of the town. The only *pīṭh* situated inside the town is that of Tripurasundarī and is to be found close to her temple.

From the outside, the temples of the *mātṛkā* look like houses. As in all traditional Newar architecture, the materials used in their construction are wood and bricks for the walls and their roofs are tiled. The plan of these "houses of divinities" is rectangular; their roofs on the facade and in the rear of the buildings, slope down at a steep angle and are sometimes dominated by what is called an *āgama*.[5] The roofs are underslung by carved wooden struts, spaced at intervals, which portray representations of the various mother-goddesses. On the top of each roof is a golden pinnacle (*gajur*): the number of *gajur* is indicative of the relative importance of the divinity (housed below) in the pantheon. As is the case with Newar domestic dwellings, these buildings have two or three storeys. The door is usually situated in the centre of the main facade (this is the case, for instance, in the *dyo chẽ* of Tripurasundarī, Brahmāyanī and Indrāyanī) or on the side wall (the *dyo chẽ* of Mahākālī). From an architectural point of view, there is no difference between a Newar domestic house and a temple of a *mātṛkā*. It is the decoration of the windows and the *toraṇa*, which are generally of wood and are placed above the windows and the doorways, which distinguish the *dyo chẽ* from an ordinary, human, dwelling-place. On each *toraṇa*, the *mātṛkā* is portrayed in the form of a standing young woman, with four or eight arms, in company with her vehicle (*vāhana*), the two principal hands holding a skull-cup, and displaying the *vyākhyā-mudrā* (exposition). Only Vaiṣṇavī alias Bhadrakālī and Mahākālī are portrayed as old women. They have, on their right, Gaṇeś, and on their left, Bhairav. Floral motifs are to be found on the *toraṇa*, and in their centres a bird similar to the Garuḍa.[6] According to Newar tradition, the bird is said to be Garuḍa's brother and is called in Newari *Chhepā*. The latter has the beak and the wings of a vulture, but the torso, the arms and the ears are those of a man.

Other religious buildings which are similar in form to a house are the *Āgama chẽ*. These private shrines are temples of a particular lineage (*phukī*) or of a particular religious association (*guṭhi*). In these *Āgama chẽ*, the decoration of the windows and the wooden *toraṇas* above the doors are the same as in the *dyo chẽ*. In Newari, the word *āgama* is compounded with the word *chẽ*, and the compound signifies an edifice where the protective divinity of a lineage or a religious association is housed. The divinity is called an *Āgam-dyo*: the name is applied to a category of divinity and is not that of a particular god. In a recent publication devoted to a study of the monuments of the Kathmandu Valley, the *Āgama* were defined in the following terms: "Similar to the *dyo chẽ* but are generally more enclosed. They contain shrines of the Kuldevatās, Iṣṭadevata and Ogamdevdas (family, patron and secret deities). No one is permitted to enter for worship without prior initiation. The enshrined images are never taken out of the building".[7] The initiated are those who have received the *dīkṣā*, the initiation is accorded only to high-caste Newars.[8] The statues which are in the *Āgama* should never leave them. However, the statues of the *mātṛkā* are taken out of their *dyo chẽ* in processions during the annual festival of the *Bisket Jātrā* and all the inhabitants of the town can see them. They are made of bronze and are kept on the upper floor of the *dyo chẽ*, the temples situated within the town limits. In the lower part of the building on the ground floor, is kept the chariot in which the deity is conveyed during its promenade at the *Bisket Jātrā*. Two of the *mātṛkā* do not have statues but are represented instead by bronze masks: these two are Indrāyaṇī and Bāl Kumārī. In this connection, we should take note of the fact that during the *Bisket Jātrā* the statues of the goddesses are taken out of their temples and worshipped in a particular order: first Bhadrakālī, then Indrāyaṇī, Mahākālī, Mahālakaṣmī, Brahmāyaṇī, Māheśvarī, Kaumārī, Vārāhī and finally, Tripurasundarī. The second big festival at which the goddesses are worshipped is Dasāī. At that time, the statues are not taken out of their *dyo chẽ* but the inhabitants of Bhaktapur go to their *pīṭh* to do worship and these *pīṭh* are visited in a certain order. People go first to the *piṭh* of Brahmāyanī, then to that of Māheśvarī, Kaumārī, Vaiṣṇavī (Bhadrakālī), Vārāhī, Indrāyaṇī, Camuṇḍā (Mahākālī), Mahālakṣmī and, on the last day of the festival, to that of Tripurasundarī. This ritual sequence highlights the relationship between the *Aṣṭamātṛkā* and Tripurasundarī and the central position of the latter. The eight goddesses are moreover considered as emanations of Tripurasundarī.

The maternal aspect of the goddesses is relatively secondary. It is not generally portrayed and they are never represented with a child as is sometimes the case in India.[9] At Bhaktapur, one finds the usual seven *mātṛkā* of India to whom are joined Mahālakṣmī and Tripurasundarī. The goddess Mahālakṣmī plays a particular role in the local pantheon, as we shall see presently. The temple of the Nava Durgā groups together some *mātṛkā*, but, in this particular case, the *mātṛkā* are not represented by bronze statues but by masks. The masks are kept inside the Nava Durgā temple and are destroyed each year at the end of the Dasāī festival. Each has a different colour:

Brahmāyanī	:	Yellow	Vārāhī	:	red
Māheśvarī	:	White	Indrāyaṇī	:	orange
Kaumārī	:	red	Mahākālī	:	red
Vaiṣṇavī	:	green	Mahālakṣmī	:	red (flesh colour)

Mahālakṣmī has no mask, she is represented in the form of a metal plate with a triangle in its centre.[10] In reality, there are nine masks for, in addition to those of the seven *mātṛkā*, there is one mask for Gaṇeśa and one for Bhairav. It should be stressed that there is here no representation of Tripurasundarī. In the course of different ceremonies, the Nava Durgā dancers sacrifice in front of the representation of Māhālakṣmī: the sacrificer is the dancer who wears the mask of Bhairav. The Nava Durgā temple is a rectangular construction, a two-storeyed building with a simple house-type roof. It is identical with the other temples of the mother-goddesses. At the main entrance there are two royal lions in stone (*rāja siṃha*). On the main facade there are six windows surmounted by *toraṇa* on which the mother-goddesses are represented. Inside the building there is a square courtyard and the masks and the dancers'costumes are kept on the first floor. The Nava Durgā dancers belong to a particular caste, the *gātha*, "gardeners". They are appointed every year to wear the masks and carry out the dance rituals. They dance in each and every *tol* (residential unit) as well as in certain localities situated around Bhaktapur which belonged in former times to the Bhaktapur kingdom: Thimi, Nala, Panauti, Deo Patan.[11]

We have stressed the fact that the goddess Tripurasundarī is to be found in the middle of the *aṣṭamātṛkā*: her *pīṭh*, which is situated inside the town, is called *madhya pīṭh*. The temple of Tripurasundarī has the same form of two-storeyed house as the other temples of the *mātṛkā*. The difference between her *pīṭh* and those of the others is a social one. Those in charge of the *pīṭh* of the *aṣṭa mātṛkā* situated outside the town are Poḍe who, in the Newar caste system, are Untouchables. The person in charge of the *pīṭh* of Tripurasundarī is a Kusle: he is also a member of an Untouchable caste, but of a higher status than a Poḍe's, and he has the right to reside within the town. The Kusle are the only category of Untouchables authorized to dwell within the town's boundaries.[12] According to learned Newar opinion, Tripurasundarī is the goddess whose residence was established at the foundation of the town of Bhaktapur. B. Kölver has drawn attention to a passage found in the fragmentary chronicle in Keshar Library and also in the Bendall *Vaṃśāvalī* which indicates that Anandamalla established Bhaktapur as a royal city with Tripurasundarī. In the ninth century, the town is said to have been called Trīpura. A Newar painting, published by Kölver, which represents a ritual map of Bhaktapur, illustrates Tripurasundarī's role as the centre of the town. As Kölver remarks "its centre is occupied by the oldest goddess of the city (i.e. Tripurasundarī). She is flanked by the two deities which stand for the most important communal ritual of the Bhaktapur year (Bhadrakālī and Ākāś Bhairav): the connection is descriptive rather than dogmatic."[13] These two divinities who are presented in the painting alongside Tripurasundarī (at Bhaktapur Bhadrakālī is the equivalent of Vaiṣṇavī) are the two principal protagonists in the *Bisket Jātrā* festival. So what is portrayed in this painting stems rather from the town's real geography than from its ideal representation in the pattern of a *maṇḍala*. In this painting, Tripurasundarī is surrounded by the Eight Gaṇeśa and the Eight Bhairava and, on the outer rim, by the Eight *Mātṛkā*. Outside the town limits, are the cremation-grounds with the usual symbols which one finds in Newar paintings of the fourteenth and fifteenth centuries: the *liṅga*, the *stūpa*, fire, and the scavenging beasts.[14] The goddess Tripurasundarī does not play as important a role in the town's life as does the goddess Taleju.

Apart from the painting, described and studied by Kölver, the inhabitants of Bhaktapur represent the positions of the *mātṛkā* in the form of two other *maṇḍala*: one is an eight-petalled lotus with Tripurasundarī in its centre; the other is formed by two *yantra*. Each *mātṛkā* represented is accompanied by a Bhairava.

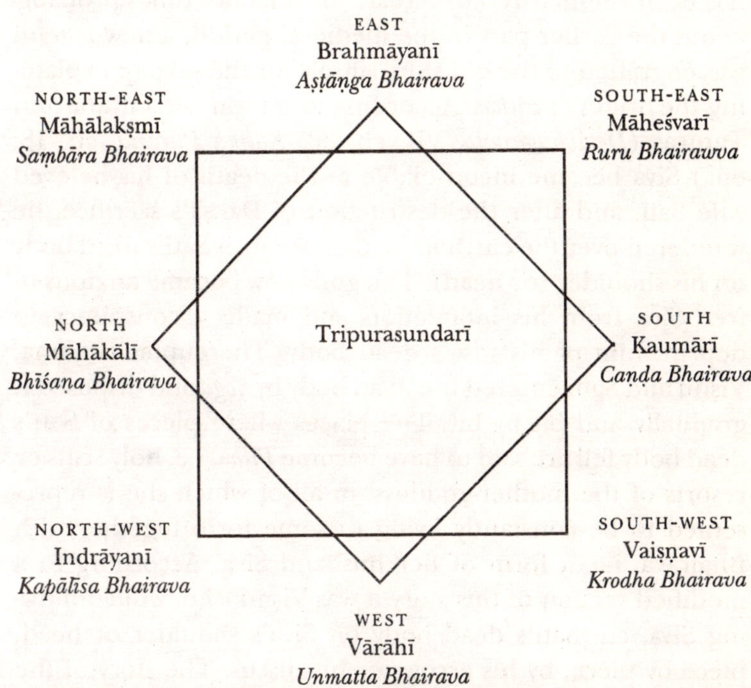

One will notice that the *Aṣṭabhairava* have neither temples nor sanctuaries. The inhabitants put a simple stone alongside each *dyo chẽ* in order to represent one of the Bhairav. Other Newar informants point to the presence of Bhairav in one of the stones which are to be found in the *pīṭh*. Elsewhere, for instance at Kathmandu, Patan and at Panauti, there are however, temples of Unmatta Bhairav which have the form of a *dyo chẽ*.

Open Sanctuaries (*pīṭh*)

The open sanctuaries, the *pīṭh*, literally altars or seats,[15] are situated outside the town limits on a hillock, surrounded by trees, and close to a river or a cremation place. The legend which explains the origin of the *pīṭh* and which is known to the inhabitants of Bhaktapur derives from Indian tradition: it has been summarized by Sircar: "In still later times probably about the earlier part of the medieval period, a new legend was engrafted to the old story simply for the sake of explaining the origin of *Pīṭhas*. According to certain late Purāṇa and Tantras (*Devībhāgavata*, VII, ch. 30; *Kālikā Purāṇa*, ch. 18, etc.) Śiva became inconsolable at the death of his beloved wife Satī, and after the destruction of Dakṣā's sacrifice, he wandered over the earth in mad dance with Satī's dead body on his shoulder (or head). The gods now became anxious to free Śiva from his infatuation and made a conspiracy to deprive him of his wife's dead body. Thereupon Brahma, Viṣṇu and Śani entered the dead body by *yoga* and disposed it gradually and bit by bit. The places where pieces of Satī's dead body fell are said to have become *Pīṭha*, i.e. holy seats or resorts of the mother-goddess, in all of which she is represented to be constantly living in some form together with Bhairava, i.e. a form of her husband Śiva. According to a modified version of this story it was Viṣṇu who, while following Śiva, cut Satī's dead body on Śiva's shoulder or head, piece by piece, by his arrows or his discus. The story of the association of particular limbs of the mother-goddess with *Śakta tirthas*, which may have some relation with the Tantric ritual called *Pīṭha-nyāsa*, belongs, as already pointed out, to the latest stage in the development of an ancient tale."[16] The number of *pīṭhas* in local tradition varies from four to thirty-two. We were assured that at Tripurasundarī's *pīṭh* in Bhaktapur one of Satī Devī's fifty important parts fell (in this case the left ribs); at Guhyeṣorī it was her genital organ.[17] All the *Māṭṛkā* too came out from the pieces of flesh which fell down. The role mythology has played in the creation of sacred spaces, such as the *pīṭhas*, has often been stressed and one of the most recent analyses is due to W.C. Beane. This author points out, quoting V.S. Agrawala, that the moral of the *śāktapīṭha* mythology is ultimately "the broad-based apotheosis of the motherland conceived in the form of encagised centres for tantric and yogic *sādhana* or for practising special meditation and spiritual discipline". In his own somewhat laboured prose Beane pursues: "What is finally remarkable about the relation between the mythic event (the Satī-Suicide) and the Birth of Sacred Space (*Śāktapīṭhas*) is another thing; that is, the Puruṣa/Prajāpati 'dismemberment' in the Vedo-Brahmanic tradition is now capable of being structurally understood within the aetiology of the *pīṭha-* motif, so that there is essentially the transformation of anthropocosmic reality into topocosmic reality".[18] Most studies of Indian *pīṭhas* published to date have been philological researches based on written sources. What is remarkable in the case of the Newar *pīṭh* is that the latter play today a vital role in the religious organization of a town such as Bhaktapur and are not matter of antiquarian, bookish interest.

Pīṭh are buildings of brick and wood and are rectangular in plan. Their base, composed of bricks and stones, is raised 30 or 50 centimetres above the surrounding ground-level. They have only one full wall; the rest of the construction is supported by wooden columns which are sometimes carved. *Pīṭh* have a tiled, sloping roof like that of a Newar dwelling; but sometimes they have two such roofs, superimposed. The inscriptions that are to be found at the different *pīṭh* are from the seventeenth century: that at the Mahākālī's *pīṭh* is dated 1661 and mentions the name of Pratāp Malla: on that of Indrāyaṇī one can read two dates, 1670 and 1791; the *pīṭh* of Māheśvarī was founded in 1746 by king Ranjit Malla; the *pīṭh* of Mahālakṣmī, in Kalacha *tol*, which is square in plan, has inscriptions which mention the gift of stone lions in 1650. In three of the *pīṭh* there is no edifice to shelter the stones: these are the *pīṭh* of Bal Kumārī, Mahākālī and Tripurasundarī. In the other *pīṭh*, the stones which are worshipped lean against the wall of the edifice. In front of each *pīṭh* there is a platform, made of stone slabs or bricks, which delimits the sacred area: at the entrance are a pair of stone lions and a bell. On the central facade there are wooden *toraṇa*, identical with the *toraṇa* in the *dyo chẽ*. The stones inside the *pīṭh* are surmounted by a stone arched buttress which reproduces the decoration of the upper part of the *toraṇa* in wood. Generally the decoration of these arched buttresses in the *pīṭh* is somewhat simpler than that of the wooden *toraṇas*. The Newar form of Garuḍa is always present: but the female personages and the *makara* are absent.

The edifices in the *pīṭh* are similar to other constructions both profane and religious: these are the *pātī* (New. phale or *phalecca*), the *sattal* and the *maṇḍap* or *maḍu* all three of which are often designated by the more general term of *dharmaśālā*.[19] Here is one definition of the *pātī*: "Characteristically the *pātī* is a partially enclosed, roofed platform (New. *phale*) constructed either as a lean-to, against and between other buildings, as a colonnaded porch built into a building (usually a private house) or as a free-standing structure with saddleback (double-pitched) roof. Frequently the *pātī* roof slopes in four directions, the hipped roof, or, reflecting the common house-roof, attaches a short pented collar to the gable-ends as a quasi-hipped roof".[20] The second type, the *maṇḍapa*, is a square platform surmounted by a roof which is supported by free-standing pillars. The *maṇḍapa* which could be described as a colonnaded pavilion has usually only one floor. It has all the functions of a *pātī* "and performs additional services as council-hall and bourse". This type of construction is more frequently found in towns. The *sattal*, which is of more imposing dimensions, serves at the same time as a resting-place and temple; inside there is an altar with an image of the divinity. A feature of this type of building is a room, a masonry-walled room,on the first floor where secret worship takes place and which the Newars call the *āgama*, Mary Slusser is right to argue that the basic difference between these three types of construction is functional: "one can scarcely establish a convincing distinction between *sattal* (Skt. *sattra* "almshouse") and common *pāṭī* and *maṇḍapa*. It shares with them both function and, essentially, form and often, in common practice, at least their names. There is a difference, however, which primarily lies in degree of function. For the *sattal*, albeit a free public shelter, caters to a more permanent occupation—often of God as well as man—than do the common *pāṭī* and ordinary *maṇḍapa*. The *sattal*, therefore, is architecturally modified to meet these new demands".[21] With regard to the temples of the mother-goddesses, we have noted that of Mahākālī has a *pāṭī* which functions as a place of rest and entertainment for travellers and also a meeting place for the residents of that particular *tol* of the town. Often, in the evenings, musicians come together there and play *bhajana*. From a functional point of view we might therefore classify this example as mid-way between *pāṭī* and *sattal*. What distinguishes a *pīṭh* from a *pāṭī* is above all its outer decoration, constituted by the wooden *toraṇa* on its central facade, their decoration being identical to that of the *dyo chẽ* of the *mātṛkā*.

A striking parallel can be drawn with the *digu dyo*, the lineage sanctuaries situated outside the town limits, and sometimes close to the *pīṭh*. These sanctuaries are composed of simple stones surmounted by an arched buttress of stone. They are identical with the stones that are to be found in the *pīṭh*. The *digu dyo* is the tutelary divinity of a lineage (*phukī*) to which a cult is rendered annually. During the celebration of this cult, the stones are decorated with all the attributes of a divinity; the divinity is invoked into the stone and is the same divinity as that which is lodged in the *Āgama chẽ*, the lineage sanctuary within the town, where the worship is reserved to the initiated (those who received the *dīkṣā*) and where worship takes place daily (*nitya pūjā*). There is the same complementary relationship between the lineage temple inside the town, which is enclosed and where worship is secret and reserved to initiates (*Āgama-chẽ*)—the temple for the mother-goddess inside the town is the *dyo chẽ*—and the open sanctuary outside the limits of the town, where the divinity is represented aniconically in the form of stones, as in the *pīṭh*. The dichotomy between what is secret and closed, *guhya*, and what is open and outside, *bāhya*, is fundamental not only in the categories of Newar religious thought but in all Newar life in society.

Nowadays, the word *pīṭh* is applied not only to the outside sanctuaries dedicated to the mother-goddesses but also to all the open sanctuaries of Gaṇeś. One particularly interesting case is that of the temple of Chumā Gaṇeś which has both a *dyo chẽ* and a *pīṭh*. The statue of Chumā Gaṇeś which is taken out from its *dyo chẽ* on the seventh day of the annual festival of *Bisket Jātrā* is kept for the rest of the year in its *dyo chẽ*. Its *pīṭh* is just next-door to its *dyo-chẽ*. Gaṇeś' role is a special one. He is invoked in every ritual and each and every quarter of the town has some form of Gaṇeś in a sanctuary: this often bears the name of the locality. Here is the list of the Gaṇeś which have, at Bhaktapur, both a *pīṭh* and a *dyo chẽ*.

Names of Gaṇeś	Name of the town-quarter where *pīṭh* is situated	*Pīṭh* attendant	Name of the town-quarter where *dyo chẽ* is situated
Chuma	Chochē	Kusle	Chochē
Balakhu	Yalachē	Kusle	Yalachē
Sala	Tacupal	Kusle	Tacupal
Dahi Binayak	Tibukchē	Kusle	Tibukchheē
Golmadhi	Golmadhi	Kusle	Golmadhi
Surya Binayak	Surje Binayak	Poḍe	Bolachē
Itache	Itache	Kusle	Itachē

It is clear from the above list that the *pīṭh* which are within the town limits are served by Kusle attendants. This was also the case of the *pīṭh* of Tripurasundarī as we have seen above. The only *pīṭh* on the list which has a Poḍe attendant is Surje

Vinayak which lies outside the town.

In each quarter of the town there must also be a temple dedicated to Viṣṇu in the form of Nārāyaṇa. The presence of these temples is linked to the fact that all Newar women after the *ihi* ceremony are the "wives" of Viṣṇu and are still bound to the divinity after divorce or the death of their mortal husbands.

The Structuring of Urban Space

The town of Bhaktapur is divided into nine sectors each of which bears the name of a mother-goddess. In the centre of the town is the temple of Tripurasundarī. It would appear that in the two other royal towns (Patan and Kathmandu) there is no temple of the goddess Tripurasundarī and so in her context at Bhaktapur she may be considered to be a local goddess.[22] Outside the limits of the town, close to each *pīṭh,* is to be found a cremation-place and a cemetery. The Newars say that each mother-goddess has her *śmaśāna* a word which designates both a burial-ground and a burning ground. The Newari names of these *śmaśāna* are not, however, well known and have perhaps been forgotten. Today four of these *śmaśāna* are well known *macha ponghale* (New. *śmaśāna*).

Brahmāyaṇī	Bhutipakho
Māheśvarī	Pasi Khyau
Hanuman	Khora
Cupī	Mudigpa

Children, who die before the age of three including those who are still-born, are not cremated but are buried close to the *pīṭh.* The *pīṭh* of Māheśvarī occupies a special function. Not only are children who die young buried there but also Kusle adults, members of the Untouchable caste who were previously Jogis, as well as Sannyasis. Buffaloes destined for sacrifice to Durgā at the Dasāī festival and who die before the festival time are also buried there. According to Brahmin and

Vajrācārya informants, there should be, in each *śmaśāna*, a *caitya*, a Bhairav, a spring of water, a *liṅga*, a tree and an image of Gaṇeś.[23]

The inhabitants of Bhaktapur must bury their children who die premature deaths, and must cremate their adult dead, in the sector of the town in which they reside. For instance, those who live in the Eastern part of the town go to cremate their dead close to the Brahmāyaṇī *ghāṭ*. At the present time three *ghāṭ* are still functioning: Hanuman *ghāṭ*, Cup'ī *ghāṭ* and Kasan Kuśi *ghāṭ*. Daily *pūjā* (*nitya pūjā*) is always done in the *pīṭh* of the *mātṛkā* or in the sanctuaries of Gaṇeś. Those who live in the Eastern part of the town will never do their *pūjā* at the *pīṭh* of Indrāyaṇī which is situated in the Western part of the town.

In Newar painting, both Buddhist and Brahmanical, one finds, from the fiteenth century onwards, *maṇḍala* with the eight *śmaśāna*. One usually finds in such *paṭa*, the *śmaśāna* arranged in a circle around a central divinity. In Nepal the different forms of *maṇḍala* which represent the eight cemeteries have been well described by P.H. Pott[24] and in the translation by S. Lèvi of the captions on the painting illustrating Svayambhunath, one finds the list of the eight mother-goddesses, of the Bhairva, and of the Eight Cemeteries, etc.[25] What is important from our point of view is that the *maṇḍala* is to be found again at the Bhaktapur town-level and that it is functional.

It would appear that this religious structuring of urban space is not ancient. If one accepts oral tradition, it seems to have been inspired by king Jitamitra Malla in the seventeenth century. This tradition receives confirmation in the dates of the temple inscriptions as these foundations generally date from the seventeenth century. While we can, at present, study buildings which go back to the seventeenth century, it is certain that the sites on which these buildings now stand were associated long before the seventeenth century with cults and rituals. The nine- fold divisions of the town of Bhaktapur must ultimately be related to traditions such as those summarized in Wright's *Vaṃśavālī* and where it is stated that Śivadeva, the last of the Licchavi "...built nine new tols, or divisions of the city, and erected nine Ganeshas.... He founded and peopled the place known as Navatol, after performing all the requisite ceremonies, and established four Gaṇeśa, four Bhairavas, four Nritya Nāthas, four Mahādevas, four Kumārīs, four Buddhas, four Khambas, four Gaganacharis, and four Chatushpathas or crossways with Bhūta images. Then, after establishing an Avarna deity in each tol or division of Deva Patan, he erected an image of Śiva. He invoked Mahāmrityunjaya to protect men from untimely death."[26] The above passage, it will be objected, refers to Deopatan and not to Bhaktapur. But this in itself is significant, for four-fold and eight-fold divisions of space in various parts of the Valley by other cultural heroes has been stressed elsewhere in our text. *Dyo chẽ* of the *mātṛkā* are also to be found in Kathmandu—for instance, those of Indrāyaṇī and Bhadrakālī: and close to the *ghāṭ* on the banks of the Bāgmatī, there is the *pīṭh* of Indrāyaṇī. However, the study of the different manifestations of the Devī in the Valley (the temples at Banepa, Harasiddhi, etc.) is still in its initial stages. And if we have chosen to draw attention to the Bhaktapur example, it is because at Bhaktapur one is still in the presence of a system of representations which is functional. Elsewhere one finds the *disjecta membra* of the system but it is no longer a living reality. Archaeology might reconstruct it: but ethnographical description elsewhere than at Bhakatpur would be suggestive of a model the existence of which could not be proven empirically.

S. Lévi wrote: "The only goddesses which deserve to be mentioned for their local function, apart from the multiple incarnations of the Devī, are the Eight Mothers (*Aṣṭamātṛkā*) who are considered as the Guardians of the Nepalese towns".[27] At Bhaktapur the mother-goddesses do play the role of guardians. And as we have seen, they determine the religious organization of the whole town. It is clear that this form of religious organization by and with *Aṣṭamātṛkā* is to found not only in Bhaktapur but in other Newar localities such as Panauti, which was formerly part of the kingdom of Bhaktapur.

At Bhaktapur the *Aṣṭamātṛkā* are grouped at the four cardinal points and at the four intermediary directions and around the central figure of Tripurasundarī. The patterns in which these nine figures are placed evokes the Buddhist pattern on which Vairocana is in the centre with the four Jina at the cardinal points and four Bodhisattvas in the intermediate directions. But this is because, both in Hinduism and in Buddhism, space, as Oldenḅerg remarked,[28] and in this case he meant "ordered" as opposed to "free" space, was conceived of as "a lotus flower the petals of which are the cardinal points and at the four intermediary points." To place a god or gods in this pattern was to order space; it was also to take the town which they protected out of the context of disordered space which surrounded it. To place towns on an eight-petalled lotus was to lift them out of ordinary time.

Pyramid Temples

In everyday speech, the Newars make a distinction between two sorts of buildings: the *dega* which are "pagoda-style" temples and the *dyo chẽ* which are temples that have the aspect of dwelling houses. The expression *dyo chẽ* is used to designate the temples of *Aṣṭamātṛkā.* Architecturally the best known of the pagoda style temples is the "five-storeyed" temple which the Newars call Nyātapola *dega.* It stands on and above a five-stepped pyramid. The five superimposed platforms diminish in size as they ascend and are linked together by a staircase which is situated on the southern facade. On the topmost platform is the temple, built from brick and wood, with five superimposed roofs of decreasing size and similar form. The *garbha gṛha* is situated within. The roofs are covered with red tiles and under their overhang are slanted struts ornamented by wooden polychrome sculptures. The construction of this temple was begun by Bhūpatīndra Malla (1690-1722) and is reputed to have been completed by 1701. According to oral tradition, the king built the temple to appease the anger of Ākāś Bhairav and he installed therein a Tantric goddess, Siddhi Lakṣmī.[29] This goddess is not allowed to be seen by the faithful masses; only Rājopadhyāyā Brahmins have the right to go inside the temple and accomplish *pūjā* at certain times in the year.

Opposite the Nyātapola temple, on Taumadhi Square, is the temple of Ākāś Bhairav. This Bhairav is said to have come to Bhaktapur from Benares; iconographically this Bhairav is represented only by a mask of his head.[30] The Ākāś Bhairav temple is a rectangular construction which rises directly from ground level. It has three superimposed roofs. This temple was erected during the reign of Bhūpatīndra Malla before Nyātapola *dega*: Ākāś Bhairav plays a special role in the religious life of the town. Along with Bhadrakālī, he is the principal personage in the festival of *Bisket Jātrā*. Moreover some of the Bhaktapur inhabitants say that just as Tripurasundarī is the centre of the *Aṣṭamātṛkā*, so is Ākāś'Bhairav in the centre of the Aṣṭabhairav.[31]

If one had the usual reflexes of an art historian, a temple such as Nyātapola Dega would bring to mind the Khmer mountain-temples, as they are called, and in particular Baksei Chamkrong (Angkor) and Prang of Prasat Thom and Koh Ker, both of the tenth century, and facing towards the east. However, what we know, through epigraphy, of one and the other does not permit us to pursue the analogy further. The structures evoke Kailāsa and the denizens of its slopes, but in a vague enough manner. At Banteay Srei (967 A.D.) two frontons represent the Kailāsa as a four-tiered pyramid, and the hosts of each of its platforms, more in accord with Indian iconography, bear only a distant relationship to those figured in this instance. However, they help us to understand that the allusions made here are to Kailāsa and the Himālaya in Indian cosmology.

Two other temples are situated on stepped pyramids and are dedicated to two tantric goddesses; one is dedicated to Bhagavatī and the other to Vatsalā Devī. They are both situated close to the Royal Palace and are of stone construction. In both cases the construction which rises from the topmost platform of the pyramid is a *śikhara*: placed around the central *śikhara* are four stone towers; in the niches of these towers are stone sculptures representing diverse images of the *Mātṛkā*. These temples were also built under Bhūpatīndra Malla at the end of the seventeenth century. It has been argued that the temple of Vatsalā Devī is a version of the Kṛṣṇa temple at Patan, but this seems unlikely when one makes a detailed architectural examination of the two.

Another temple, dedicated to Śiva in Khauma *tol*, previously rose above five-stepped terraces. Today the base alone remains, consisting of five-stepped terraces. The upper part, where the *garbha gṛha* used to be, was destroyed by earthquakes, the most devastaing of which took place in 1934. According to the inscription which is to be found close by the temple, it was built in 1667 by Jagatprakāś Malla.

One should also draw attention to another temple which is known as Phasi Dega and which is also dedicated to Śiva. It has the same five-terraced, pyramidical base. The upper part was destroyed in the 1934 earthquake. Phasi *Dega* and the Khauma *tol Dega* have bases of stone, and not of bricks as is the case of Nyātapola.

All the above-mentioned temples have entrances situated on the southern facade and a staircase which links the terraces together. On either side of the staircase on the southern facade of Nyātapola *dega* are to be found ranks of huge guardians: "At the bottom are the giants Jaya Malla and Phata, athletes in the king's service and reputed to have the strength of ten men; above them are two elephants ten times stronger yet; then, continuing this decimal progression in muscular vigour, two lions, two tigers and the goddesses Siṅghinī and Vyāghriṇī".[32] The same guardians are to be found at the entrance to the temple dedicated to Śiva in Khauma *tol*. The two wrestlers, or royal athletes, are to be found also at the entrance to Dattatreya temple, another temple of royal function erected by Yakṣa Malla (1426-80) in the fifteenth century.[33] The significance of these guardians and the symbolism of the mythical animals are no longer known. In certain paintings, dragons, elephants and other animals surround the principal personage on his throne and to some extent seem to support the latter. One might suggest that these animal-guardians were associated with royal power. Various stories are told about the two athletes. For instance, they are said to have arrived in Bhaktapur from Jaipur at the time when Bhūpatīndra Malla was in the process of building the Nyātapola *dega*. At that time considerable difficulty was being experienced by the workmen in installing the *gajur* on the summit of the top-most roof, and huge scaffolding had been erected for this purpose. When they saw the difficulty of the other workmen, the two athletes themselves climbed up and put the *gajur* in place. The king was so astonished by their prowess that he decided his daughters should marry them. That is why it is sometimes said that these two huge statues represent the king's sons-in-law.

The temple dedicated to Bhagavatī has also two ranks of guardians but these are not the same as those at Nyātapola: in this case we find a camel, a horse, a rhinoceros, a dragon and a statue of guardian (New.: *Kutuwa*), with a child. According to local informants, these animals are the vehicles of Durgā. Karmakar writes that animals of fabulous variety can be associated with the Devī: "Birds, tortoises, alligator, fish, nine species of wild animals, buffaloes, bulls, he-goats, ichneumons, wild bears, rhinoceros, antelopes, iguanas, rein-deer, lions, tigers".[34] To the best of our knowledge, this is the only temple in the Valley which has such animals as rhinoceros and camel on the entrance facade.

These temples with pyramidical bases at Bhaktapur date from the seventeenth century and are without exception

Śaivite; they are dedicated either to Śiva or to a particular Śāktī. Staircase entrances are situated on the southern facade, with one exception, that of the temple of Vatsalā Devī, the entrance to which faces east. The ranks of guardians on the staircases are one of the characteristics of the temples of Bhaktapur, compared to other temples in the Valley.

Notes

* First published in *Newar Art: Nepalese Art during the Malla Period*, Westminster, Aris and Phillips, 1979.

1. It seems that Bhaktapur (or Bhatgaon) is the most recent of the three principal towns of the Valley of Kathmandu: according to oral tradition it was founded in the ninth century A.D. At the end of the fourteenth century, the status of the locality changed and it became the capital of the kingdom of Bhaktapur. The religion of the inhabitants is predominantly Hinduism: 80 per cent of the population is Śaivite. The monuments which one sees today were built between the second half of the fifteenth century and the eighteenth century. Religious edifices are still numerous despite the succession of earthquakes (1808, 1833 and 1934). Despite a few economic and social transformations the town retains its ancient way of life, which is to a great extent regulated by religion.
2. Taleju was the tutelary divinity of the Malla kings: the image of the goddess was brought, it is said, from India by king Harisiṃha-deva in the first half of the fourteenth century. After the division of the Malla kingdom into three separate kingdoms in 1482, other temples for Taleju were built, one in Kathmandu Mahendra by Malla in 1576, one at Patan by Siddhinara Simha (1620-1661). At Bhaktapur and at Patan both temples form part of the palace complex.
3. H. Jorgensen, *A Dictionary of the Classical Newari*, Levin and Munksgaard, Copenhague, 1936, p. 111, *pīṭhu* outside or *pi-thya*, outside.
4. The other Hindu inhabitants of Kathmandu Valley—the Chetri, the Parbatiya, the Brahmins—ignore these Tantric cults and practices.
5. M. Shepherd Slusser and G. Vajracarya, "Two Medieval Nepalese Buildings: An Architectural Study" in *Artibus Asiae*, Vol. XXXVI, No.3, 1974, pp. 169-218. The authors point out that other religious edifices known as *sattals* are surmounted by an *āgama*: "a rather unusual feature of the upper storey is the presence of *āgama*, or secret shrine, a masonry walled room in front of which is the screened sleeping area".
6. This form of Garuḍa which constitutes one of the main features of

Newar art is found not only in wooden and stone sculpture but also in paintings, especially in the *paṭa* of the fifteenth and sixteenth centuries. The same form of Garuḍa is to be found in Thai and Khmer art. See J. Boisselier, *La Sculpture en Thailande*, Paris, Bibliothèque des Arts, 1974, and P. Pal, *Vaiṣṇava Iconology in Nepal*, The Asiatic Society, Calcutta, no date, p. 120

7. *Kathmandu Valley: The Preservation of Physical Environment and Cultural Heritage. A Protective Inventory*. Vienna, A. Schroll, 1975, Vol. I, p. 35. We do not understand the expression Ogamdevda. Perhaps it is a printing mistake for *Āgam-dyo*.
8. This ritual of initiation is known by both Buddhamārgi and Śivamārgi Newars. For the *dīkṣā* among the Buddhist Newars, see M. Allen, "Buddhism without Monks. The Vajrayana Religion of the Newars of Kathmandu Valley", *Journal of South Asian Studies*, No. 3, 1973, University of Western Australia, pp. 1-14.
9. B. Sahaī in *Iconography of Minor Hindu and Buddhist Deities*, Delhi, Abhinav Publications, 1975, p. 210, writes: "Next stage in the development of the *Mātṛkā* figures is furnished by the relief in which four of the Divine Mothers have each a child in the left arm". See also the chapter on "The Old Goddesses in Tantric Cults" in R.N. Nandi, *Religious Institutions and Cults in the Deccan*, Delhi, Motilal Banarsidass, 1973 and T.A. Rao, *Elements of Hindu Iconography*, Madras, 1914, Vol. II, Part II, pp. 356-82.

   Profesor Boisselier points out that the sanctuary South East of Pre Rup (961 A.D.) had, on each side of the doors and frontispieces, images in stucco of *mātṛkā* of which identifiable remains are those of Brahmāyaṇī in the North-East and Vārāhī in the South-West; this seems to be the only example from Cambodia.
10. P. Pal, "Paintings from Nepal in the Prince of Wales Museum", *Bulletin of the Prince of Wales Museum of Western India*, No. 10, 1967, mentioned a manuscript of Devī Mahātmyā (XV) where Māhālakṣmī is represented: "The two covers are illuminated with the images of Śiva dancing on the bull, Mahishasuramaridini, Kālī, the Seven *Mātṛkās*, Mahālakṣmī and Gaṇeśa. With two of her hands, each goddess displays the *vyākhyāna-mudrā* and holds a skull-cup. The remaining hands exhibit attributes peculiar to the particular form of the Devī. Each is seated on her respective mount" (p. 5). For the cult of Mahālakṣmī in India, see R.N. Nandi, *op. cit.*, pp. 137-41.
11. N. Gutschow and B. Kölver, *Bhaktapur. Ordered Space, Concepts and Functions in a Town of Nepal*, Kommissions Verlag Franz Steiner, Wiesbaden, 1975, p. 44: "Between Dasaiṃ and May, before the monsoon, the *gāthā* (woodcutters) impersonating the Nava Durgā, perform dances, part of which is the playful attempt to catch children: hence the name of the rite. They dance in altogether forty places, twenty-one of which are located within the precinct of

Bhaktapur proper, while nineteen others lie in villages or little towns which belonged to the Kingdom of Bhatgaon during the 16th century. The ninth place within the Bhaktapur series is in front of the big Bhairavnāth temple in Taumadhi Square: the twelfth is on Gahhiti." S.Lévi, *op. cit.*, Vol. II, p. 377: the list given by the author does not correspond to that of the Nava Durgā of Bhaktapur.

12. The residential layout of the castes within the town is connected with their position in the social hierarchy. Even today the Untouchables remain outside the limits of the town at Patan as well as Bhaktapur. The Kusle are former Yogi who carry out certain funerary rites. G. Singh Nepali, *The Newars: An Ethno-Sociological Study of a Himalayan Community,* Bombay, United Asia Publications, 1965, writes about the *pīṭh* attendants (*dyo pālā*): "A very important fact to note in connection with these malignant female deities of the lower order is that their *deva pālās* are invariably drawn from the untouchable castes such as Pore, Kusle, Kasai, and Chyame, who are entitled to touch these deities. During the annual festivals, however, the Vanra priest or an Achaju or Joshi may perform the priestly functions" (p. 311).
13. B. Kölver, "A Ritual Map from Nepal" in *Folia Rara,* F. Steiner, 1976, pp. 68-80.
14. P. H. Pott, *Yoga and Yantra: Their Interrelation and their Significance for Indian Archaelogy.* The Hague, M. Nijhoff, 1966. See the chapter: "The Sacred Cemeteries of Nepal", pp. 76-101. On p. 77, the author writes: "It may seem rather unexpected that a cemetery should play the part of a sacred ground. But in Tantrism such regions are *par excellence* the places where the highest ritual initiations in the esoteric doctrine are carried out".
15. D. C. Sircar, *The Śākta Pīṭhas,* 2nd edition, Delhi, Motilal Banarsidas, 1973, p. 3.
16. D. C. Sircar, *op. cit.*, pp. 6 and 7.
17. S. Lévi, *op. cit,* Vol. I, p. 376: "Under the name of Guhyeśvarī, Our Lady of the Secret, she is the ancient patroness of Nepal. Mañjuśrī discovered her and venerated her, hidden in the root of the lotus which bore Svayambhunāth, yet manifest in the limpid spring coming out of the ground....The Brahmins, who do not admit the story about Mañjuśrī, have nevertheless a reason for worshipping the goddess at the same place. When Devī, in a previous existence, was the daughter of Dakṣa, her father slighted shamefully Śiva, her husband; the goddess, offended in her love and her dignity, killed herself, while vowing to be re-born with better parents: she then became the daughter of Himalaya. Learning of the suicide of his beloved, Śiva abandoned his ascetic mortifications and hastened towards the funeral pyre on which Devī had voluntarily mounted, giving thus, to virtuous wives, a shining example; he picked up in his

arms the half-burnt body and returned, burdened by his precious load, towards the peak of Kailasa, but the scorched limbs fell one by one along the way. The secret parts (*guhya*) of the goddess happened to fall on the bank of the Bāgmatī: the earth closed jealously over the holy relic; but a temple marks the site, and, within the sanctuary, a lotus with eight petals decorated with mystic syllables bears the emblem of a triangle which the Brahmins worship as the symbol of the generative organ, while for the Buddhists it expresses the holy Triad, the Three Jewels."

18. W. Ch. Beane, *Myth, Cult and Symbols in Śākta Hinduism*, Leiden, E.J. Brill, 1977, p. 206.
19. M. Shepherd Slusser and G. Vajrācārya, "Two Medieval Buildings: An Architectural and Cultural Study," *Artibus Asiae*, Vol. XXXVI No. 3, 1974, pp. 169-218.
20. M. Slusser and G. Vajrācārya, *ibid.*, p. 172.
21. M. Shepherd Slusser and G. Vajrācārya, *ibid.*, p. 176: "Three architectual types of *sattal* may be distinguished, even though functionally they are one. These are: (1) a small, rectangular building corresponding to the common *pāti*, except for its additional second storey, usually laticed, frequently richer decoration, and occasional inclusion of one or more enclosed shrines. (2) a medium to large, two or three storey structure each floor basically a columned *maṇḍapa* in diminishing size and one or more of which is screened; it may be well decorated and usually incorporates a shrine. (3) a medium to large, two and a half storey structure of a rectangular plan, the ground floor devoted to one or more brick walled shrines surrounded by a columned porch, the intermediate half storey walled, and the top storey an open or partially open pavilion."
22. Tripurasundarī is of course well known in many districts of India and elsewhere in Nepal, for instance at Tibrikot. See D. Snellgrove, *Himālayan Pilgrimage*, Oxford, Bruno Cassirer, 1961, pp. 27-28.
23. P. H. Pott, *op. cit.*, p. 80: "Various texts mention the eight *mahāśmaśānas* in passages dealing with cosmogony. These are mentioned thus in the dPag-bSam-LJon-bZang; and the *śricakrasambaratantra* also considers them expressly in connexion with the Śricakra as a cosmic symbol; not only are the names of various *śmaśānas* given but various deities are also named as their inhabitants and furthermore, various things such as trees and clouds, etc. have a place". Also M. Th. de Mallmann, *Introduction à l'iconographie du Tantrisme bouddhique,* Paris Maisonneuve, 1975, p. 359.
24. P. H. Pott, *op. cit.*, pp. 82-83.
25. S. Lévi *op.cit.*, pp. 82-83.
26. D. Wright, *History of Nepal,* Calcutta, Susil Gupta, 1958, p. 74.
27. S. Lèvi, *op. cit.*, Vol. I, p. 386.

28. H. Oldenberg, *Die Weltanschaung der Brahmāṇa-Texte*, Göttingen, Bandenhoeck and Ruprecht, 1919, p. 38.

A temple consecrated to Siddhilakṣmī is found at Patan; the temple is in the form of a *dyo chẽ*; see the photo in *Kathmandu Valley*, Vol. II, p. 188. The catalogue *Nepalese Art*, Department of Archaeology, Kathmandu, 1966, p. 15, states: "Historically the *Vaṃśavalis* were eloquent about a Kiranti dynasty as perhaps the earliest rulers of Nepal, and there are even people, composed of a section of the Limbus and Rais, who call themselves Kirantis and on a specified day, the occasion of Dewali, gather in large numbers and offer worship to their tutelary deity called Siddhi Lakṣmī in Patan".

30. G. Singh Nepali, *op. cit.*, p. 299: describes the temple of Ākāś Bhairav of Kathmandu at Indra Cok: "This deity derives its name from the belief that its face is always upturned towards the sky because if its eyes were to fall on any object, that object would be destroyed at once. Ākāś Bhairav is also identified with Eklabya, the Bhilla prince mentioned in the Mahabharat.... Another tradition refers to this deity as a Rakshasa prince who had gone to witness thebattle of Mahabharat. This tradition goes on to say the Rakshasa prince was asked by Krishna on whose side he would fight. To this he replied that he would fight on the losing side. Krishna there upon fearing that he was sure to assist the Kauravas, beheaded him with his discus, *Sudarshan cakra*, and caused his head to be thrown back to his home in the Valley of Nepal. This legend also explains the tradition of representing Bhairava in the form of its mask."

31. B. Kölver, *ibid.*, p. 71: "In theory, they might be, indeed by some are, referred to the Bhairava of the central triangle, who is said to stand for the big Bhairavnāth temple immediately south-east of the Nyatapol pagoda. In the present state of our knowledge, this attribution seems somewhat uncertain: I do not know of a ritual observance that would solely link the Aṣṭabhairava to the Bhairavnāth temple."

32. S. Lévi, *op. cit.*, Vol. II, p. 11; the goddesses Siṅghiṇī and Vyāghriṇī are linked with the *Mātṛkā*: on the occasion of the Nava Durgā dance, their masks are to be found in some dance performances. With reference to the *Naipalya Devata Kalyana Panchaviṃśatika*, B. H. Hodgson points out that Siṅghiṇī and Vyāghriṇī "are inferior spirits attached to the *Mātṛkās*" in his article "Notices of the Languages, Literature and Religion of the Bauddhas of Nepal and Bhot", published in *Asiatic Researches*, Vol. XVI, 1828, p. 465. He gives an interesting drawing on p. 464 of Vajra Yoginī between Siṅghiṇī and Vyāghriṇī. The drawing of the two goddesses corresponds closely to the statues that one can see today in front of Nyātapola.

33. M. Shepherd Slusser and G. Vajracarya, *ibid.*, pp. 212-16, give a good

historical description of Dattatreya temple which was originally a *sattal* for Śaiva ascetics. However they say nothing about the two wrestler-guardians at the entrance; the fact that they occupy this position today does not of course mean that they are contemporary with the foundation of the temple.

34. A. P. Karmakar, *The Religions of India*. Vol. I, Lonvala, Mira Publishing House, 1950, p. 212. W. C. Beane, *op. cit.*, suggests that "the affinality of such creatures with the realm of Durgā- Kālī as the Earth-Goddess meant a religious orientation of persons to a divinity who demanded such animals as votive offerings for the welfare of her subjects" (p. 54).

Ritual Planning of the Bhaktapur Kingdom*

Urbanization in Kathmandu Valley became reality at the time of the Malla dynasties (1200-1768). The urban character of agglomerations of settlements becomes clear at that period. The plans of the three towns of the Valley, Kathmandu, Patan and Bhaktapur, today guard traces of previous villages which were incorporated in them at the time of their foundations.[1] These three towns were, in former times, capitals of three different kingdoms after the Valley was divided up at the end of the fifteenth century on the death of king Yakṣamalla (1428-1482).[2] The territories occupied by these "kingdoms" were quite small. The Malla sovereigns did not, it seems, devote much of their activity to extending the frontiers of their domains. However, they did concentrate on the religious organization of their territories. That religious organization, planned some centuries ago, is still functioning today despite the political changes which have occurred in the interim. In this article, I will deal mainly with the former kingdom of Bhaktapur, situated in the Eastern part of the Valley.

It has been claimed that the whole social and religious organization of Nepal was established according to the norms of Hindu texts (*dharmaśāstra*). Brahmins from India, particularly from Mithila and the Deccan, became *purohita* and *rājguru* of the kings of the Malla dynasty who themselves claimed to be of Rajput ancestry. Some royal rituals have been performed in Nepal in the same manner from the thirteenth century up-till modern times despite the fact that the Malla dynasty came to an end in 1768. The Shah dynasty, which has ruled Nepal since 1768, took over ritual practices from the Malla in order to legitimize its own power. For instance, the Shah dynasty adopted the tutelary goddess of the previous Malla rulers: Taleju. From family records studied by M. Witzel, it can be shown for Bhaktapur that some Brahmin families have been active as *rājguru* over long periods.[3] The lack of change in the rituals as well as the "Indianness" can be ascribed not only to the presence of these Brahmin families in the Nepal Valley but also to the existence in Nepal of the major Sanskrit texts of rituals. As is well known, Nepal claims to be the last Hindu kingdom in the world.

From 1970 onwards, a number of scholars have studied the religious organization of the towns of the Valley. The study of Bhaktapur was begun by B. Kölver and N. Gutschow.[4] Since then other studies have been undertaken in Kathmandu, during the restoration work on the Royal Palace at Hanuman Dhoka, by John Sanday and W. Korn,[5] and in Patan by N. Gutschow.[6] In Panauti, a French team has published a detailed analysis of the town.[7] The study of the town plans and place names showed that the planning of the towns of the Valley followed rules imposed by a king. In local ideology, it is always the king who is responsible for the organization of the town or kingdom. Moreover, religious edifices were sited with care and formed a network at ground level which was well known to the local inhabitants. The network, the relationships between different temples and gods residing therein, formed and form part of local knowledge. Preoccupation with the organization of urban space is not only characteristic of Nepal: one finds the same preoccupation in northern India, as recent studies on Benares and Puri have shown.[8] In the late medieval period, throughout India local *māhātmyas* are preoccupied with similar ideas.[9] In Nepal, we are faced with space organized in a manner that no known text enables us to identify but which fieldwork reconstitutes and analyses. However, the fact that the texts "behind" this organization are not yet identifiable should not lead to the conclusion that the construction of the Nepalese religious buildings in questions was inspired by non-Hindu, non-Indian influences.

One of the worthwhile ways of studying the religious organization of the former Newar kingdoms is to concentrate on their rituals. The latter maintain traditions over long periods of time, particularly in Nepal. Recent studies have shown that the whole town of Bhaktapur was thought of by its inhabitants as forming a vast *maṇḍala.*[10] The study of rituals has shown how the kingdom itself was controlled through the propagation of such ideas– and not only the town of Bhaktapur. The foreigner who arrives on foot at Bhaktapur is not at first aware of its plan, is not struck by its symmetry. Nevertheless the inhabitants see it as based on a plan oriented in space, a *maṇḍala*, the centre and the cardinal points of which are indicated by the presence of divinities. At the centre is situated the goddess Tripurasundarī, who is considered as being the first deity established in the town by the king. According to local tradition, it was she who helped the king to found the town and thus the kingdom. Eight goddesses called *mātṛkā* are linked to her, are indeed emanations of her: their temples are situated on the outer rim of the *maṇḍala* and are thought of as protecting the town. Between Tripurasundarī and the *mātṛkā* are situated three circles of divinities comprising ten Mahāvidyā, eight Bhairava and eight Gaṇeśha.[11] The town is divided into nine sectors; each bears the name of a mother goddess. The divinities which figure in this *maṇḍala* do not constitute the whole pantheon. The great Hindu gods, Śiva and Viṣṇu Nārāyaṇa, are also worshipped; but their localization in the town's *maṇḍala* are difficult to determine. Mention must also be made of a feminine divinity Taleju also called Bhagavatī and Śrī, who dwells in a temple within the walls of the Royal Palace and whose cult links the town divinities to that of the king. Taleju, as I have already pointed out, was adopted as tutelary divinity (*iṣṭadevatā*) by the kings of the Malla dynasty. Through her links with Viṣṇu, she is a royal goddess[12] and, in certain legends, she is the king's wife. Only the king, the *rājguru*, the *karmācārya*, and the *jośi*[13] were entitled to see her image, which is kept on the first floor of the temple. The link between the town divinities and the royal goddess Taleju can be observed at certain festivals, for instance, at the *Bisket Jātrā*, considered as the New Year Festival (March-April) and at Dasāim, the festival of the goddess (October-November).[14] At the *Bisket Jātrā* the divinities of the *maṇḍala* are taken out in procession in a precise order. The order is hierarchical. The divinities do homage to Tripurasundarī, then to Taleju. On the last time the processions go out, the ninth and last day of the festival, it is the goddess Tripurasundarī who does homage to Taleju. The same order of precedence is followed at the festival of the goddess, Dasāim, when all the local divinities do homage to Taleju; it is again Tripurasundarī who is the last divinity during the festival to do so.

Moreover all town-divinities in course of the various processions render homage to Taleju. For instance, the Dīpaṅkara Buddha, during their outings, stop in front of Taleju temple to worship. However, the image of Taleju never goes out in procession. Only the goddess Duimāju, represented in the form of a simple stone, and considered as a substitute of Taleju, is taken out at the time of the *Bisket Jātrā* and goes around the Durbar Square.[15] The difference between Taleju, who never moves out of the temple– yet controls the whole town– and the town divinities, which do go out and follow itineraries which signify the parts of the town which are under their control, is clear.

Control of space both inside and outside town-limits is attributed to another group of divinities called Nava Durgā. According to the inhabitants of Bhaktapur, the Nava Durgā must be distinguished from the Aṣṭa Mātṛkā despite the almost identical names of the two groups' members. The Nava Durgā are represented by nine masks worn by dancers who are members of the gardeners' caste, called *gāthā*. Their dances (New. *phyaka*) take place throughout eight months of the year from October to June. According to the oral tradition and chronicles,[16] it was the king Ananda Malla (1147-66), the founder of the town of Bhaktapur, who was instructed by the Nava Durgā to set their images in proper places to ensure the security and protection of the town of Bhaktapur both internally and externally. In fact, Ananda Malla restructured the existing villages when he chose Bhaktapur as the capital of his realm. The dances are reputed to have been inaugurated by king Suvarṇa Malla in 1513 as part of measures he took to put an end to a famine.[17]

Each year, in the month of August (Śravan), new masks are made in secret by a painter (*citrakār*). The masks are made of clay, mixed with bits of cotton, and a gum-like paste made from wheat flour. Once the mixture is ready, it is separated into thirteen parts by a painter. Each part is placed over a low-relief mould (New. *thasa*) covered with a clean black cloth. The mask-making painter kneads the clay with his fingers to make it fit into the contours of the mould. The clay mask-forms are left on the moulds to dry for about four days. When dry, the masks are painted with a mixture of boiled wheat flour, water and animal glue. When dry this paint results in an almost opaque finish. In making the masks, the painters consult a book containing drawings of the original Nava Durgā masks and notes on the colours to be employed.[18] Colour in this context has several symbolic functions. Red, blue and white are considered to be the most powerful colours. At the popular level, red stands for sacrificial blood and anger. Blue-black represents energy and power. White stands for male semen, purity and death.[19] The masks portray the frightening aspects of the goddess.

The masks are destroyed by burning at the beginning of the rainy season. The ashes from this fire are hidden in a clay pot (*kalaśa*) which is put into the river Hanumante. The masks are in fact treated like human dead whose ashes are also put in the river. These ashes will later be incorporated in the new masks made in the following months of August and September, usually one month before the festival of the goddess called, in Nepal, Dasāim.

The goddesses in the Nava Durgā group are: Mahākālī, Vaiṣṇavī, Brāhmayaṇī, Indrāyaṇī, Maheśvarī, Kaumārī and Vārāhī. Mahālaksmī, the eighth goddess, is not represented by a mask but by a small silver *yantra.* Tripurasundarī, the ninth, is not shown to the public: her mask is kept inside the Nava Durgā temple. The goddesses whose names figure in the Nava Durgā are also to be found in other combinations in India. They are to be found in lists in various *Purāṇa.*[20] What is important here, is the local interpretation of the role of the goddesses. In Bhaktapur the so-called Nava Durgā include in fact five other masks, also worn by the dancers; Bhairava, Gaṇeśa, Seto Bhairava, a mask of a lioness called Sinhā, and a mask of a tiger, Dunia. To these is added a mask of Śiva which is carried by Gaṇeśa but not worn. Śiva is considered as the lord of the Nava Durgā. When the dances are not performed, the masks are kept in a temple, located in the northeast part of the town, at Ga-che.

The masks of Nava Durgā are connected with the agricultural cycle and, in particular, with rice production. The power represented in the masks helps farmers to get good harvests as a result of their labours. The Nava Durgā dances start on the last day of Dasāim, the great autumn festival which commemorates the mythic victroy of Durgā over the demon Mahisāsura. On the eighth day of Dasāim the masks of the Nava Durgā are placed in the open sanctuary of the goddess Brāhmayaṇī, situated in the northeastern part of the town. The dancers then put on the new masks for the first time and go to Taleju's temple, at night-time. There, in the principal courtyard, they meet the image of Taleju which is, in fact, covered by a red cloth and carried by farmers, Suwal Jyapu, who cook the rice for the goddess Taleju. They are followed by two Brahmins who carry the sword of the Malla kings, also covered in red cloth, which is normally kept on the first floor of the temple. Around midnight, a white stallion, the king's mount, is led into the courtyard of the temple. It is said that, at that moment, a Rājopādhyāya Brahmin gives the dancers the power (*siddhi*) to act and dance throughout the eight coming months.[21] Life is thus given to them under royal patronage. The group of masked dancers carry with them , in a basket, the severed head of a buffalo, signifying in this manner Durgā's victory.

I have mentioned earlier that the masks are burnt at the beginning of the rainy season in the bright fortnight of Āsāḍha. At that time, the town's inhabitants worship, for the last time in the year, the masks of the Nava Durgā. A few days before this, they must visit the Taleju temple and the Brahmin then, with the help of a *mantra*, extracts life from the masks so that what is subsequently burned are, so to speak, their dead bodies. When people come back from the Taleju temple and the masks have not yet been burned, a ram is sacrificed in the temple of Viṣṇu Nārāyaṇa (Wakupathi Nārāyaṇa) in the eastern part of the town. In the Newar context, a sacrifice to Viṣṇu Nārāyaṇa is exceptional: it can only be explained in this instance by the links between the Nava Durgā and the king. It is a well-known fact that the king identifies himself with Viṣṇu in the form of Nārāyaṇa. The dances begin under royal control since it is the royal goddess who gives them the power to dance. The dances take place first within the boundaries of the town. The town is divided, from an administrative point of view, into 24 quarters (Nep. *tol* or New. *twa*). "The visits to the quarters of Bhaktapur, however, start on a very auspicious date. Within the calendar of the Nava Durgā it is the only date which is not scheduled according to the lunar calendar but according to the Indian solar calendar, which is sidereal." "They move through the streets and lanes of the quarter they are supposed to visit according to a fixed schedule, the processional movement being divided by 3 to 9 stops."..."the distribution of the routes well reflect the spatial organization of the town into specific quarters with identifiable edges".[22] They do not perform in the westernmost quarters; they dance in 21 quarters. They must dance in each part of the town to renew the links between that part of the town as a whole. Their role while distinct from that of the Aṣṭa Mātṛkā is also more dynamic.

The dances are performed not only inside the limits of the town but also in a number of localities outside and around the town. I was able to compile a list of fourteen localities (see the map).[23] When we put together the names of these localities, we realize that they are all situated within the limits of the former kingdom of Bhaktapur. The first places visited outside the town are Deopatan and Paśupatināth. Like the kings of Kathmandu and Patan, those of Bhaktapur held political power from Paśupatināth. As for Deopatan, the first place they visit is the "stele" marking the foundation of the old royal palace. Throughout the centuries, Deopatan has been an important political centre. Today, the first place visited by the dancers in each locality is the former residence of its territorial chief. Such chiefs were previously subordinate to the Malla kings.[24] The dancers then go to the temple of the local manifestation of the goddess, considered as the religious centre of the locality. In the villages of the countryside, space is organized in a more simple manner. There is usually just one main temple of the goddess as, for instance, at Nala, Thimi or Bode. The small town of Panauti is exceptional by the complexity of its organization which has been stressed in the French work mentioned above (note 7).

The inhabitants of Bhaktapur claim that the dancers represent divinities which ensure the success of the rice-harvest as well as the protection of the town.[25] This interpretation is valid not only for the capital town, but also for the kingdom. Yearly, each district of the kingdom was ritually re-connected to its centre by the Nava Durgā dances which thus had an integrating function. As the boundaries of each locality are well known, the assemblage of all localities enables us to trace the former boundaries of the state. So it can be said that the itineraries followed by the Nava Durgā dancers draw attention to the limits of the former kingdom of Bhaktapur.

Notes

* First published in *Shastric Tradtions in Indian Arts,* F. Steiner, Verlag, 1986.

1. L. Petech, *Medieval History of Nepal,* Roma Is. M.E.O., 1984, p. 184. For Bhaktapur see N. Gutschow and B. Kölver, *Bhaktapur, Ordered Space: Concepts and Functions in a Town of Nepal.* Wiesbaden, F. Steiner, 1975, p. 20: "The town of Bhaktapur probably developed from two or more villages which at some time grew together. This process is anything but unique in South Asia: vide, e.g. Chittagong, the old name of which was, in Sanskrit, Saptagrāma (of) seven villages. When separate settlements were fused to become a city, there arose the necessity to delimitate the new foundation, to set signs which marked the unity recently established".
2. L. Petech, *op. cit.*, p. 181.
3. M. Witzel, "Zur Geschichte der Rājopādhyāya von Bhaktapur", in *Folia Rara,* Wolfgang Voigt LXV Diem Natalem Celebranti, Wiesbaden, F. Steiner, 1976, pp. 159-79.
4. N. Gutschow and B. Kölver, *op. cit.*
5. W. Korn, *The Traditional Architecture of the Kathmandu Valley,* Kathmandu, Ratna Pustak Bhandar, 1976.
6. N. Gutschow, *Stadtraum und Ritual der newarischen Städte im Kathmandu-Tal.* Stuttgart, W. Kohlhammer, 1982. See Patan: pp. 148-67.
7. V. Barré, P. Berger, L. Feveile, G. Toffin, *Panauti, une ville au Népal,* Paris, Berger Lavrault, 1981.
8. D.L. Eck, *Banaras, City of Light.* Princeton, Princeton University Press, 1982.

   H. Kulke, "Legitimation and Town Planning in the Feudatory States of Central Orissa", in *Ritual Space in India, Studies in Architectural Anthropology,* edited by J. Pieper, London, AARP, 1980, pp. 30-40.
9. H. Kulke, *Cidambaramāhtmya. Eine Untersuchung der religionsgeschichtlichen und historischen Hintergründe für die Entstehung der Tradition einer südindischen Tempelstadt.* Wiesbaden: Harrassowitz, 1970.

   M.C. Porcher, 'La représentation de l'espace sacré dans le *Kāñcimāhātmya*' in *Puruṣārtha. L'Espace du temple* 1. Paris, 1985, No. 8, pp. 23-53.
10. A. W. Macdonald and A. Vergati Stahl, *Newar Art– Nepalese Art during the Malla Period.* Warminster: Aris and Phillips, 1979, pp. 86-87. M. Shepherd Slusser, *Nepal Maṇḍala: A Cultural Study of the Kathmandu Valley,* Princeton, Princeton University Press, 1982, pp. 83-127; the author showed that all the Valley was conceived as a *maṇḍala.*

11. B. Kölver, "A Ritual Map of Nepal", in *Folia Rara,* Wolfgang Voigt LXV Diem Natalem Celebranti, Wiesbaden, F. Steiner, 1976, pp. 68-80. B. Kölver, "Stages in the evolution of a world picture", in *Numen,* Vol. XXXII, 1986, No. 2, pp. 131-168; "house, temple, town or country is placed under the guardianship of a group of deities who are distributed over the Four or Eight Quarters; they surround the territory thus protected; they are worshipped by the usual means, including circumambulation; and this circumambulation serves to set off the lands so protected from their surroundings" (p. 138). "Thus, we find systems of shrines or statues or struts: Eight Bhairavas, or Mothers, or even Gaṇeśas, who ideally occupy the eight regions of the compass. These configurations can again be used to ward off a territory: the ideal line connecting the deities forms a ritual boundary which sets the enclosed 'field' (*kṣetra*) off from the unprotected world outside" (p. 139).
12. A. Vergati Stahl, "Taleju, Sovereign Deity of Bhaktapur" in *Asie du Sud. Traditions et Changements,* Paris, Ed. du C.N.R.S., 1979, pp. 163-67.
    G. Toffin, "Dieux souverains et rois dévots", *L'Homme,* 99, 1986, Vol. XXVI, No. 3, pp. 71-95.
13. A. Vergati, 'Les associations religieuses (*guṭhi*) des temples de la vallée de Kathmandu (Népal), in *Puruṣārtha. L'Espace du temple II,* Paris, Ed. du EHESS, 1986, pp. 97-123.
14. For detailed descriptions of these two *jātrā* see M. Anderson, *The Festivals of Nepal,* London, George Allen and Unwin,1979; N. Gutschow, 1982, *op. cit.*
15. M. Shepherd Slusser, *op. cit.*, p. 67: "Taleju was widely worshipped in Mithila and in other parts of India, and, with the Maithilī influx into the Valley in the 14th century, Taleju's cult received new impetus.Her popular association with Mithila is illustrated by one of her nicknames, Domāju, the Mother Goddess of the Ḍoya (Maithilī)".
16. B.J. Hasrat, *History of Nepal as Told by its Own and Contemporary Chronicles,* Hoshiarpur, V.V. Research Institute Press, 1970, p. 50.
    D. Wright, *History of Nepal,* Cambridge University Press, 1877, p. 163: "He established his court at Bhaktapur, where he built a Durbar; and having one night seen and received instructions from the Nava Durgā, he set up their images in proper places, to ensure the security and protection of the town both internally and externally."
17. B.J. Hasrat, *op. cit.*, p. 58: "In the Nepali Samvat 633 (A.D. 1513) a dreadful famine occurred which caused the inhabitants of Bhatgaon to be scattered in the country. In the meantime Raja Svarṇamalla having quarrelled with his brother was reigning in Bhatgaon and Banepā. In that very year he heard from many wise men that the Rajah of Kantipur had constituted or rather caused to be peformed the Nava Durgā festival. In order to outdo him, Svarṇamalla caused to be

performed and established the Ikhuncha Pyakun nāch and also annually a nāch of Mahālakṣmī at Bore".

18. A. Vergati, "Sketchbook of Viṣṇu Bahadur Citrakar" in *Buddhist Iconography in Nepalese Sketch-Books*, edited by Lokesh Chandra. New Delhi, 1984, pp. 1-59.
19. J. H. Teilhet, "The Tradition of the Nava Durgā in Bhaktapur, Nepal' in *Kailash*, Vol. VI, No. 2. Kathmandu, 1978, pp. 81-98; her article gives a detailed description of the process of mask-making and iconographic details of the masks. See also for the symbolism of colours and of masks: R. Levy, "How the Nava Durgā protect Bhaktapur, The effective meanings of a symbolic enactment", paper presented at the conference on the Heritage of the Kathmandu Valley, Lubeck, June 1985, pp. 24-28.
20. N.N. Bhattacharya, *History of Śakta Religion*, New Delhi, Munshiram, 1973, pp. 102-03; D.C.Sircar, *The Śakta Piṭha*, 2nd edition. Delhi, Motilal Banarsidas, 1973.
21. J. H. Teilhet, *op. cit.*, p. 93.

    N. Gutscow, "The Nava Durgā of Bhaktapur– Spatial Implications of an Urban Ritual", paper read at the conference on the Heritage of the Kathmandu Valley. Lubeck, June, 1985. The author gives a detailed description of the ceremonies performed by the dancers inside the town and then followed in different quarters.
22. N. Gutschhow, *op. cit.*, 1985, p. 10.
23. The list I made in Nepal during fieldwork is less complete than those to be found in K. Stürzbecher, *Bhaktapur, Architektur und Stadtentwicklung im Kathmandutal*, Saarbrücken, Breitenbach publisher, 1981, pp. 174-75 and N. Gutschow, *op. cit.*, 1985, p. 3. I was not able to follow the dancers throughout the eight months.

    Paśupatināth-Deo Patan, Thimi, Nagdes, Bode, Kabilas, Chaprigau, Gokarna, Sankhu, Cangu, Sanga, Dhulikel Nala, Banepa and Panauti. Five more localities are mentioned by these authors; Bhulankhocho, Tokha, Tingal, Choukot and Khampu.
24. K. Stürzbecher, *op. cit.*, p. 173.
25. R. Levy, *op. cit.*, p. 36: "The pattern traced by dances both outside and within the city are considered to form protective *yantras*, in the same way as the pattern of the dance performance in a local area out a protective space. Only few specialists in the city among the Brahmans and among the Gatha performers are aware of the places and sequences in the largest cycle. All that the vast majority of the spectators to the local performance know is that somehow this local performance weaves their locality into a larger pattern of temporal and spatial relationships during the annual cycle, a pattern centering on the city".

The Killing of the Snakes or the Founding of the Town of Bhaktapur*

The ancient towns of Nepal—at least those which have more than five thousand inhabitants (the official criterion of the Nepalese Government for classifying a locality as a town)—are all situated in the Valley of Kathmandu.[1] They were founded by Newars and are still inhabited, mainly, by the Newars, an ethnic group whose language is classified as Tibeto-Burman and who form the old substratum of the population of the Valley. Other ethnic groups, settled in the Valley from the sixteenth century onwards, are, for instance, the Khas whose language was Nepali. However, even the change of dynasty in 1768, when the Gorkhas took political control, did not succeed in making Newar culture disappear. One of the major differences between the Newars and the other ethnic groups of Nepal is that the former live in towns and the urban nature of their civilization is predominant.

Today, there are three important towns in the Valley. All three, at different moments in their history, were royal capitals: the present-day capital Kathmandu, Patan (or Lalitpura) and Bhaktapur (or Bhadgaon). Among these three towns it is Bhaktapur which has retained its traditional character: the population is still 98 per cent Newar and is in majority Hindu (Śaivite). Kathmandu, on the other hand, since the eighteenth century, sheltered diverse non-Newar populations. The town of Patan, considered to be the most ancient town in Nepal, is above all Buddhist by tradition.

Towns really existed only from the start of the Malla period (1200-1768) onwards. This urban growth corresponded to an important increase in trade and handicrafts.[2] Nevertheless one must stress that the Valley served as warehouse on one of the roads from India to China: the towns of the Valley have never subsisted entirely, nor even principally, on trade nor on handicrafts, the latter being however of great repute.

In 1975, about 80 per cent of the population of Bhaktapur was composed of farmers. Patan, the cottage industries of which are still famous, is also inhabited in majority by farmers. The plans of these three towns bear traces of the old villages which were incorporated in them at the time of the foundation as well as of the ancient routes crossing them. In Nepal the difference between towns and villages is not so much a question of types of buildings as of social organization: only the towns have a population where all the castes are represented. Recent studies (Toffin 1982: 81-93) have shown that even today several villages of the Valley have populations of only one caste: their inhabitants are thus forced to summon priests living in the towns for their religious ceremonies.

The most ancient chronicle of the Valley, the *Gopālarājavaṃśavali*, which goes back to the fourteenth century refers to the founding of towns.[3] So do two other texts, one Hindu and the other Buddhist, which were compiled in the nineteenth century making use of older materials.[4] The three chronicles in question are dynastic lists (*vaṃśavali*): they give the dates of reigns: they are concerned above all with political events and the construction of religious edifices, etc. The founding of towns is mentioned in these texts as the glorious act of a king. In the Buddhist chronicle, edited by D. Wright at the end of the nineteenth century, the creation of the Valley is attributed to the Bodhisattva Mañjuśrī and the protective divinities of the kingdom, installed by kings, the cults they inaugurate, are, in majority, Buddhist.

In the nineteenth century Hindu chronicle translated into English by Hasrat, the creation of the Valley is Viṣṇu's doing; Hinduism attributes an eminent role in the creation of the world to him: the protective divinities of the kingdom are almost all Hindu. Let us remember that the Newar population was composed of Buddhists and of Hindus in proportions which varied from place to place but that the Newar kings were all Hindus and that Hinduism was the state religion.[5] Let me add two important points. The first is that the two nineteenth century chronicles contain many dates which, at first sight, seem exact but which, when one examines them carefully, are more often than not wrong. The second point is that there are two phases in the legend of the peopling of the Valley. First, there is the "creation" of the Valley by a divinity who, for Buddhists, is Mañjuśrī and for Hindus, Viṣṇu. More precisely it is not a question of a creation *ex nihilo* but of provoking conditions which allow the Valley to be inhabited: the Valley is depicted as having been originally a lake the waters of which were drained away by the divinity (Lévi 1905, II: 47). The founding of towns comes next : such as it is described in the chronicles, it is a royal undertaking. The name of the king to whom the foundation is attributed can vary; the date of the founding can change; but the foundation is always a royal work. The founding comprises the construction of religious edifices: temples, sanctuaries, monasteries, etc. A locality acquires the status of a town when, through the act of foundation, the protective divinities of the site have been installed *inside* and *outside* its limits. The organization of a town's sanctuaries and temples takes place initially from its centre and, ideally, the divinities are disposed in concentric circles around this centre. The limits of a locality are also ritual limits. The gods are "installed" not only at the level of the capital town but also at the level of the kingdom.

Here, for instance, is how the chronicle translated by Hasrat describes the foundation of the town of Naubali at

Deopatan. The foundation is attributed to king Śivadeva of the Licchavi dynasty (c. 3000-750 C.E). It is probable that the account is fictitious. Moreover, it will be noticed that it is a case of the foundation of a town inside a town or in place of a town (*sic*): it is then, a historically fanciful story. For this very reason it reveals more clearly the ideology which lies behind the concept of "foundation" for the Newars: "Śivadeva also built a city, on the four crossroads, which was named Naubali, and in which were formally placed the images of the following deities with respective *vahana* or carriages and *ganas* or followers: 4 Ganeś, 4 Bharaiva, 4 Nrityanath, 4 Mahadeva, 4 Kumari, 4 Khandita Buddhas, 4 Khamba, 4 Gaganachari. He then placed at the door of each temple the image of Mahādeva to guard the entrance of it. Again he placed nine different Devīs in nine directions of the city and also built and placed, where required, doors, wells, streams, Nrityanāthas, etc. and named the city Gullo or Svarnapuri. He also re-established the images of Vana Kali and Vana Vinayaka which lay hidden in ruins and also to the west of Vajresvari he built a masan (*smaśana*) or a place to burn the dead (Hasrat 1970: 41).

Although the notion of orientation is not mentioned formally, it is clear that the installing of the divinities takes account of an oriented spatial schema. The brahmin who wrote this chronicle (or part of it) did so with an oriented view of the spatial situation of the town's sanctuaries and of their mutual relationships.

The founder king does not act on his own initiative. He receives from a goddess the advice, that is to say, the order to carry out the foundation in a particular site. The goddess belongs to the group of the goddesses called "Vaisnavite". They are Mahālakṣmī at Kathmandu, and Annapurna Devī, who came from Benares, at Bhaktapur; in Patan, a Buddhist town, there is the Buddhist goddess Sareśvara (Wright 1877: 135; Hasrat 1970: 44). Here is how the chronicle translated by Hasrat recounts the founding of the town of Kathmandu: "Guṇakāmadeva was a fervent adorer of Mahālakṣmī, or the goddess of riches, who consequently was very kind to him. One night when he was sleeping he had a dream in which he was commanded by the said deity to build a city in the shape of a *khadga* (sword) near the confluence of the rivers Vāgmati and Viṣṇumati where the God Kāmeśvara resides and the place is pure. After the above mentioned dream, the Rajah (king) built the city of Kantipur where he settled the image of Lakṣmi. The city consequently became a place of trade and wealth peopled by 18,000 inhabitants" (Hasrat 1970: 46).

The foundation of a town implies therefore an order given miraculously by a goddess; the installation in its centre of the principal feminine divinity; the installation of other divinities in an oriented schema (*maṇḍala*); sometimes the fortification and then the construction of a large number of houses (12,000 houses when Bhaktapur was founded by the king Ananda Malla; and 18000 houses when Bhaktapur was founded by the king Guṇakāmadeva); and lastly the inauguration of an annual festival of the locality (*yatra*) in honour of the goddess who helped the king at the time of the foundation.

According to the texts which are available to us, different origins are given when explaining the founding of the town of Bhaktapur. According to the inscriptions, Ananda Malla (1147-1166) built the Royal Palace in the Eastern part of the town: this Palace was called Tripura (name of a Vaisnavite goddess) and the town was known as Tripura until the sixteenth century (Petech 1984: 66); the act of Ananda Malla was not therefore one of founding a town *ex nihilo* but of changing the status of an agglomeration which, through the construction of the Royal Palace, became a royal town. Yet it will be noticed that the oral tradition, to which I will return later, makes the goddess Tripurasundarī the most ancient goddess in the town. Her temple constitutes the religious centre of the town of Bhaktapur.[6] The Buddhist chronicle, edited by D. Wright, which, in the matter, does not differ from the Hindu chronicle, tells a tale in conformity with the ideological schema I have already sketched out: "This younger brother, being very generous and wise, gave up the sovereignty over the two cities; and having invoked Annapurna Devī from Kasi, founded a city of 12,000 houses which he named Bhaktapur (Bhadgaon) and included sixty small villages in this territory" (Wright1877:163) According to this chronicle, the king was not satisfied with founding the capital of the kingdom; he also founded seven towns which, we are led to believe, formed the entirety of the various localities in the ancient kingdom of Bhaktapur: Banepa, Panauti, Nala, Dhulikel, Khadpu, Chaukol, Sanga (Wright 1877:163). The goddess, who authorized the founding of these towns, is not Annapurna (the goddess at the origin of the founding of Bhaktapur) but Candeśvarī, the principal goddess of Banepa, the most important of the seven towns mentioned above.

In all of this there is, undoubtedly, a mythic element reminiscent of similar Indian texts. Numerous Indian texts indicate the ideal spatial layout of edifices within a royal capital, in particular in that of a universal sovereign, the *cakravartin* of Buddhist tradition.[7] The medieval chronicle of the kings of Kashmir, the *Rājatarangini*, points out that when the king of Kashmir founded the town of Pravarapura, today called Śrīnagar, he did so with the help of a local goddess who showed him the place where it should be founded and indicated the moment propitious for doing so. But the Kashmiri legend is not exactly similar to the Nepalese legends.[8]

Today, there still exists in Bhaktapur an oral tradition the contents of which differ from those of the written chronicle but the conceptual basis of which is similar. I collected several versions of it from a dozen or so informants in 1975 and 1979. This oral tradition connects the founding of the town with the town's main festival, the *Bisket Jātrā*. Bisket is a Newar compound which one can translate as the "killing of the serpents": *sket* from the verb *syako* "to sacrifice or to put to death", to kill; and *bi* "serpent". This festival takes place each year at the beginning of the month of April, and this corresponds with the beginning of the Nepalese and Indian New Year.[9] The festival lasts nine days: it is the only one of the town's festivals which brings into play all the local pantheon. Its principal actors are the goddess Bhadrakali (known during the rest of the year by the name of Vaiṣṇavi) and Akaśa Bhairava, a terrible form of Śiva: they are taken out in procession on two different chariots. According to the oral tradition, this festival was inaugurated by a king in honour of the goddess Bhadrakali, whose name varies according to different informants. The masculine divinity Akaśa Bhairava would have arrived later from the town of Benares in order to calm the anger of the goddess.

Here is the most widespread version of the legend. "A prince of the future Malla dynasty came one day to hunt in the jungle near the town of Bhaktapur. At Lhaku Lache, he watched a cat and a rat which were fighting. The rat won the fight; and the prince followed the rat into a tree trunk. Inside this trunk the prince saw the elephant-headed god Gaṇeśa who asked him what he wanted. The prince answered that he wished to found a town. The god Gaṇeśa replied: 'I cannot ensure the success (*siddhi*) of the town's founding. That is beyond my power. Go towards the South-west: there you will find an old woman who is looking towards the south and drying her hair. Stay behind her and ask her permission to build the town'. The prince followed the god Gaṇeśa's instructions. He found the old woman who was none other than the goddess Bhadrakali (or Vaiṣṇavi). After having listened to him, she asked him to move around in front of her and said to him, 'Go and take a bath in the river at Hanuman ghat; there you will find in the river a sword (*khadga*). Take that sword and go into the jungle: there you will meet a serpent that you must kill; this serpent is the serpent of the princess (*rāj kumārī*)'. The prince carried out her instructions. He found the serpent who said to him: 'If you kill me, you must promise to kill next the serpents who come out of the nose of the princess, and marry her'. The prince found the princess asleep in her Palace. Close by her he saw a stretcher on which lay the body of a young man. Suddenly the goddess appeared to the prince in the Palace and explained to him that each night a young man who wanted to marry the princess (or who was the lover of the princess) was killed by the serpent demons which came out of the nose of the princess when she was asleep. The prince followed the advice given by the goddess. He took the sword and killed the two serpents when they came out of the nose of the princess. He was thus able to marry the princess, became king and founded the town of Bhaktapur". The first goddess to be installed in the centre of the town was Tripurasundarī. Then the king inaugurated the festival of *Bisket Jātrā* in honour of the goddess Bhadrakali. In other versions the founding prince is called Bhadra: after having married the princess, he becomes, like his descendants, "King of the serpents".

These versions of the legend of the foundation of the town of Bhaktapur can be reduced to the following schema: a goddess gives to a foreign prince the two means necessary for becoming a king who possesses a kingdom: (1) a sword (*khadga*), symbol of martial power and, later on, sceptre of the Malla kings; (2) a territory represented by a princess who is unmarried (or who cannot keep a husband), prisoner of the fiendish forces which impede the good government of the kingdom and from which the prince must deliver her. The prince comes from the "outside"; he hunts in the forest and meets the goddess there. The site of the future town is a deserted place: often the inhabitants, when they tell this legend, emphasize: "before the coming of the Malla kings there were neither houses nor temples" which does not stop the prince from meeting the princess of the legend in the "Palace". The goddess Bhadrakali, who helped the king to find the sword and to kill the serpents,is usually called Vaiṣṇavi and only bears the name of Bhadrakali during the festival of *Bisket Jātrā.* She is then a goddess linked to Viṣṇu; and every Indian king is a partial incarnation of Viṣṇu. The king's main spouse is likewise identified with the goddess Śrī, the wife of Viṣṇu. In Indian royal ideology, the kingdom, or the space of the kingdom, is considered also as being the goddess Śrī. Thus the king is at the same time the master and the husband of the land, which is considered as a woman. In Nepal, the king who founds a town is also the first king of the Malla dynasty and so its founder.

The South-westerly direction, indicated by the god Gaṇeśa, is that in which today we find the open sanctuary (*piṭh*) and the temple of the goddess Bhadrakali. Let us remember that the town of Bhaktapur is conceived ideally as a *maṇḍala* and is surrounded by the sanctuaries of the eight goddesses: to each goddess is assigned a cardinal point or an intermediary direction.

The foundation involves a murder: the prince must kill the serpent demons and thus deliver the princess.[10] The conquest of the princess assures him the kingdom.[11] The theme of the two serpent-demons coming out of the nostrils of the princess is found also in the Tibetan version of the *Tales of the Vampire.*[12]

In the Tibetan story too the prince comes from the "outside": it is after the predictions made to him by Buddhist divinities such as Vajrapāṇi that he learns how to take possession of a territory by killing two serpents. Although in the Tibetan story it is not a question of founding a town, the hero nevertheless takes possession of a palace and of a kingdom by freeing the princess. It is then possible that the legend of the founding of Bhaktapur includes also elements which came from Tibet, which is nearby, or from High Asia.

This legend of the founding of a town which is so steeped in Hinduism, makes apparent an aspect of the concept of royalty which has not yet been studied. In it, the sovereign is, first of all, a founder and, from this act of founding, the brahmin is absent. The priest is in no manner associated with the act of taking possession of a territory. At the most, one can suppose that he makes his entry when sanctuaries and cults are inaugurated. In this respect the Kashmiri chronicle is no different from the Newar legends : in this case too the king founds the kingdom with the help of the divinity and without the intervention of a priest.

In Newar ideology, to found a town is also to establish the sanctuaries which organize space in the town and the kingdom.[13] In the historical and geographical conditions prevailing in the Valley of Kathmandu, Newar kings have accorded more importance to the religious organization of their kingdoms which, in the fifteenth century, seldom occupied more than a third of the Valley, than to the conquest of new territories.

The myth of the founding of the town of Bhaktapur is thus a lively and vital element in religious life: it is written in the topography of the town and the location of its sanctuaries. It has inspired the town's great local festival, the *Bisket Jātrā*, in which, each year, the founding of the town is re-enacted.[14] The participants and the spectators of the festival are fully conscious of its implications. The festival is an annual rehearsal of the founding myth.

Like many festivals in the Valley of Kathmandu, *Bisket Jātrā* is a succession of processions (New. Jātrā) in the course of which statues of divinities are taken through the town following precise itineraries which allow very little place for innovation or personal initiative. The festival takes its course in function of the local hierarchy of the divinities and thus is a reflection of this hierarchy. *Bisket Jātrā* takes place every year at the beginning of the month of April; as the calendar is lunar the date for it is fixed by astrologers in function of the phases of the moon: it corresponds more or less to the Nepalese New Year. The festival lasts nine days. This period can be divided into two parts: the first lasts four days and is concerned with the procession of the chariot of Akaśa Bhairava and of the chariot of the goddess Bhadrakali; the second is devoted to the procession of the other divinities of the town. This is a Śaivaite festival but all the inhabitants of the town are concerned by it and participate in it whether they are Hindus or Buddhists. One of the kings to whom the inauguration of the festival is attributed is Bhupatindra Malla (1696-1722) who is also considered to have had Taumadhi Square, where the festival takes place, reconstructed.

The first act is staged in the centre of the town on Taumadhi square, where two important temples are situated—Nyatapola and that of Akaśa Bhairava. The temple of Nyatapola, famous for its five superposed roofs, was built at the end of the seventeenth century by king Bhupatindra Malla : it is dedicated to the goddess Siddhi Lakṣmī (Success Prosperity) who, in fact, takes no part in the procession: the worship carried out in the temple is secret and the inhabitants have not the right to see the statue. The temple of Akaśa Bhairava is more ancient than that of Nyatapola: its foundation goes back to the fifteenth century. Akaśa Bhairava ("the frightener of the sky"), one of the terrible aspects of Śiva, is the principal actor in the festival; he is accompanied by the goddesses Bhadrakali (or Vaiṣṇavi). The presence of Akaśa Bhairava at Bhaktapur is explained as follows: "Śiva had come from Benares to Bhaktapur to watch the Jātrā of the goddess Bhadrakali. Nobody recognised him but the Goddess Bhadrakali made known to her faithful that Śiva was in the town in human form, that she wanted to keep him in Bhaktapur and that he had to be caught: he could be recognized because he was a head taller than anyone else. When people tried to catch hold of him, Akaśa Bhairava tried to flee under ground. But his head remained above ground level: it was cut off and that is why Akaśa Bhairava is represented in the form of a mask, that is to say, a head without a body. The head fell in the southern area of the town between the river Hanumante, at Ciupin *ghat*, a cremation place, and Taumadhi square, in a place which is today signalled by a ditch surrounded by stones. It is in this part of the town (between Taumadhi and the river) that the two chariots, those of Akaśa Bhairava and of the goddess, are drawn in procession. On the third day of the festival, it is at the site of the ditch surrounded by stones that the chariot of Akaśa Bhairava is stopped and blood sacrifices are made. The legend of Akaśa Bhairava implies that the festival of the goddess Bhadrakali existed before the festival in its present form. It is probable that the festival of *Bisket Jātrā*, at the start, did not unfold in its present-day form: it was principally Bhadrakali's festival. Previously, at Kathmandu, the king used to visit the sanctuary of the goddess Bhadrakali, accompanied by the living goddess called Kumari: that points to the special links which these two goddesses have with royalty" (Shepherd Slusser, 1982: 317).

At the end of the previous year's festival, the chariots of the divinities are in part disassembled and stored in two little edifices (*pati*) on Taumadhi square. A few days before the start of the procession, they are made ready and are repainted: they are decorated with figures of spun copper which, throughout the year, are kept inside the temple. When re-assembled these chariots have the form of a temple with three superposed storeys: at the time of the procession they are decorated, in addition, with leaves, flowers and fruits.

At the front and at the back of each of the chariots four long ropes are attached. Bhairava's chariot stays at Taumadhi: that of the goddess Bhadrakali is brought close to the temple of the goddess in the south-western part of the town so that the statue of the goddess can be installed in it before the start of the festival.

On the first day of the festival, late in the afternoon, people crowd together, whatever their caste, in front of the temple of Akaśa Bhairava. At nightfall, two Rajopadhyaya brahmins, priests of the temple of the royal goddess Taleju, go, accompanied by a retinue, to the temple of the goddess Taleju which is situated in the enclave of the royal palace, two hundred metres north of Taumadhi square. They wear long white skirts and their heads are covered by little white hats. They are accompanied by *karmācārya* (priests in charge of the temples of the goddess and executants of the blood sacrifices) who are dressed in the same costumes as the brahmins but red in colour. It is on the first floor of the temple of the goddess Taleju, in the inner sanctuary (*garbha gṛha*), that the sword of the ancient Malla kings, symbol of royal power, is kept. In principle only the brahmins attached to the royal temple of the goddess Taleju have the right to take this sword out. As elsewhere in the Valley of Kathmandu, the coming out of the royal sword is the signal for the start of the festival. When the brahmins come out of the temple of Taleju the procession forms up: the brahmins who carry the sword are preceded by musicians and followed by the *karmācārya*. They go to Taumadhi square and climb into the chariot of Akaśa Bhairava. It is clear that we are in presence of an adaptation of a more ancient rite: in previous times the Malla kings were indeed obliged to be present at the festival and took their place inside the chariot.

The *karmācārya* of the temple of Akaśa Bhairava take out of the temple a box which contains the mask of the god and place it inside the chariot. It is then that the farmers take hold of the chariot ropes, those from the upper part of the town at one end, those of the lower part at the other. There then begins a tug of war where each group tries to pull Akaśa Bhairava's chariot into his own part of the town. It is not a game the result of which is a foregone conclusion but a manifestation of the rivalry between the two parts of the town which is to be observed in all localities in the Valley whether urban or rural at festival periods. This division of the locality into "high" and "low" exists in all Newar localities in the Valley: the division is fixed in relation to the direction of the flow of the nearest river (Toffin 1982: 200; Gutschow 1982: 81).

The struggle lasts all the second day: but the result does not really have any influence on the course of the procession: whatever the outcome, on the third day, the chariot of Akaśa Bhairava must arrive at Lakulache, situated between Taumadhi and the river Hanumante, in the south part of the town.

On the morning of the third day, which in Newari is called *sya tyako* (to sacrifice), the mask of Akaśa Bhairava is taken out of the chariot and is installed on a platform at Lakulache, situated between Taumadhi and the river Hanumante: the chariot itself is dragged a little bit further on into the Ga hiti quarter. Throughout the day, sacrifices are also made in front of the image of Betal (Skt. *vetāla*) who serves as mount for

Akaśa Bhairava: this image is normally attached to the front of the chariot. Great quantities of goats and cocks whose throats are cut by a *karmācārya* are offered in sacrifice. The carcasses of the animals are carried off by the faithful and eaten in the evening in the course of a large meal which brings together all the lineage members.

On the fourth day, the festival takes place in the southern part of the town. The two chariots must be pulled towards the river, following a very precise itinerary: both stop at a place called Yakshimkel. A few days previously, members of the caste of oil-pressers (Manandhar) go into the forest to cut a tree which they fashion, transforming it into a mast: the mast is deposited close to the river, nearby an open edifice called Cyaslim Mandap. The erection of the mast takes place at nightfall. On the top of the mast are hung two long red banners (Skt. *paṭaka*) with gold brocade which symbolize the two serpents killed by the prince when he delivers the princess.

This is the interpretation advanced by the inhabitants: when they are questioned about these banners, they evoke the legend I recounted earlier and add that the king ordered that the bodies of the serpents be strung up on a mast (*viśvadhvaja*) so as to be visible to everyone. He inaugurated also a festival to commemorate the victory over the the serpents. The raising of this mast is clearly one of the crucial moments of the festival: it is only once it has been erected that the statues of the divinities begin to be taken out of their temples in order to exhibit them during three days in the open sanctuaries (*piṭha*) situated outside the limits of the town. The exhibition of the divinities can only take place after the killing of the serpents: by killing the serpents the king re-established order in the kingdom. Around six o'clock in the evening, an important crowd forms close to the Cyaslim Mandap. The mask of Akaśa Bhairava is placed there previously: the inhabitants of the town go to pay homage to it throughout the night. The next morning, that is on the fifth day, the inhabitants go to the banks of the river Hanumante in order to take a purifying bath.

Hierarchy of Divinities and Territory

On the evening of the fifth day begins the procession of the statues. Around six o'clock in the evening, the priests of the temple of the goddess Taleju take out in a palanquin (*khat*) the mobile form of the goddess Taleju, called Duimaju: this is a stone decorated with jewels. They make it go around the square in front of the Royal Palace. At the same moment, the priests of the temple of the goddess Indrayani, paredra of the god Indra, sovereign divinity, take out the statue of that goddess in procession: the two processions meet on the square in front of the Royal Palace.

After these processions, the inhabitants receive *prasād* (the part of the offerings dedicated to a divinity which is eaten by the devotees) and go down to the southern part of the town to be present at the felling of the mast (*viśvadhvaja*). Two goddesses linked to royalty therefore inaugurate the procession. Even today it is said that the Malla Kings, whose dynasty had ceased to exist since 1768, used to go, on the fifth day of the festival, to pay homage to the goddesses Duimaju and Indrayani receiving their *prasād* on the royal sword; then, with the sword in their hand, they went down to the bank of the river Hanumante in order to give the signal for bringing down the mast. Nowadays the king's role is played by his sword, the only subsisting material symbol of the Malla monarchy. This sword, taken out of the Royal Palace on the first day of the festival, is taken back there by the brahmins, whose duty is to watch over it, on the same day. They take it out again on the evening on the fifth day and carry it in procession up to the river, passing in front of the mast. The mast is brought down by undoing the ropes which hold it upright. When the mast touches the ground the New Year begins.

The sixth day is devoted to the joint procession of the statues of Mahakālī and Mahālakṣmī. Their temples are situated in the north part of the town: the inhabitants of the northern quarters are the sole participants in the procession. The goddesses and the processions which accompany them turn around the northern quarter and then go to render homage to the goddess Taleju.

On the seventh day, the festival takes place in the Eastern part of the town. The statues of the goddesses Brahmayani, Kaumari, Maheśvari and Varahi are taken out in procession, meet one another on the square in front of the temple of Dattatreya and, in a joint procession, turn around the eastern part.

The eighth day is that of the procession of Chuma Gaṇeśa. This Gaṇeśa is the only one of the numerous forms of Gaṇeśa of Bhaktapur which the population identifies with the Gaṇeśa whom the prince met in the forest and who taught him how to find the goddess Bhadrakali. The statue of Gaṇeśa also goes to pay its respects to the goddess Taleju at the end of the procession.

On the ninth and last day of the festival, all the statues of the divinities with the exception of that of the goddess Duimaju are taken out individually in procession. The last goddess to pay homage to the goddess Taleju is Tripurasundarī. On the evening of the ninth day, the statue of the goddess Duimaju is taken in procession around the centre of the ancient town. The temple of Tripurasundarī can be considered as the religious centre of the town, just as the temple of the goddess Taleju, in the enclave of the Royal Palace, can be considered as its political centre. Late at night on the ninth day, all the statues return inside their respective temples and the festival is over.

The course of the festival of *Bisket Jātrā* such as I have just described it, highlights a certain number of elements which I shall recapitulate here in ascending order. It is a festival where the spatial categories, the internal divisions of the town, play an essential role. These divisions are represented by their respective deities in separate processions. At the same time, this division into quarters corresponds to the dispositions operated inside the *maṇḍala,* which represents the religious organization of the town. "A house, a temple, a town, or country is placed under the guardianship of a group of deities who are distributed over the Four or Eight Quarters; they surround the territory thus protected: they are worshipped by the usual means, including circumambulation; and this circumambulation serves to set off the lands so protected from their surroundings" (Kölver1968: 8).

A hierarchy of the divinities was made manifest in the course of the festival: all the goddesses are subordinated to the royal goddess Taleju. The festival is closely linked to the Malla royalty as the inaugural role played by the king, on the first and on the fifth days, demonstrates. Today there is no longer a Malla king but his sword represents him and all the divinities of the town manifest their subordination to the goddess Taleju, the king's tutelary deity.

In the minds of the town's inhabitants, the festival is linked to the myth of the founding of the town, which it represents annually. Several elements clearly show this: for instance, the two banners hung on the mast erected in the south part of the town bring back to memory the killing of the serpents; and the procession of the elephant god Chuma Gaṇeśa recalls that it was he who helped the prince to find the goddess and the princess.

The links between the festival and the myth of foundation are emphasized by another episode in the festival which I have deliberately taken out of its chronological context. On the fifth day of the festival, the statue of the goddess Bhadrakali is transported on its chariot up to its open sanctuary, situated in the south-west part of the town, close to the place where the mast will be erected. In the evening, prior to the erection of the mast on the bank of the river, a stretcher is brought (in former days it was the the oil-pressers, Manandhars, who had to carry it). Behind the stretcher, is carried an earthen pot full of rice: this is the offering (New. *bhog*) which is usually made in funerary ceremonies. At the same time, fire is brought, as well as straw to burn "the body". During the night, the stretcher is taken, in the utmost secret, from the temple of the goddess Bhadrakālī up to the cremation place (*ghat*), close to the river Hanumante.

Even if the festival of *Bisket Jātrā* contains aspects which link it to widespread notions of fertility and fecundity (Gutschow and Kölver: 1975:46) such as the couple formed by Akaśa Bhairava and the goddess Bhadrakali, the mast thrust into the earth at the moment which marks the beginning of a New Year, its major significance, for me, lies elsewhere. In the first place, *Bisket Jātrā* is a mythical evocation of the founding of a town, the ancient capital of a kingdom, which, in a certain way, is the microcosmos of the entire territory of that kingdom. This foundation is "re-played" each year at the festival; the town is thus "renewed" at each New Year and the forces re-generated which condition the fertility and prosperity of the kingdom.

Notes

1. Caplan, L.1975. *Administration and Politics in a Nepalese Town.* London, Oxford University Press, p. 2: "In Nepal, the sole census criterion for an 'urban' designation is size, i.e., a population of 5000 or more inhabitants. In 1952-4, when the country held its first census using modern enumeration techniques, only ten settlements contained more than this number: half of these were in the Valley of Kathmandu, and the remainder were in the Terai, a belt of plains forming the kingdom's southern border with India. By 1961, although the nation's population had increased by approximately one million to a total of some 10 millions, there were still no 'urban' localities in the hills, which contained well over half the country's inhabitans".
2. Petech. L. 1984. *Medieval History of Nepal* (750-1482), Roma, ISMEO, p. 184: "The rise of actual towns, of urban life, was a later development. It was due, as suggested already by S. Lévi, to a shift in the economy of Nepal from a purely agricultural to a mixed one, in which trade and crafts played an increasing role: the beginning of this process was roughly contemporary with the beginning of the period treated in the present work".
3. Vajracarya. D. and Malla K.P. 1985, *The Gopālarājavaṃśāvalī*, Wiesbaden, F. Steiner Verlag p. 128: "King Śrī Anandadeva (ruled for) 20 years. He commissioned a copper-roof over the temple. He

consecrated two deities at the temple of Śivagla in Bhaktapur. He built and consecrated the capital-city, including the Tripura palace".

4. Wright, D. 1877, *History of Nepal,* Cambridge University Press; Hasrat, B.J., 1970. *History of Nepal,* Hoshiarpur (India), Research Institute Press.
5. Petech, L. 1984, pp. 202-203: "Since the early Licchavi times the political position of religion may be defined as the rule of Hindu kings over a mixed Hindu and Buddhist society. This general frame never changed during the whole course of Nepalese History . . . solitary exceptions strongly underline the general principle that the king in his public capacity was bound to follow the Hindu rites and to uphold the Hindu social order".
6. Macdonald, A. W. and Vergati Stahl, A. 1979, *Newar Art. Nepalese Art during the Malla Period.* Warminster: Aris and Phillips, p.91: "The town of Bhaktapur is divided into nine sectors each of which bears the name of a mother goddess. In the centre of the town is the temple of Tripurasundarī. It would appear that in the two other royal towns, Patan and Kathmandu, there is no temple of goddess Tripurasundarī and so in her context at Bhaktapur she may be considered to be a local goddess".
7. *Mahāvastu,* translated by J. Jones, 1949, London, Sacred Books of the Buddhists, No. 17-18, Vol. I, pp. 152-153: Vol II, p. 221.
8. Stein, M.A., 1961. *Kalhana's Rājatarangini. A Chronicle of the Kings of Kashmir,* Delhi, Motilal Banarsidass, Vol. II: p. 442: "When king Pravarasena II had returned from his victorious expeditions abroad, he desired to found a new capital which was to bear his name. He was then residing in the city of his grandfather, Pravarasena I, i.e. in Purāṇādhiṣṭahana. From there the king went forth at night in order as the text says 'to ascertain in a supernatural way' the proper site and the auspicious time for the foundation of the new city. On his way he reached a stream which skirted a burning ground and was illuminated by the glow of funeral pyres. Then on the other bank of the stream there appeared to him a demon of terrible form. Promising him fulfilment of his desire, the demon invited the king to cross over to his own side by the embankment he was preparing for him. Thereupon the Rākṣasa stretched out his own knee from the other bank, and thus caused the water of the Mahāsarit to be parted by an embankment (*setu).* The courageous Pravarasena drew out his dagger (*Kṣurikā*), cut with it steps into the flesh of the Rākṣasa, and thus crossed over to the place which has since been known as Ksurikabala. The demon then indicated to him the auspicious time and disappeared after telling him to build his town where he would see the measuring line laid down in the morning. The line (*sūtra*) of the Vetāla the king eventually discovered at the village of Saritaka at which the goddess Sarika and the demon Atta resided. There he built

his city in which the first shrine erected was the famous one of Śiva Pravareśvara".

9. A brief description of the festival is given in Anderson, M. 1971, *The Festivals of Nepal*, London, Allen and Unwin, pp. 41-46. See also Gutschow, N. and Kölver B., 1975, *Bhaktapur, Ordered Space Concepts and Functions in a Town of Nepal*, Wiesbaden, F. Steiner, pp. 46-48.
10. Another legend of foundation is given in Regmi, D. 1966, *Medieval Nepal*, Calcutta, K.L. Mukhopadhyay, Part II, p. 651: "According to another chronicle the two poles are also said to represent the spiritual tutor and his wife of a king named Śivadeva in ancient history of Nepal. This spiritual guide knew the art of transformation through spells. He, by name Shekara Acarya, has saved his kingdom on many occasions by these stratagems. These had helped even to defeat alien invasions. One day his wife asked him just for fun to show himself like a python, which he did, telling her she should not get panicky at the sight and after some time when her curiosity was satisfied she should throw a grain of rice on him to bring him back to human form. However just in the nick of time she got so panicky that she began to run away and instead of throwing the rice upon the husband she herself took it, which at once transformed her into a she-python. This was a great tragedy befalling the couple. There was still a ray of hope, the king knew the charms and if the pythons were recognised he would surely restore them in their original form. The two pythons therefore waited before the Royal gate, every morning and evening while the king was to come out. They went there daily. As they would not harm any one they attracted popular curiosity but nobody recognised them. Then out of desperation they committed suicide. It came to the king's knowledge that they were his tutor and his wife only when someone in the neighbourhood conveyed the story of the couple's transformation. The king felt sad and commemorated the event by erecting two poles on the last day of the year". This version which explains the origin of the festival of *Bisket Jātrā* is recent: the two serpents which must die at the origin of the festival have been retained but in this case the *raj guru* who sacrifices himself is present (in other oral versions he is killed by the king).
11. Porcher M.C., 1985, "The Princess and the Kingdom: On the Representation of Kingship in Dandin's *Daśakumaracarita*", *Journal Asiatique*, t.CCLXXIII, pp. 183-207, p. 189: "For in spite of their initial poverty the *kumāra* obtain for themselves, after their exploits, possession of a (sometimes several) kingdom (s). To reach this result they invariably have recourse to the same means, that is to say, the conquest of a woman, of a princess (sometimes even of a queen) which puts them in a position of heir to a royal throne. All the tales are woven on a common woof, they are tied to the tale of seduction about which it must be stated at the outset that it is depicted as mutual. The hero

finds himself at once seized by the passion he has aroused in the woman of his choice. This intention to seduce never implies duplicity or domination let alone violence".

12. Macdonald, A.W. 1967, *Matériaux pour l'étude de la littérature populaire tibétaine*, I. Paris, PUF, p. 99: "The day passed. The lady made a small, swift movement. Again his knife came out of the sheath. Then the lady got up, staggering. Among the beams were heard two sounds: *tin tin*. From the lady's nose came out two squiggling snakes. At the sight of the snakes, the prince was frightened and got up. The *'dre* said: 'Prince! Don't move!' The point of the knife moved. When the two snakes had emerged, the prince's knife came out of the sheath and cut their necks. Once the two demons, male and female, had been subdued, the lady approached the king and said 'Sir, Sir' and touched him with her head." See the chapter pp. 93-101. See also *Taranātha's History of Buddhism in India*, 1979. Translated from the Tibetan by Lama Chimpa and A. Chattopadhyaya. Simla, Indian Institute of Advanced Study, pp. 257-259.
13. Gupta, S. and Gombrich, R. 1986, "Kings, Power and the Goddess", *South Asia Research*, no. 2, pp. 122-138: "The Goddess is invariably conceived as seated at the centre of the cosmogram, *cakravartinī*, thus she is literally in the centre of the circle but the predominant meaning is 'cosmic sovereign', *cakreśvarī*. She is thus conceived at the controlling centre of the world whether she is literally depicted there or not and this applies to exoteric as well as esoteric worship".
14. The description which follows is based on the analysis and classification of a series of observations made during my field-trips to Nepal in 1975 and 1978. The festival occurs in several places simultaneously, so my description may be imcomplete. I have tried to rectify possible omissions by consulting the observations of my colleagues N. Gutschow and M. Shepherd Slusser and by questioning the local people.

References

Anderson, M. 1971, *The Festivals of Nepal*. London: Allen and Unwin. Caplan, L,1975, *Administration and Politics in a Nepalese Town*. London: Oxford University Press.

Gupta, S. and Gombrich, R. 1986, "Kings, Power and the Goddess." *South Asia Research 2* (Vol. 6), pp. 123-138.

Gutschow, N. and Kölver, B. 1975, *Bhaktapur, Ordered Space- Concepts and Functions in a Town of Nepal*. Stuttgart: W. Kohlhammer.

Hasrat, B.J. 1970, *History of Nepal—As Told by its Own and Contemporary Chronicles*. Hoshiarpur (India): Research Institute Press.

Kölver, B. 1980, "Aspects of Nepalese Culture: Ancient Inscriptions and Modern Yatra" in *Proceedings of the First Symposium of Nepali and*

German Sanskritists 1978. Kathmandu, pp. 152-172.

Kölver, B. 1985, "Stages in the Evolution of a World Picture" *Numen* 32, pp. 131-168.

Lévi, S. 1905-1908. *Le Nepal, étude historique d'un royaume hindou*. 3 vol. Paris: E. Leroux.

Locke, J. 1980, *Karunamaya. The Cult of Avalokiteśvara- Matsyendrānth in the Valley of Nepal*. Kathmandu: Sahayogi Prakashan.

Macdonald, A. W. and Vergati Stahl, A. 1979, *Newar Art. Nepalese Art during the Malla Period*. Warminister: Aris and Phillips.

Macdonald, A.W. 1967, *Matériaux pour l'étude de la littérature populaire tibétaine*, vol. I. Paris: PUF.

Malamoud, Ch. 1976, Village et forêt dans l'idéologie de l'Inde brahmanique. *Archives Européennes de Sociologie* 17, pp. 3- 20.

Marize, J.C. Bisket Jātrā, la fête communale de Bhaktapur *Objets et Mondes*, 24, pp. 7-20.

Petech, L. 1984, *Medieval History of Nepal* (750-1482). Roma: ISMEO.

Porcher, M.C., 1985, La princesse et le royaume. *Journal Asiatique*, t. CLXXIII, pp. 183-207.

Regmi, D. 1966, *Medieval Nepal*, Part II. Calcutta: Firma Mukopadhyay.

Slusser Shepherd, M. 1982, *Nepal Mandala. A Cultural Study of the Kathmandu Valley*. 2 Vols. Princeton: Princeton University Press.

Stürbecher, K. 1981. *Bhaktapur. Architektur und Stadtentwicklung im Kathmandutal*. Saarbrücken: Verlag Breitenbach.

Toffin, G. 1977, *Pyangaon, une communauté néwar de la Vallée de Kathmandu: la vie matérielle*. Paris: Éd. du C.N.R.S.

Toffin, G. 1984, *Société et Religion chez les Néwar du Népal*. Paris: Èd. du C.N.R.S.

Vajracarya, D. and Malla, K.P. 1985, *The Gopālarājavaṃśāvalī*. Wiesbaden: Steiner Verlag (Nepal Research Centre Publications no. 9).

Wright, D. 1877. *History of Nepal*. Cambridge University Press.

The Worship and Iconography of Dīpaṅkara Buddha in the Valley of Kathmandu*

The Buddhism of the Newars of the Valley of Kathmandu has been little studied,[1] although Buddhist texts found in Nepal have helped towards the reconstruction and the understanding of ancient forms of Indian Buddhism. In Nepal, Buddhism seems to have been known since the fourth century B.C. The birth place of the historical Buddha is situated in the south of the country in the plains, at Lumbini. We have proof that, in the Licchavi period (300-750 A.D.), both Buddhist currents, the Mahāyāna and the Hīnayāna, were known. From the twelfth century onwards, at the start of the Malla period, Mahāyāna Buddhism, strongly influenced by Tantrism, predominated. Today it is the Mahāyānist school known as Vajrāyāna which holds a dominant position in Nepal. However during the Malla dynasty, around the fourteenth century A.D., monks gave up celibacy and monastic life. Monks were thenceforth known by the population as *bare* or *banra* (venerables) and they formed a separate social category. From the fourteenth century onwards, their life was regulated by royal decrees. The *banra* caste was composed of two sub-castes: the previous monks (*śākya)* who are today goldsmiths, and the *vajrācārya,* Buddhist priests who alone are permitted to enter the sanctuaries (in Newari: *āgama chẽ*) and carry out the consecration rituals (*dīksā*).

I want to focus on one particular aspect of Newar Buddhism: the worship of Dīpaṅkara Buddha and his iconography. I observed the worship of Dīpaṅkara at Patan, an ancient royal town where Buddhism has always been dominant, and also at Bhaktapur (or Bhadgaon) where the majority of the population is Hindu, Buddhists constituting only a small minority there (roughly 20 per cent of the population) composed mainly of artisans such as painters, dyers, potters.

The worship of Dīpaṅkara Buddha is still current in the Valley; it would seem that, in earlier days, it was also widespread in Tibet and China.[2] In Nepal, Dīpaṅkara is only one of the Buddhas of the past to whom a cult is addressed and representations of whom can be observed frequently. He is the only Buddha who is taken out in procession during the Buddhist ceremonies which take place in Nepal in the month of August (Newari: *Guñla*), the holy month for Newar Buddhists. Generally, in the Sanskrit tradition, Dīpaṅkara is considered as the first of the twenty-four predecessors of the Buddha Śākyamuni. A. Foucher wrote in his *Étude sur l'iconographie bouddhique de l'Inde* that in Nepal "there seems to be a tendency to put Dīpaṅkara Buddha closer to the Buddha Śākyamuni and to make him the first of the seven or nine earthly Buddhas."[3] The triad "Śākyamuni-Dīpaṅkara-Maitreya" to which A. Getty draws attention in Nepal and Tibet called "the Three White Buddhas"[4] can be seen during the Buddhist ceremonies in the month of August when the statues of these three are on show in the courtyard of Buddhist monasteries. Every morning in the month of *guñla,* Buddhists visit, one after the other, all the monasteries and stūpa of the Valley. "Each day a procession of *banras* forms up carrying little wax trees with flowers of white paper: at the time of these visits, the vihāras exhibit their paintings, images of gods, of saints, of Buddhas, of Bodhisattvas, religious or legendary scenes".[5] The week-long period when in monastery courtyards the sacred images kept inside the sanctuaries are put on show is called *bahi-boye* in Newari, the expression deriving from the word *bahi* (or *bahal*) (Skt. *vihāra*, meaning "monastery") and from the verb *boye*, meaning "to exhibit".

The images of Dīpaṅkara Buddha which are known are late, the earliest ones being from the end of the seventeenth century. Despite the many studies which have been done on Buddhist statues of the Licchavi period (300-750A.D.) no image from this period has been identified as Dīpaṅkara Buddha. P. Pal in his study of the sculpture of Nepal devotes an important chapter to the images of the Buddha[6] but none of them represents Dīpaṅkara. One should perhaps take up again the hypothesis suggested by A. Foucher according to which a certain number of Indian statues making the gesture of the *abhayamudrā* and the *varamudrā* with the right hand are perhaps the images of Dīpaṅkara. This hypothesis must be considered with great prudence and A. Foucher himself wrote: "I do not set out to claim, on the unique basis of a similitude in the pose, that they are all statues of Dīpaṅkara".[7] J. Boisselier when re-examining Foucher's suggestion with regard to a statue at Tuol Ta-Hoy (Cambodia) noted: "The evidence from post-Gupta reliefs leads us in another direction: in the compositions the interpretation of which is certain, it is always the *varamudrā* which is preferred. So it would be tempting to admit that the statues of the Buddha standing, making the *varamudrā*, wearing a garment leaving the right shoulder uncovered, which are a series few in number at the period we are considering, could represent Dīpaṅkara Buddha."[8] I do not know of any image of Dīpaṅkara in Nepal dating from the first Malla period (1200-1482), a period in which the arts flourished and from which we know many images of the Buddha Śākyamuni and of the future Buddha Maitreya.[9] P. Pal identifies several images of the Buddha Maitreya dating from the ninth and eleventh centuries. Nonetheless an inscription published by D. Regmi concerning Itum *baha*, one of the most important monasteries of Kathmandu dated 502 N.S. (1382 A.D.), testifies that the king Jayasimharana paid homage to Paśupatināth, the great god of Nepal (Nepalādhipati), and erected, with his brother Jalasayana Narayana, statues of Dīpaṅkara and of Aryāvalokiteśvara at Bungamati.[10] One should emphasize that Bungamati (or Bunga), a small locality six kilometres from Patan, is of great importance for Newar Buddhism. One of the temples of Matsyendranāth, who is a form of Avalokiteśvara (Lokanāth), the most important Buddhist deity in the Valley as he is believed to bring rain, is situated in Bungamati. From June till December the statue resides at Bungamati, and from January till June at Patan.

Several texts, the best known of which are *āvadāna* and the most widespread of which is the *Avadāna* of the *Mahavastu,* recount the legend of Dīpaṅkara Buddha.[11] The manuscripts known today are fairly recent but they are often copies of old texts. The manuscript of the *Mahākarmavibhaṅga* (the Great Classification of Acts), found in Nepal and published by S. Lévi dated 531 N.S. (1410 A.D.), mentions the name of Dīpaṅkara Buddha in connection with the qualities which one acquires if one makes the gift of a lamp.[12] The images of Dīpaṅkara in the manuscript of the *Aṣṭaṣahasrikā Prajñapāramitā* analysed by A. Foucher carry inscriptions: two are from Ceylon and two from Java.[13] But no Newar painting of the Malla epoch represents Dīpaṅkara, and this despite the fact that we know today a considerable number of Newar paintings representing Buddhist subjects which are indeed more numerous than the paintings dealing with Hindu subjects.

The statues of Dīpaṅkara we know of from Nepal date from the seventeenth century. A statue of which I publish a photograph is to be found in the Patan Museum: it dates from the end of the seventeenth century. It is the classical representation of Dīpaṅkara Buddha standing, draped in a robe leaving the right shoulder uncovered, wearing a crown and making the gesture of the *abhayamudrā* and the *varamudrā.* These gestures are directly influenced by Pāla tradition. The statue is in many-coloured wood, the robe and ornamentation are in embossed copper. The crown reminds one of that of the Newar kings of the Malla period. It can be compared to certain representations of the king as, for instance, the painting which depicts the legend of Lokanātha (Matsyendranāth) and, at the same time, the ornaments are similar to those of other Bodhisattvas such as Amoghapāśā (a fifteenth century painting)[14] or Buddha Śākyamuni. The clothing worn, leaving the right shoulder uncovered, reminds one of a monk's attire but its lower part, with the folds in the skirt and the decoration of the material, is similar to the costume of the Malla kings of the seventeenth century such as they are represented in the paintings of that epoch. The jewellery and the clothing only draw attention to the regal appearance of this statue of Dīpaṅkara Buddha. According to P. Pal, these images of Dīpaṅkara Buddha would be of Tibetan origin but he gives no bibliographical reference in support of this affirmation.[15]

In several monasteries in the town of Patan, which is par excellence the town of Buddhist tradition in the Valley, one finds images of Dīpaṅkara Buddha in gilt bronze. During the ceremony of the Five Gifts (*Pañcadana*) or *Banra jātrā*, which I was able to watch at Patan in the month of August in 1978, the only Buddha images taken out in procession were those of Dīpaṅkara Buddha. On this occasion the images are carried by Śākya around the quarter where the monastery is situated. The procession stops at the principal cross-roads and, in front of private houses, important gifts of rice are made to the Śakya and to the Vajracārya. In the inner courtyard of the monastery of Oku bahal, I was able to observe the gifts made by the faithful: rice, lentils, oil, sweetened water, money. According to certain Newar Buddhists, in previous times only boiled rice was distributed throughout the festival. However today because of prohibitions imposed by the system of castes adopted officially in Nepal in the fourteenth century, the Vajrācārya and the Śākya no longer wish to accept boiled rice from the hands of people of lower social status. G. Singh Nepali gives this description of the *Vanra Jātrā*: "The celebration starts early in the morning with the Buddhist Newars visiting the temples of Svayambhu and Machendranath. Kathmandu town becomes far busier on this day than any other town in the Valley because of the temple of Svayambhu. People from all corners of the Valley flock in to pay their homage at the temples of Buddhist divinities. The main event is the offering of the alms to *Vanras* and feasting them. This takes place on two days. First the *Vanras* go from shop to shop or door to door and beg for alms. The Buddhist sections of the Newars offer them a mixture of rice and paddy in a copper bowl. The *Vanra* in return touches the forehead of the alms-giver wth the sacred book which he carries.[16] Individual offerings are often followed by a collective offering. According to S. Lévi, the procession of the *Vanras* can start up again at any time if there is a charitable purse to pay the costs. It consists basically in a distribution of money and food to the *banra* and puts in memory the time when the residents of the *vihāras,* as true *bhikṣus,* lived from alms. If it is a private individual who offers the *yātrā,* he summons by personal invitations the *banras* of the town or even of the whole Valley to a *samyak sambhojana* (body-feast). The expenses can be heavy as sometimes the number of those present can be as many as ten thousand. Moreover the festival includes amusements and illuminations. The King must be present or send a personal representative and this is again an honour which has a price for he must be offered a silver throne, a parasol and cooking utensils. Facing the house of the donor is erected a wooden scaffolding with a shelter opening on to the road; the whole is decorated with hangings and brilliantly lit. The helmet of Amitābha from Svayambhunāth, which the *vajrācārya* come to worship, is brought. Then the procession starts: beforehand, along the houses that the cortege of the *banras* is to pass, is made a covered path, separated from the road by a wooden barrier and which crosses each cross-roads by a bridge. The wives of the Buddhists who want to join in the festival arrived beforehand in their best dresses, flowers stuck in their hair and with baskets filled with foodstuffs, to take up position on the road the procession is to follow: each *banra* who passes in the file receives fruit, grain or money. When the baskets are emptied, it is up to the patron to fill the gaps. Here and there groups of grown men or young boys pour water respectfully onto the feet of the *banras*."[17]

In the east of the Valley at Bhaktapur (or Bhadgaon) in the town's principal monasteries, Dīpaṅkara Buddha is represented by a big effigy 2 metres 50 in height.[18] The face is figured by a red-coloured mask, the body of the divinity is formed by a wooden framework with arms : and the effigy is dressed in clothes of different colours. The clothes are like those worn by *Vajrācārya* during certain ceremonies. The ornaments are in gilt bronze and made of five parts (*pañca mukura*). Images of Dīpaṅkara Buddha are to be found in the five main monasteries of Bhaktapur (*mu baha*). The other monasteries are considered secondary and are dependant on the former. The five main monasteries of Bhaktapur are:

(1) Dīpaṅkaravihāra or Prasanaśilamahāvihāra, situated in the North-West part of the town (Kwathandau *tol*).
(2) Caurabahi situated at Gomadhi *tol.*
(3) Caturvarṇamahāvihāra situated close to the royal palace.
(4) Kutu bahi.
(5) Tatu bahi.

The last two monasteries are situtated outside town-limits and are royal foundations from the end of the sixteenth century.

It seems important to draw attention to the red colour of Dīpaṅkara's face. The masks for the effigies are repainted every three years. In Nepal the Bodhisattva Avalokiteśvara is also red in colour, and this is not only the case of the form of Rato Matsyendranāthā of Patan, called, according to certain documents, Lokanāth and, by the Newars, Bungadyo, but also in different Nepalese paintings : I am thinking primarily of the illustrations in the eleventh-century manuscript of Cambridge which was published by A. Foucher.[19] At Thimi, a locality situated at four or five kilometres from Bhaktapur, I have visited several monasteries where we found the same effigies of Dīpaṅkara as at Bhaktapur but smaller in size. In the monastery of Yaceñ the effigy of Dīpaṅkara is to be found on the first storey in front of the entrance to the Tantric sanctuary (*āgama*).

When each day the faithful enter the courtyard of the Caturvarṇamahāvihāra at Bhaktapur they pay their respects and make offerings of flowers, rice and money to Dīpaṅkara Buddha who is placed on the left, in a small sanctuary, and not to the Buddha Śakyamuni, whose *cella* is situated opposite the main entrance.

According to oral tradition, in Kathmandu Valley Dīpaṅkara Buddha came from the East, from Great China (Mahacina), from a town called Dipavati Nagar. Other Buddhist divinities such as Mañjusri, the creator of the Valley, came also from great China. The Bodhisattva Mañjuśrī, possessed of the perfection of wisdom, knew that a *Svayambhū*, a spontaneous manifestation of divinity, had appeared in Nepal: he was then staying beyond the country of China in the country of Great China (*Mahacīna*), which is surrounded by a sevenfold wall, on the mountain of the Five Peaks (Pañca Śirsa Parvata).[20] Images of Mañjuśrī in Nepal are old: the first dates from the end of the tenth century or from the beginning of the eleventh century.[21] Rāto Matsyendranāth, the divinity who brings rain and assures successful harvests, came from North India, from Assam, from the region called Kamarūpa. According to the legend, king Narendra Deva and his spiritual guide the recluse Gorakhnāth caused the image of Matsyendranāth to come into the Valley of Kathmandu.

In the Sanskritic tradition, Dīpaṅkara Buddha symbolizes light whereas in the Pali tradition the word *dvipa* signifies "island": moreover, in the text of the Mahāvastu, Dīpaṅkara is born in an "island" which appeared before he lit the wonderful lamp to which he owed his name.[22] Newar Buddhists still associate Dīpaṅkara Buddha with a lamp. The *Mahākarmavibhaṅga*, in the paragraph devoted to the ten qualities which one acquires if one donates a lamp, explains that Dīpaṅkara reached the stage of Buddha by giving a garland of lamps.[23] Moreover A.C. Soper while writing on Buddhist art in China has emphasized that Sanskrit texts from the North manifest special interest in Dīpaṅkara and that they underscore his connexions with the themes of light and fire.[24] In August 1978, when the Dīpaṅkara Buddha of Patan came out in procession, I was able to watch what Newar Buddhists call "the festival of lights", *mata yâã,* the word *mata* means "light" in Newari and *yâã* is the Newar form of the word *yātrā.* During this festival, young boys, wearing small lighted lamps on their shoulders and around their legs, have to visit the principal monasteries of the town: they always move in groups of between four and ten people. One can ask oneself whether this festival of lights is not linked to the worship of Dīpaṅkara. In his *Etude sur l'iconographie bouddhique de l'Inde,* A. Foucher already drew attention to "the association of ideas which would make Dīpaṅkara still preside at certain festivals in High Asia celebrated by illuminations".[25]

At Bhaktapur, the images of the five Dīpaṅkara Buddha, called locally *Pañca Buddha,* are taken out in procession at the end of the month of August. At Bhaktapur the festival of the *banra* occurs three weeks later than at Patan. The difference between the dates when the ceremony takes place in these towns could perhaps be due to the fact that in former times the two towns were the capitals of separate kingdoms. These five Buddhist priests (*vajrācārya*), who choose the future royal Kumārī at Kathmandu, are called *Pañca Buddha.*[26] The five *vajrācārya* wear long robes: and each robe is of a different colour : yellow, blue, white, red and green, which corresponds to the colours of the five Buddha Tathāgata. The five effigies of Dīpaṅkara Buddha at Bhaktapur which are carried by Śakya go around the town; they stop several times, the last halt taking place opposite the platform situated in front of the temple of Bhairavnāth at Taumadhi. All processions which circumambulate (pradakṣiṇa) the town stop at this point. This ceremony is observed only by Buddhists, who live above all in the north-western part of the town. All along the circuit, the effigies of Dīpaṅkara Buddha stop to receive offerings (fig. 5) and to listen to the musical interludes. The varied offerings made to the divinities (rice, flowers, lentils, cash) will be shared as equally as possible between the *Śakya* and the *Vajrācārya*.

To judge by the images of the Buddha from the Licchavi epoch, it seems that the historical Buddha was then very popular, but clearly, today, in the Buddhism of the Valley, the historical Buddha now only plays a fairly secondary role. A change took place in the Buddhism of the Valley with the spread of the Vajrāyana and its ritualsfrom the tenth and eleventh centuries onwardswhich resulted among other things in transforming the pantheon. Today the most popular divinities are Avalokiteśvara, in the form of Matsyendranāth, Mañjuśrī, Vajrapāṇi and Dīpaṅkara Buddha. In 1935, P. Mus noted that in Northern Buddhism (Mahāyāna) worship of the historical Buddha was replaced by "a multicoloured pantheon of Buddhas and Bodhisattvas. . ."[27] The expression might well be applied precisely to the special case of Newar Buddhism, as I hope to have shown.

Notes

* First Published in: *Arts Asiatiques*, xxxvii - 1982

1. Valuable information on Newar Buddhism is to be found in the work of S. Lévi, *Le Nêpal, Etude historique d'un royaume hindou*, Paris, E. Leronx, 1905, but the best study is, at present, that of D.L. Snellgrove, the chapter "Buddhism in Nepal", pp. 92-120, of *Buddhist Himālaya*, Oxford, Bruno Cassier, 1957. Mention must also be made of the study by J.K. Locke, S.J., *Rāto Matsyendranath of Patan and Bungamati*, Kirtipur, Institute of Nepal and Asian Studies, Historical series No. 5, no date.
2. A. Getty, *The Gods of Northern Buddhism*, Oxford, Clarendon Press, 1928, pp. 12-15.
3. A. Foucher, *Etude sur l'iconographie bouddhique de l'Inde d'après des documents nouveaux*, Paris, E. Leronx, 1900. He devotes a chapter to Dīpaṅkara Buddha, pp. 77-84.

4. A. Getty, *op. cit.*, p.14.
5. S. Lévi, *op. cit.*, Vol. II, p. 51.
6. P. Pal, *The Arts of Nepal, Part I, Sculpture*, Leiden, Brill, 1974. See the chapter "Buddhist Sculpture".
7. A. Foucher, *op. cit.*, p. 83.
8. J. Boisselier, "Le Buddha de Tuol-Ta-Hoy et l'art bouddhique du Sud-est asiatique", *Annales de l'Université Royale des Beaux Arts*, Phnom Penh (1967), pp. 121 -156.
9. P. Pal, *op. cit.*, pp. 103 126.
10. D.R. Regmi, *Medieval Nepal, A History of the Three Kingdoms.* Calcutta, K.L. Mukopadhyay, 1966, Vol. I, p. 540.
11. Rajendralala Mitra, *The Sanskrit Buddhist Literature*, Sanskrit Pustak Bhandar, Calcutta, 1971 (revised edition). E. Senart, *Le Mahavastu*, Paris, Imprimerie Nationale, 1899, Vol. I, pp. 193-252.
12. S. Lévi, *Mahākarmavibhaṅga* (La grande classification des actes) et *Karmavibhaṅgopadeça*, Paris. E. Leronx, 1932.
13. A. Foucher, *op. cit.*, p. 79.
14 A.W. Macdonal and A. Vergati Stahl, *Newar Art, Nepalese Art during the Malla Period*, Warminster, Aris and Phillips, 1979, p. 128; see the *paṭa* of Amoghapāśa.
15. P. Pal, *Nepal, Where the Gods are Young*, New York, Asia House Gallery, 1975, published an image of Dīpaṅkara, p. 34, ill. 12, similar to the one in the Patan museum. In describing the statue, he writes: "In Nepal, the majority of his images are rather late in date and his cult may have been introduced from Tibet after the sixteenth century, when Tibet began to exercise considerable influence on Nepali Buddhism. Stylistically, as well, this image reveals influences from Tibet, particularly in the manner in which the garments are delineated. The iconography of the figure is essentially the same as that of Śākyamuni" (p. 73). See also Waldschmidt, *Nepal, Art Treasures from the Himalaya*, Calcutta, Oxford Publishing Co.,1969, p. 26, ill. 40.
16. Gopal Singh Nepali, *The Newars, An Ethno-sociological Study of a Himalayan Community*, Bombay, United Asia Publications, 1965, p. 357.
17. S. Lévi, *op. cit.*, Vol. II, pp. 52-53.
18. D. Snellgrove (ed.), *The Image of the Buddha*, Paris, UNESCO, Serindia Publications, 1978, p. 344: "A cult of the former Buddha Dīpaṅkara persists in Nepal, and of him there are many beautiful effigies, some complete statues but others put together for the occasion using masks and heads fitted on a frame and they are dressed." He publishes two images of Dīpaṅkara Buddha : ill. 273, where the image is dated 1680, and ill. 275.
19. A. Foucher, *op. cit.*, p. 79 and also A. Getty, *op. cit.*, p. 69.
20. S. Lévi, *op. cit.*, Vol. I, p. 332.
21. P. Pal, *op. cit.*, Vol. I., p. 122: "Although Mañjuśri is associated with the

formation of the Kathmandu Valley, no image of Mañjuśri has so far come to light that can be attributed to the Licchavi period."

22. E. Senart, *op. cit.*, Vol. I, p. 217. A Foucher, *L' Art Gréco-Bouddhique du Gandhara*, Paris, Imprimerie Nationale, 1925, t. 1, chapter: Dīpaṅkara Jātaka, pp. 273-83.
23. S. Lévi, *op. cit.*, p. 149.
24. A. Soper, *Literary Evidence for Early Buddhist Art in China*, Artibus Asiae, Ascona, 1959.
25. A. Foucher, *op. cit.*, p. 79. I watched the festival of lights at Patan rapidly in 1978 and I am only suggesting a simple hypothesis. This festival is different from *dīpavali*, the official festival which takes place in the month of *Kartika* (October-November) and celebrated in all localities in the Valley: the victory of Viṣṇu over the demon Naraka is celebrated at that time.
26. M. Allen (*The Cult of Kumari*, University Press, Tribhuvan University, Kathmandu, 1975) writes: "The Pancha Buddha are five Buddhist priests of Vajracarya caste who officiate during the annual Kumari *jatra* and have various other ceremonial duties in connection with the goddess. They consist of two Raj Gubhajus, one from Sikhamu Baha and the other from Saval Baha in central Kathmandu and three other Gubhajus of Sikhami" (p. 8).
27. P. Mus, Barabuḍur, *Esquisse d'une histoire du Bouddhisme fondée sur la critique archéologique des textes*; Hanoi, Imprimerie d'Extrême Orient, 1935, 1, p. 9.

The King as Rainmaker: A New Version of the Legend of Red Avalokiteśvara*

One of the most venerated gods of the Valley of Kathmandu is Red Avalokiteśvara, whose cult is in the hands of Buddhist priests (*vajrācārya*). Nevertheless as distinct from other Buddhist divinities of Nepal such as Dīpaṅkara, Vajrapāṇi, Tārā, the worship of Red Avalokiteśvara is by no means limited to the members of the Nepalese Buddhist community. As distributor of rain, prosperity and abundance in a country whose principal richness is its agriculture, he is one of the kingdom's great gods worshipped as much by Hindus as by Buddhists. The king supervises and participates in the celebration of the god's festival which takes place each year at Patan, so that the correct ordering of the procession guarantees the good government of the country. The chronicles of the kingdom of Patan make regular mention of donations made to the temples of Red Avalokiteśvara at Patan and at Bungamati for the celebration of the festival.[1] In the circumstances it is not surprising that this Avalokiteśvara became the chosen divinity (*iṣṭa devatā*) of the king of Patan Śrīnivāsa Malla in the seventeenth century.[2]

To judge from the archaeological remains of the Licchavi epoch (c. 350-700 C.E.), the worship of Avalokiteśvara was very widespread in the Valley from the sixth century onwards. The most ancient image is in the old monastery Gana Bahal at

Kathmandu. What is particularly surprising is the great continuity of worship and the conservatism in the iconographical representations.[3] Today several temples and statues of Avalokiteśvara are to be found in the Valley. Among the manifestations of Avalokiteśvara which are worshipped throughout the Valley are white Avalokteśvara (New.: *Yamala,* Skt.: Samantabhadra) whose principal residence is the monastery of Jana Baha at Kathmandu[4] and the one with which we are concerned in this article: Red Avalokiteśvara (New.: *Bunga Dyo*). This Red Avalokiteśvara is known by the following Sanskrit designations: Lokeśvara, "the lord of the world" or Rāto Lokeśvara "the red lord of the world", Lokanātha, "the master of the world", Karuṇāmaya, "made of compassion", Padmapāṇi, "who holds a lotus in his hand". In spoken Newari he is called Bunga Dyo or Vunga Dyo, "the divinity of Bunga". In Newari the word *bunga* means "place where there is water". The non-Newaris of the Valley call the god Matsyendranāth, "the master of the chief of the fish", assimilating him in this way to a god very popular in Bengal and in North India. The name of Matsyendranāth surfaces for the first time in Nepal in an inscription from Patan dated 1748. The name is only frequently employed after the conquest of the Valley by the Gorkhas in 1768.[5] Throughout the nineteenth century, the chronicles use only the name of Matsyendranāth for the divinity at Patan. All authors agree that the transformation of the divinity Avalokiteśvara-Bunga Dyo into Matsyendranāth took place recently, round about the seventeenth century.[6]

The first known iconographical document representing Rāto Lokeśvara is an eleventh-century (1015) manuscript published by A. Foucher. He wrote: "Among the images of Avalokiteśvara, standing and in human form, we must take account of the two idols in the miniatures 1.6 and 11.4. They have in fact in common that, exceptional and unique, they are red: this difference and this similitude cannot be a pure accident. Obviously in Nepal the red colour of Amitābha had passed on to his *Dhyāni Bodhisattva* [....] One cannot fail to recognize in the other the no-less famous idol which, as Bhagvānlāl Indrājī testifies, ensures the processional connection between Lalitpattanan and the village of Bungamati".[7] Two centuries later the Tibetan monk Dharmasvamin who stayed in Nepal from 1228 to 1234 indicated that this cult of Avalokiteśvara was one of the most important in the country and was known as far off as India. He describes ceremonies analogous to those which take place even today: "In Nepal, in the monastery of Bu-kham there is a miraculous image of Avalokiteśvara (*svayambhu*) made in sandal-wood, red in colour, with the aspect of a five year old boy. This Ārya Bu-kham is very famous in India; in Tibet, the Svayambhu-caitya is very famous. On the eighth day of the month of Aśvin this image of the lord (*ārya*) of Bu-kham is taken out: offerings are made to it and there is a great show. The people, specially the king and the rich, make offerings to the image and all invite it to their houses and present to it offerings which are the five *amṛta*, that is yoghurt, milk, unrefined sugar, honey and sugar. They pour these substances onto the head of the image and bathe it. They then consume the bath-water and the food offerings. For half a month they worship it in this manner. During these washings, the vermilion (colour of the image) fades. Then on the seventh day of the following month, young tantric priests called *Hang-du,* carrying fly-whisks and musical instruments, conduct the image back to the temple in the middle of a great show. On the eighth day (of the month) they repaint the image in red."[8]

Red Avalokiteśvara-Bunga Dyo is the only divinity in the Valley which has two residential temples: the principal residence is at Bungamati where he stays for six months each year from June till November or December and the other is at Patan where he resides the rest of the year. The village of Bungamati is situated six kilometres from Patan (previously called Lalitapatana): it has a population of roughly three thousand. The image of the divinity is carried from Bungamati in a palanquin (New.: *khat*) and then deposited in its temple of Ta-

Baha close to the Royal Palace. The temple of Red Avalokiteśvara at Patan is in the form of a pagoda with three tiers of roofs in the classic style of the Valley's temples. At Bungamati the present-day temple of the divinity is in the form of a śikhara and was built at the end of the sixteenth century on the foundations of an older temple. According to inscriptions found in the village of Bungamati, worship of the divinity would have been popular there during the reign of Narendra Deva, that is to say, in the first half of the seventh century.[9] The manuscript quoted by A. Foucher shows that from the eleventh century onwards the divinity of the village of Bungamati was known as Avalokiteśvara. The *Gopālarājavaṃśāvalī*, a chronicle which has been proved to be trustworthy for this period, calls it Vugama Lokeśvara.

Several authors have written that Red Avalokiteśvara was originally a mother-goddess (New.: Ajima)[10] for his ritual includes specifically feminine aspects. Each year when the statue is ritually renovated on the occasion of one of the ten *saṃskāra* (or *daśa karma*), she is married (New.: *ihi*) to a *bodhisattva* in a ritual normally reserved for young Newar girls, carried out before puberty. In addition, during the consecration of the statue, an eleventh ritual, *barhatayegu,* reserved for young girls at puberty, is carried out.[11] The girl is then shut in a dark room for ten days at the time of her first period. This isolation would correspond to the moment when the statue is shut in the eastern part of the temple of Ta-Baha. However in Great Vehicle Buddhism representations of the Bodhisattva Avalokiteśvara not only in Northern India but also in Tibet and in China are often sexually ambiguous.[12] The possibility cannot be excluded that a local divinity was adopted by Buddhists and transformed into Avalokiteśvara.

The annual festival and the chariot procession *ratha jātrā,* during which the divinity is taken out, takes place at Patan each year around April-May which coincides with the end of the dry season and the approaching monsoon. But once every twelve years the divinity is left at Bungamati throughout the entire year: the annual ceremonies of bathing and reconsecrating the statue are then carried out at Bungamati as in the annual procession. The festival lasts roughly two months for the chariot of the divinity, accompanied by the chariot of another divinity, Mīnanātha, whom the local inhabitants consider to be the younger brother of Avalokiteśvara. Matsyendranāth must circumambulate the town of Patan and stop in certain quarters of the town (Nep.: *tol*). Each of these stages only concerns the inhabitants of Patan and particularly those of the quarter in which the chariots stop over. But, during the last three days of the procession, the festival is not purely local but becomes national. From all the towns and all the villages of the Valley of Kathmandu, Buddhists and Hindus, Newars and Nepalese come to pay homage to the divinity. At the end of the three days, in the presence of a huge crowd, the Buddhist priests (*vajrācārya*) show to those present the divinity's shirt (Nep.: *bhoto*; New.: *palvakulan*).[13] This is the culminating point of the festival. The king of Nepal even today comes in order to pay homage to the divinity. Moreover all the incidents which occur in the course of the procession are interpreted as presages of national importance involving the future of the Valley as a whole. Yet the priests and the executants who carry out the rituals during the two months of the procession are all Buddhists: *vajrācārya* and *śākya*, natives of Bungamati. They belong to the religious association (*guṭhi*) of the temple of the divinity Bunga Dyo.

In all the versions of the legend which are to be found in the Newar chronicles, the cult of Avalokiteśvara - Bunga Dyo is linked to the king Narendra Deva (664-680). The most ancient chronicle, the *Gopālarājavaṃśāvalī* which was set down during the reign of Jayasthiti Malla (1381-1395), mentions king Narendra Deva and his priest (*ācārya*) as inaugurators of the annual festival of Bunga Lokeśvara. In a version of the *Svayambhūpurāṇa* (fifteenth century) there is a rapid mention of the fact that the king of Bhaktapur, Narendra Deva, and his spiritual guide, Bhandhudatta Ācārya, brought Ārya

Avalokiteśvara from Mount Potalaka so as to put an end to a twelve-year drought which was ravaging the country. In other versions of the legend, the divinity could have been brought from Kāmarūpa (Assam) by a king and his spiritual guide.

Since the end of the seventeenth century, the legend of Avalokiteśvara is linked with the name of the Śaivite Hindu saint Gorakhnāth who is considered as having been the disciple of Matsyendranāth. In his work, J. Locke has shown the historical changes which the legend has undergone during the Malla epoch (1200-1768).[14] A certain number of features are common to all the versions of the legend. To begin with, let us note that the statue of the divinity was brought from abroad in difficult circumstances by the king with the help of his spiritual advisor. Now most Nepalese divinities are Indian but they are considered as being divinities of the country as is manifest in the cult and in the legend. Even the royal goddess Taleju came from outside, from India too: but in that case we are confronted by an event which can be considered as truly historical.[15] Among Buddhist divinities, local tradition has the creator of the Valley come from the East, from Mahācīna; but there is no special festival for Mañjuśrī. The Buddha Dīpaṅkara who is worshipped by Newar Buddhists would also have come from Mahācīna.[16] One should also recall the numerous legends which depict the Buddha Śākyamuni or some other Bodhisattva as a tamer of serpents (Skt.: *nāga*) assuring in this manner the country's prosperity.

Let us note too that the introduction of the divinity Avalokiteśvara is linked with the need to put an end to a drought which was ravaging the country for twelve years past. According to the Indian notion of royalty, it is the king who is responsible for the prosperity of the country and for rain: he is the god Indra on earth. In Indian representations, *nāga*, serpents of the subterranean waters, control also the rain.[17] In the Nepalese legends of Red Avalokiteśvara it is because the serpents are tied up and unable to act that the king has to find a means of setting them free. That is why he leaves for

Kāmarūpa accompanied by his *guru* Bandhudatta so as to look for the statue of Avalokiteśvara, a divinity capable of freeing the serpents. Dictionaries identify Kāmarūpa with Assam but as its name indicates ("which takes forms as it wishes"), it is rather a question of a mythical country situated somewhere to the east of Nepal. In the legend the king's *guru* is a Buddhist priest (*vajrācārya*). He alone knows and can carry out the rites (*sādhana*) which fix the divinity in a vase, a *maṇḍala* or a statue and oblige it to act according to the will of the *vajrācārya* who is, at the same time, a *siddha*. In Newar society the *vajrācārya* are indeed magicians capable of mastering evil spirits and of acting as healers. In the legend in this respect the king can do nothing without his *guru* who, although he is a Buddhist, in reality plays the role of *purohita* of a Hindu king.[18]

It must be emphasized that Avalokiteśvara plays his role of rainmaker as the protector of the kingdom. The protection which he accords is linked to the carrying out of the festival and of the procession. If, despite this protection, a drought occurs the Newars, whether they be Buddhists or Hindus, ask a *vajrācārya* (a Buddhist therefore) to undertake special ceremonies to make this rain come. Even today, when there is a drought, the *vajrācārya* do a *pūjā* on the *maṇḍala* of Varuṇa, a divinity whose connection with waters is known since the *Vedas*.[19] Such rites are collective, often organized by a village or a town-quarter, and their participants are above all farmers (*jyāpu*).

Here I wish to discuss an illustration of an unpublished version of this legend of Red Avalokiteśvara. Up to the present, no text has been published which gives us the same details. This version of the legend is painted on a scroll 2.20 metres in length and 64 cms. in width. This type of painting of which we possess quite a few examples dating from the seventeenth and eighteenth centuries are called in Sanskrit *paṭa*. They are put on show in monastery courtyards or in Buddhist Tantric sanctuaries (*āgama-chẽ*) during the month of *guñla* (July - August) which Newar Buddhists consider as being particularly sacred and during which very important ceremonies take place. S. Lienhard when publishing a similar but much longer scroll, preserved in the Museum of Berlin,[20] has explained how with the help of a stick the story-teller points to and comments on the various episodes in the legend represented in the painting.

The scroll which I study here (Pl. 1-IV) is painted in dominant reds and greens. A comparison with a scroll with a similar subject kept in the Prince of Wales Museum, Bombay, dated 1617 and of purely Newar fabrication, shows the importance of the Indian influences on this painting.[21] These influences are manifest in the conception and in the portrayal of the landscapes and above all in the costumes which are those worn by Indian Princes in North Indian miniatures at the beginning of the eighteenth century. By contrast the images of divinities decorated with jewels are purely Newar.

The Bombay museum holds two Newar paintings the study of which has helped me a lot towards understanding certain scenes in the scroll I publish here. A scroll dated 1619 illustrates scenes from the *Kāraṇḍa vyūha,* a text very popular among Buddhist Newars and which vaunts the merits of Avalokiteśvara. The second scroll, dated 1617, is composed in a manner completely identical to the one on which I comment here. It only differs by the way in which the personages and the landscape are treated. That is why I have given two photographs of it. It allows one to affirm that the version of the legend of Avalokiteśvara, which is our present concern, goes back at least to the seventeenth century. The two scrolls are mentioned by P. Pal who does not describe them in detail and unfortunately does not decipher the legend they carry which would have been of great help to me in understanding certain episodes which are obscure. He only indicates that they were painted in 1619 and 1617 respectively at the request of Kāśirāja Bharo, an inhabitant of Byam Vihāra.

The scroll I have chosen to illustrate and of which there exist partial shots in colour in *Les Royaumes de l'Himālaya* was made in 832 Nepal saṃvat = 1712.[22] This date is to be found in the third line of the inscription: the statue of Lokeśvara was damaged so the festival could not take place. The painting commemorates the event. One will note on the left at the bottom a panel showing ten personages worshipping the statue of Red Avalokiteśvara being carried on the processional chariot. Inscriptions give the names of these personages. Among them are Mahendra Malla, his son Yoga Narendra Malla and Śrīnivāsa Malla. We know that the king of Patan, Śrīnivāsa Malla, whose *iṣṭa devatā* was Red Avalokiteśvara, had decided that the ritual bath, a very important moment in the festival, must take place in the presence of the king.[23] Now a Newar chronicle points out that "the first day of the dark fortnight of the month of Caitra (March-April of 832 N.S. = 1712) when the moment arrived for the ceremonial bath of Bunga Deo (Red Avalokiteśvara), the king Mahendra Malla stayed at Kathmandu. Finally the ceremony took place without him. He did not go to the festival at Bungamati either. As a result the image was brought back in his absence."[24] The painter has however decided to represent the king and the court (at Patan, it is true) because without their presence the ceremony would not have been complete and perhaps because a similar scene was depicted in the 1617 scroll.

To interpret the scenes in the scrolls of 1617 and 1712 is often difficult. The Newari caption does not give all the indications and details which one would like to have. That on the scroll from Bombay (1617) has been neither transcribed nor deciphered. That of the 1712 scroll is written in an elliptical old Newari, from a semantic as well as a syntactic level. The transcription of the inscription was made by Thakur Lal Manandhar. I fixed the translation of it after long discussions with Śrī Bhadri *Vajrācārya* but uncertainties subsist, particularly with regard to the right-hand side of the second register. Examining the Bombay scroll, the content of which is identical but sometimes better conserved, helped me to understand better certain details and it is a pleasure for me to be able to thank here M. Sheti, the Conservator of the Prince of Wales Museum in Bombay, who helped me to obtain photographs of this scroll and permission to publish them. Other items which helped my understanding were the published descriptions of the festivals of Patan and Bungamati, field notes taken in 1978 and 1981 on fieldwork financed by grants from the Laboratoire d'Ethnologie et de sociologie comparative of the University of Paris X—Nanterre and conversations with learned Newars, particularly those whose names I have just mentioned.

In order to simplify the understanding of the scenes, I give first of all a synopsis of the episodes.[25] The panel is divided into two parts by a wide band decorated with flowers. Each of the three registers in the scroll is divided in this way into two parts (left and right) which, it is clear, when one examines this scroll or other paintings using this partition technique, that they bring together episodes which have a thematic unity. There are in all six main series of episodes. Top left, two kings of Magadha (so says the caption) Dharmaketu and his son Candraketu are carrying out rituals prescribed for kings. Top right, they are fighting and the country experiences drought and desolation.

The second panel is enigmatic in various respects. On the left, two monks and two women have gone to the paradise of Amitābha whence they bring back Avalokiteśvara the compassionate; back on earth they deliberate with a king who wears the head-dress of the kings of Nepal. On the right two monks are chastised in Yama's hell: then one of these two monks is in a palace on a bed, in gallant company; finally water flows forth from Svayambhu hillock: the drought is over; prosperity has returned.

Below, left, the panel depicts the Patan procession: on the right are represented the statue's consecration and the ritual bath to which I referred previously.

The detailed description of the diverse episodes employs a fictive numbering of them. A Roman number stands for the register; a letter (a,b,c...) for the place of the episode in this register starting from the viewer's left.

In part 1 a, two kings, accompanied by their wives, on a chariot drawn by dragons and preceded by Red Avalokiteśvara render homage to Amitābha, the head of the family (*kula*) of Avalokiteśvara. Amitābha, red in colour, is seated on a peacock, his usual mount.[26] Both kings wear crowns. The first, slightly taller, the father, has a very pale skin; the other, who seems to be the son, is of darker complexion and wears clothing of a darker colour. In 1b the same two kings are carrying out the ritual of *aṣṭamī-vrata* in honour of Amoghapāśa (written *Amukapāśa* in Newari) Lokeśvara depicted in a medallion. In 1c the *maharṣi* and the (king's) *guru*, in the company of the two kings and their wives, listen to the "*dharma* of Lokeśvara" (says the caption). The great *ṛṣi* is carrying a book in his hand; the *guru* has a beard. In 1d, this same *guru* and the two kings, kneeling down, pay homage to an image of Red Avalokiteśvara.

The first part of the top register is therefore centred on the royal worship of Avalokiteśvara, worshipped in this case in his form of Amoghapāśa ("he of the unfailing noose"). His worship was very popular. Many works of art depict him.[27] Several paintings of the fifteenth and sixteenth centuries represent him as white with six or eight arms (as in this instance). In his hands he holds on the left (the viewer's right) a running noose, a flowering lotus and a vase; on the right, a rosary and a jewel: one of the right hands makes the gesture of favour (*vara-mudrā*). In certain paintings[28] Amoghapāśa is represented with the appearance of an ascetic, with a tiger-skin round his kidneys and an antelope-skin on the left shoulder: his hair-dress is ornamented by an image of Red Amitābha.[29] His worship is still very popular. It is celebrated on the eighth day of each month, whence the name of *aṣṭamī-vrata* given to the ceremony. It is carried out at one of the twelve *tīrtha* in the Valley. The place of residence of those who participate is not taken into consideration: the priest brings together those who wish to take part in the ceremony and indicates to them the date and the place where the ritual will be celebrated. Apart from these *tīrtha*, this ritual is still celebrated every month on the eighth day of the clear fortnight in the monastery of Bungamati, the residence of Lokeśvara.[30] During this ceremony, a particular *maṇḍala* is drawn with white lines on a red back-ground, the same as the one which is visible on 1b alongside the image of Amoghapāśa.[31] The *aṣṭamī-vrata* ritual includes a fire sacrifice (*homa*) which can be seen in 1b: this *homa* is usually made by a *vajrācārya*. This *vajrācārya* is depicted here as an ascetic (coiled top-knot, ear-ring, rosary) and in the caption bears the name of *maharṣi* (*mahārikhi-na* in the Newar writing). *Ṛṣi*, according to Tibetans, was used for priests celebrating a *homa* and *vajrācārya* have told me that, in previous days, on the occasion of great ceremonies, they used to wear the clothes of *yogin*.[32]

In the right-hand part of the first register (1c) two kings are at war. They face each other, both being on a chariot—one of which is drawn by elephants, the royal animal par excellence, and the other by horses. In the centre, Avalokiteśvara (takes position between them ?). In 1f, we see the battle-ground: dogs and ravens are eating the dead.[33] In 1g, a dried up fountain symbolizes the drought which has struck the country. In 1h, the two kings discuss what they should do to put an end to the drought.

This series of episodes therefore links in a relation of cause and effect, the war which the two kings, father and son, are waging and the drought which is devastating the country. This drought lasts for twelve years, a traditional figure for great calamities resulting from the *adharmic* behaviour of a king.[34] The type of fountain portrayed in 1g is typically Newar, but the costumes of the kings and of the soldiers and the chariots are Indian; moreover the caption stipulates that these events are taking place in Magadha and thus, in theory, in Bihar. This name probably refers back to a mythical past: the scene takes place in very far-off days at a time when the Valley of Nepal was supposed to be an integral part of Gangetic India. The life of the Buddha, the legend of Aśoka have given this name of Magadha to Newar Buddhists as the name of a glorious ancient country, governed by powerful kings. The names of the kings are more interesting: Dharmaketu "who has for flag Law or Religion" and Candraketu ("who has for flag the moon") These names do not appear in the latter-day published versions of the legend of Red Avalokiteśvara. Let us recall that in these the drought is provoked by the fact that serpents, divinities of the waters, are "bound" by Gorakhnāth: King Narendra Deva (643-679), with the help of his *ācārya* Bandhudatta, brings back to Nepal the statue of Avalokiteśvara and thus puts an end to the drought. In this case, there are no snakes, no Gorakhnāth, no Narendra Deva. But the name of Candraketu is not unknown. He is one of the legendary kings whose reign would have preceded that of Narendra Deva. Sylvain Lévi has this to say about his legend: "Candraketu who is also absent at Kathmandu [does not reign at Kathmandu] reigns at the time of troubles: enemies attack the country from all sides and rob the people. Grief-stricken, the king shuts himself up with his two wives and spends twelve years bewailing his misfortune. Supernatural assistance, due to the intervention of the *vajrācārya* Bandhudatta, restores prosperity in the country: the kings who had devastated Nepal hand back their loot. Becoming old, Candraketu Deva hands on the crown to his son Narendra Deva and goes to heaven."[35]

The legend recorded by S. Lévi is definitely connected with what the scroll represents: there is no question of a drought but the name of the *ācārya* Bandhudatta figures in the "traditional" legends concerning this drought. According to S. Lévi, the king at whose time the drought began, and also finished, was Candraketu. On our scroll, it is not stated to which of the two kings the benefit was due; and it is difficult to recognize Candraketu: the two kings, father and son, have the same clothes and the same features. But in 1a and 1b, the two kings are shown one behind the other. We can suppose that the one in front, and who is moreover taller, is the father. Now another significant detail (*lakṣaṇa*) seems to be the colour of the face (since the clothes change): Candraketu's face is dark. This is confirmed when we look at 1e: Dharmaketu, the first-named in the caption, must be on the left; Candraketu, named in second, must be on the right: now the personage on the left has a pale face, that on the right a dark face. I consider therefore that Candraketu's face is dark and I will use this detail to try to explain the enigmatic second panel.

In 11a, we see a representation of the couple Bhairava Śakti embracing each other. Bhairava, whom the Buddhists of the Valley call Mahākāla, has his statue at the entrance of all Buddhist Newar monasteries and he is often represented in union with his śakti in Buddhist paintings and sculptures.[36] 11b shows the paradise of Amitābha. 11c represents the Buddha Amitābha, looking to the right, that is: 11d. In 11d, Avalokiteśvara, two monks and two women are seated on a heavenly chariot (*vimāna*), the *lakṣaṇa* of which is the cloud which carries it. In 11e, a king and his spouse are enthroned in front of the seated monk, followed by his two wives.

The first part of the second register is therefore devoted to the intervention of Avalokiteśvara leaving the paradise of Amitābha to visit the earth. But the events in their detail are obscure for the caption is not sufficiently explicit. It gives the names of the divinities who figure in the paradise of Amitābha, an important detail aimed at avoiding a loss of memory by the recitant. The gods of this paradise are grouped around a monument with a *śikhara* roof inside which is placed the image of Red Avalokiteśvara. He is represented in his human form, in an image identical to that which is taken out in procession at Patan. This monument is quite similar to the present-day sanctuary at Bungamati. The painting from Bombay, of 1617, shows another type of monument (Pl. V-VI). The list of the gods does not necessitate any special comment: according to my informants, it is traditional and modelled on a text which is very popular in Nepal, the *Kāraṇḍa vyūha*.

Avalokiteśvara in the form of Mahākaruṇa is represented as descending from the sky on the god's vehicle, the *vimāna.* On what summons does it descend to earth? The caption which mentions monks (*bikhu*) and nuns (*bikhuni*) does not furnish the details we would like to have: the Newar plural form is vague and the caption does not give the name(s) of the *bihhu* nor of the *bikhuni.* Nor are facial features individualized. There is therefore no indication allowing this episode to be connected with that of the first register. But this connection must exist and one can try to imagine it. One can suppose that one of the kings (perhaps both of them) has retired to a monastery and that it is after this on his intervention that Avalokiteśvara came down to earth. Let us recall what S. Lévi wrote about Narendra Deva, the king who would have brought the statue of Red Avalokiteśvara to Bungamati: "Narendra Deva only held royal power for seven years, just long enough to build a few *vihāras;* then, having renounced the things of this world, he abdicates and enters a convent. His elder son Padma Deva and his younger son Ratnadeva had already done so. It is there that Vara Deva comes to beg him to save Nepal which is being devoured by drought (here is the episode of Narendra Deva and Bandhudatta). In dying Narendra Deva leaves his crown to his two daughters along with a copy of the *Prajñā-pāramitā,* and his soul passes into the left foot of Matsyendra Nātha."[37] It would not be difficult to interpret this left part of the second register in function of this legend, which is given in a Buddhist chronicle. But the caption on our scroll usually gives the names of the gods and the personages. If a new personage as important as the king Narendra Deva were to intervene, one would expect his name to be mentioned. We shall also see that the monk or monks represented in 11d are perhaps the personages who suffer chastisement for their evil acts in Yama's hell in 11d. This also seems to exclude Narendra Deva. We must therefore look for a personage who has already been mentioned in the legend. The choice is limited to Candraketu and Dharmaketu. Candraketu is known as the "saviour" of Nepal in a like circumstance. Now the personage represented behind Avalokiteśvara on the *vimāna* has a dark face. He could then be Candraketu. But who is the second personage? The women could be the wives of the monk (Candraketu ?): it has for long been known that Newar monks are married.[38] As for Avalokiteśvara, his appearance is exactly that which he has in 1a and where the caption indicates his name. So there is therefore no doubt as to his identity.

The interpretation of the scenes which follow is even more difficult. Who is this king of Nepal who appears suddenly in 11c, and whom the caption does not name, and this monk who is facing him? Certain details are important: the monk is dark in colour, like Candraketu in 1, like the monk of Avalokiteśvara's *vimāna*; he wears jewels; he is followed by two women (let us remember Candraketu's two wives in S. Lévi's text) and by a personage with the top-knot of the ascetics in the 1617 scroll. As for the king, he is not a king of Magadha: he wears the traditional costume and head-dress of the Malla kings, those we can see, for instance, on the painting dated 1643 and which represents the king of Kathmandu Pratapa Malla (1644-1674) weighing his son against gold. In the scroll from Bombay, dated 1617, the king has neither turban nor crown but he too carries a book in his hand.[39] This detail is therefore important. We can compare it with the book figured in 1c in the hand of the great *ṛṣi* who, the caption tells us, is listening to the "*dharma* of Lokeśvara", that is to say, the rituals to be carried out in his honour, a partial illustration of which we see in 1d. We can then suppose that once Avalokiteśvara has been brought back to earth by the monk, the king pronounces the edict inaugurating the festival and that his instructions are symbolized by the book he is holding in his hand. But all this is hypothetical and remains obscure.

Even more obscure is the right hand part of the second register. In 11d, Yama, the lord of hell, and his servant, Yamadūta, "the messenger of Yama", chastise the two monks watched by two women. In 11e, one of (these two?) monks is lying on a bed in a house or a palace in the company of his wife. In 11g water spouts out of the mountain of Svayambhunāth (New.: *Go-śṛṅga*) where the gods have gathered: two farmers (*jyāpu*), one dark-skinned and the other light-skinned, collect it.

In 11g, the situation has clearly become normal once more. The gods have reoccupied their place on the sacred hillock of Svayambhu, water flows abundantly; sins have disappeared (*nirmala* says the legend). Among the gods featured on Svayambhunāth, around Red Avalokiteśvara, there are also Mañjuśrī, creator of the Valley, precisely at this point, and Gaṇeśa, a god who is extremely popular in the Valley and who is the god of material well-being.[40] The method of interpretation, which I have adopted, and which is based on the idea of a unity of theme in each half of the register, encourages me to think that the two episodes which precede 11g (11d, scene in hall; 11e, erotic scene) bear some relationship to this return to normal. 11d would be the punishment of the guilty, 11e the return of the monk-king to his palace. We would then have a sequence *dharma* (punishment in hell), *kāma* (erotic scene), *artha* (water and peasants). But I do not understand why the monk or monks who have seemingly brought Avalokiteśvara down to earth to put a stop to the drought are tortured in hell nor why one of the monks, whom we see being tortured in hell in 11d, is next found in bed in gallant company in 11e. The 1712 scroll is slightly damaged at this point, but on the Bombay scroll the scene is clear: in both cases the personage is one and the same. As for the text of the caption, it is so elliptical that I have some doubts about my translation of the second part of the second line.

However obscure for us may be the events which precede and those which follow the episode of the hells (11d) this episode nevertheless teaches us a lot. In them we see the lord of hell Yamarāja and his servant Yamadūta torturing two monks who, the caption tells us, have done evil deeds. The role of the women is not clear. Yama, throughout the Indian world and for Newar Buddhists also, is charged with punishing those who have carried out bad actions; he is also called Dharmarāja. But in Nepal he has special links with Avalokiteśvara. One of the versions of the legend of the white Avalokiteśvara of Jana Baha at Kathmandu makes Yama the spiritual guide of Avalokiteśvara.[41] The first storey of Tā Baha, the temple where Red Avalokiteśvara resides at Patan, is decorated with several images of Yamadūta. The scene of punishment in the hell is not therefore a simple depiction of punishment; in the mind of Newar Buddhists there is also a connexion—very difficult to specify, it is true—between this scene and the compassionate Avalokiteśvara.

The text of the caption does not seem to correspond exactly to what is represented on the scroll; on it Yamadūta who is white is beating one of the monks with a hammer; Yamarāja, who is red, holds his sword above a second monk who is caught by a snake (*nāga*). In the best known episode of the legend of Avalokiteśvara, it is the serpents which are bound, and the drought is the consequence of this "binding".

But here the serpent is not bound: he is the instrument of punishment. He is not the cause of drought: on the contrary he intervenes only in the final episode of the legend, at the moment when water will again pour out. I have already given examples of the connection between snakes and rain. Snakes are always associated with the underworld. King Pratapa Malla (1641-1674) of Kathmandu, during a terrible drought, took the place of a *vajrācārya* in Śāntipura, a cave at Svayambhu. In contemporary times Buddhist priests descend into certain caves near Svayambhunāth and invoke the snake-like divinities of the Valley in order to cause rain-fall. The chronicle relates that king Pratapa Malla, after a terrible fight with the demons, succeeded in seizing a book written with the blood of the snakes. As soon as he emerged, it began to rain. The divinity invoked by Pratapa Malla, a Hindu sovereign, is not Avalokiteśvara but Śiva accompanied by his wife Śakti.[42] The story about king Pratapa Malla is very significant: a king can take the place of a priest and he can put an end to drought without the help of a spiritual guide. He acts as absolute master. As in the painting of 1712, the king descends into the subterranean world where *nāga* live.

The third register represents the procession of Avalokiteśvara. The caption indicates that the statue had been damaged. the procession could not therefore take place. Its repair was carried out at the expense of a personage whose name has disappeared at the beginning of the third line but could be Bhīma Bharo, mentioned at the end of the line. *Bharo* in fact is an epithet of seemliness. The person who ordered the Bombay painting was Kaśirāja Bharo; and a Tibetan translated Bharo by "rich".[43] Once the repairs had been made the *guṭhi* of the Bungamati temple was able to carry on with preparations for the procession of NS 832 (1712) which the third register portrays. The initial espisode (111a) has disappeared, but can be reconstituted by comparing it with the scroll from Bombay: it is the *maṇḍala* of the moon-god Candra, very popular among the Newars. The allusion to Candraketu is clear: Candra plays no part in the legend of Avalokiteśvara. By putting his image at the beginning of the register homage is also paid to the king's victory.

In 111b two Malla kings and their wives are present at a *pūjā* being celebrated by a *vajrācārya* who is wearing a metal head-gear. In 111c, the kings and the court (the names are given in the caption) are watching the arrival of the chariot, figured in 111c. To the right of the flowered strip, in 111d, is depicted the ceremony of *kalaśa-pūjā* and in 111e the bathing (*mahā-snāna*) of the statue in the presence of musicians. The differences with the ceremony described in detail by J. Locke[44] are slight. The story seems to be organized here more on a spatial than a chronological principle. The events are to be read from right to left so that the chariot can arrive on the left in front of the court who are kneeling.

The ceremony starts with a *kalaśa-pūjā,* 111d. A *vajrācārya* takes the god out of his statue and shuts it in a large silver urn (*kalaśa*). In addition he consecrates eight smaller silver pots, two for the bath and six containing protective divinities whose names are never revealed. Henceforth the divinity is no longer in the statue but in the silver urn which remains in the temple of Tā Baha at Patan. The statue is transported into another quarter of Patan, at Lagan Khel, is placed on a platform and bathed (1 should say "showered") by Nyekhus (members of the Newar caste of painters of religious images) in the presence of the *vajrācārya* and of the king who has arrived with a suite. This is the scene we see on 111e. The statue is on the platform; on the right, the king and his family are kneeling, followed by musicians; on the left, the *vajrācārya,* also kneeling.

After having bathed it, the Nyekhus bring the statue back to Tā Baha and repaint it during a fortnight. Then it is again consecrated by a *vajrācārya* from Bungamati[45]: he once again transfers the divinity from the silver urn, where it was situated, into the statue which has been renovated and where it will henceforth reside. This ceremony necessitates a large clay pot, and sixty-three little pots of which only eighteen are represented on the image 111d. This is a *kalaśa-pūjā* which precedes the marriage ritual which is not represented on our scroll but to which the caption makes reference. The marriage is part of the *daśa karma,* "ten ritual acts", carried out at the consecration of a statue. These are the ten *saṃskāra* which punctuate the life of an individual. The ninth (*pāṇi-graha* or *vivāha*) corresponds to the marriage of young Newar girls to a divinity (New.: *ihi*), a ritual which is probably very important as the caption makes precise mention of it. In former times another *saṃskāra,* the *barha tayegu,* which I have already mentioned, used to take place, during which the statue was shut up in the dark, and which corresponds to the seclusion which young Newar girls undergo at the time of their first period.

The procession itself which nowadays takes place in *Vaiśākha* (April-May) and which took place in *Śrāvaṇa* (July-August) in 1712, after a more or less long interval (which is function of whether or not the chariot breaks down and other incidents) arrives at Patan Jawalakhel where the last part of the festival takes place, that which is today the most important: in the presence of the king the shirt (*bhoto*) of Matsyendranāth is then displayed. The presence of the court in 111c makes certain that it is indeed the final episode in the procession which is represented. But we do not see the divinity's shirt, nor any other detail which would make us think of this ceremony. On the image which I call 111d, we see only, on the right, Mīnanātha's chariot, on the left that of Avalokiteśvara, such as they still exist today, one following the other, the smaller (Mīnanātha) behind the taller. Each of the wheels represents a Bhairava. The shaft of the chariot is the *nāga* Karkoṭaka; at its end is figured the mask of Hayagrīva ("horse-necked"), a Bhairava who, like Avalokiteśvara, belongs to the family (*kula*) of Amitābha. The chariot of Avalokiteśvara has stopped in front of the *guru* of the king, seated in front of the royal sword. Personages climb onto the *śikhara* of the chariot of Avalokiteśvara, probably in order to carry flowers to the personage perched right at the top of it: we see him throwing flowers to the crowd. Today, this ceremony does not take place at Jawala Khel but at Pode Tol, a month before the chariot starts out towards Jawala Khel. A member of the *guṭhi* climbs to the top of the chariot, and, as image 111c shows, throws to the crowd rice, flowers, red powder, sweetmeats, coins and a coconut. Whoever grabs this coconut is certain to have a son within the year. It is impossible to know whether 111c is a summary showing at the same time what takes place at Jawala Khel and what takes place at Pode Tol or whether in former days the procession ended with the distribution of flowers, coins, etc. I would tend to opt for the latter since the painting does not show the ceremony which is today considered to be the most important, the one that attracts the crowd which has come from the entire Valley: the brandishing of the shirt of Matsyendranāth. There is nothing of all that on the 1617 scroll, no display and no distribution either. At the chariot's pinnacle there is only an image of white Avalokiteśvara.

The analysis I have just undertaken, while insufficient as far as discovering all the details of this new version of the legend of Avalokiteśvara is concerned, reveals nonetheless certain important facts. First, may I recall that this painting was ordered by the *guṭhi* of Bungamati, that is to say, by the association of Buddhist clergy whose particular responsibility was the worship of Red Avalokiteśvara. For instance, it is from Bungamati that comes the *vajrācārya* in charge of the *kalaśa-pūjā* prior to the procession. The version which I have just studied is then the official version of the Bungamati *guṭhi*. With versions previously known it has certain points in common: a twelve-year drought, the role of the king as responsible for the prosperity of the country, the role of the king's *guru*, the unfolding of the festival and of the procession. However the differences are much greater. That the king involved is not Narendra Deva is of little importance. What strikes one is the exclusion of any episode or incident concerning Gorakhnāth, Matsyendranāth, and the displaying of the god's shirt. In this case it is the war between the kings which provokes the drought and the "misfortunes" and not the *nāga*. In 1712 the Bungamati *guṭhi* kept a version of Avalokiteśvara's legend containing no allusion to the intervention of Gorakhnāth but in which ascetics have a definite role in the cult rendered to Avalokiteśvara. If one judges from the 1617 painting, we can affirm that the ascetics are Kānphaṭa for they have the long ears pierced by long ear-rings according to the fashion of the *nātha*.[46] Twice in the inscription of the 1712 painting we find the word *nātha* associated with the name of Lokeśvara. The first inscription, which shows the presence of *nātha* ascetics in the Kathmandu Valley, dates from the fourteenth century: it is (to be) found inside the Kāṣṭhamaṇḍapa at Kathmandu. But the influence of the *nātha* and their religious activity developed considerably only in the seventeenth century. We can suppose that the association of ascetics with the cult of Avalokiteśvara-Bunga Dyo was very considerably prior to the transformation of the legend and of the divinity Avalokiteśvara-Bunga Dyo into Matsyendranāth. It is very likely that the transformation took place at the end of the eighteenth century when, during the reign of Prthivi Narayan Shah, first king of the new Shah dynasty and conquerer of the Valley in 1768, the cult made fresh progress. All that explains why the Hinduized version of the legend has ultimately prevailed over the Buddhist version. We can deduce from this that if the legend of Avalokiteśvara is undoubtedly very old, the version of it which is promulgated today is certainly fairly recent.

First Line

sva . . . bhumi . . . nehmaṃ. . . nehmaṃśu . . . yāṅā/maharaka ṛṣi nehmasena śrī amukapāśa sake dharmma danakā śukla aṣṭami dhaarma dana rājāpani sena jima neda punyā yāṅā thana vāgāka subhuk.sa jura/ maharaka rikhina guru bon'āva śuklaṣṭami dharmma kha kaṅā rājā nehma bākāyā/śrī maharaka rikhina śrī lokeśvara sake gvapala yāka/lokeśvarana dharma upadesa kaṅā/dharmmaketu cabdraketu rājāpani nehma bākāyā rathasa daṅāva lvāka śrī magāṅāva jyoti hava the the lvāka bākāyā phukija sika dhora khica kokhana nava/magaha desayā rājā dharmaketu candrakety nehma vāyu thva desasa jemaneda va magāka . . . tise phukhulisa rājā yā aṃdora/

Second Line:

. . . yā saktāṃ sahita/śrī ma (harikina) śrī lokeśvaranātha yā śrī mahādeva brahmā viṣṇu lokapanī sahita sabhā/śrī mahādeva śrī brahmā vajrapāni śrī amitābha yā sabha krakuchanda tathāgata śrī lokeśvarana śrī kārana bibhu kha bikhu bikhuni sakha nihma survarṇa vimāna thakāra amitābha loka sa yā śubha vaj(r)asattva/ kārana bibhu upākṣāna bikhu . . . toṛa tāva punyā cita vaṅāva prathama bikhuni va hoñāva . . . karma dhararapu/bikhuna khata karmma torata godha yāṅāna yāma dūtana nugarasa mugarana vāṅā nāgapāśana ciyā prathama tiriyā vairajña/bikhuna thava prathama tiritoratāva akuri gādha yā ka . . . dhua . . . hākuhijyā hiku joparanirmal tirthasa /śrī svayāmbhu parvata sa samasta devaloka . . . gośṛnga cakra . . . na yāka

Third Line:

. . . ka tvakāhāra vyūha . . . śrī kā . . . bhāro . . . na bugamaṃ...ohna va maphu hloṆā pratiṣṭhā yāṅā/vimuni purāna majiyāva hira thva varasa sukrija yāka guṭhisa nohatayo cakā va dhunakā dina thva samvat 832 śrāvana kṛṣṇa caturdasi magha nakṣatra buddhavāra /śrī tailokanātha rathasa bijyācakaṃ/ jātrā yāṅā aneka dīpa aneka/dhvajā lohana/raka pholu pakvānaṃ ruyā śrī mīnanātha yā ratha svadani yāṅā ācāryana pāthakana śrī brahmā kalaśa yajña yāṅā śrī tailokanātha vivāhā yāṅā yātrā yāta/śrī gaṅgā jara saṃkhasa piva samudra oha kalaśa sa snāna pañcāṃṛta sahita mahāsnāna nānā vādya thāṅāva sugaṃdha dhūpa thaṅāva ghaṇṭa vādya śrī bhimarabho sahitana / śrī tailokyāṅātha mahāsnāna yācake bijackā/

Third Line on the left:

1. vajrācārya
2. Jasavantaju
3. Mahesvaraju
4. Kāyasṭha Viṣṇugovinda
5. Śrī Śrī Mahindra Malla deva thākura
6. Śrī Śrī Yoganarendra Malla
7. Śrī Śrī Nivāsa Malla jūjū

I Together. . . together . . . the great *ṛṣi* (*maharaka ṛṣi*) (with the population) carries out the rites (*dharma danaka*) in honour of Śrī Amoghapāśa (Amukapāśa) the eighth day of the bright fortnight. (As a result) of the rites (*dharma dana*) and of meritorious actions (*puṇya*) accomplished by the kings and population (*sena*) every twelve years, in the country there was rain (*va*) and abundance of food (*subhukṣa*). The great *ṛṣi* (and) the *guru* ask the two kings, father and son, to carry out the rites of the eighth day of the bright fortnight. The great *ṛṣi* ... *does*...*all the (?)*... for Śrī Lokeśvara. Lokeśvara teaches the dharma. The two kings, Dharmaketu and Candraketu, the father and the son, fight each other, each on a chariot (*rātha*). Śrī Lokeśvara tries to get the king Candraketu to give up (the fight) ... In Magadha, throughout twelve years, there is no rain. The sun (*jyoti*) burns (everything) (because) the father and the son and all the people of the same lineage (*phuki*) are fighting one another. They massacre each other. The dogs, the ravens devour them. In Magadha, the kings Dharmaketu and Candraketu are in conflict and for twelve years it does not rain ... all the reservoirs of water (are dried up?) ... The two kings do no know what to do.

II ... they are reunited. Śrī le grand *ṛṣi*, Śrī Lokeśvaranātha, Śrī Mahādeva, Brahmā, Viṣṇu, Lokapani, in assembly (*sabha*) are reunited (*sahita*). (Here are) Śrī Mahādeva, Śrī Brahmā, Vajrapāṇi, Śrī Amitābha in the assembly (here is the tathāgatā Krakucchanda. Śrī Lokeśvara (composed entirely of compassion? *karuṇa vibhu*?), the monk(s) (and) the nun(s) are together, carried aloft on a heavenly vehicle (*vimāna*) made of gold (*suvarṇa*), and are leaving the paradise of Amitābha (*Amitābhaloka*) and of the auspicious (*śubha*) Vajrasattva. The compassionate (*kārana*?) monk has renounced ... praiseworthy thoughts (*puṇya-citta*) ... He has done several bad actions and he has rejoined the first nun(?) ... The monk has renounced the six *karma* and committed several bad actions (*akuri godha*). Yamaduta has struck his chest with the hammer and has tied him up with the serpent-noose (*nāga-pāśa*). The first wife (*prathama tiriyā*) has become disgusted (*vairajña*). The monk has abandoned the first woman who had committed bad actions (*akuri godha*) ... Both ... have cleaned (*nirmala*) their clothes at the *tīrtha.* The mountain of Svayaṃbhu; the gods have come together (*samasta*) there. At Svayaṃbhu (*okuśriṅga*) ... they have caused water to flow out...

III . . . the disposition (*vyūha*) . . . Śrī . . . Bharo . . . at Bungamati . . . has repaired and then installed (*pratiṣṭḥa*). A part of the god was damaged. (The members) of the *guṭhi* have done a good action and have repaired it. In this day of the year 832, in Śrāvana, the fourteenth day of the dark fortnight, in the constellation Magha, a Wednesday, they have announced the end of the repairs and have made Śrī Trailokanātha Avalokiteśvara "protector of the three worlds" ride in a chariot. They went in procession (*yātrā*), they lit many lamps (*dīpa*) they hoisted banners (*dhvajā*) of copper (*lohana*), various kinds of garlands of flowers and of sweetmeats. They made a chariot for Śrī Mīnanātha. The ācārya recited (*pāthaka*). He carried out the ceremony (*yajña*) of the *kalaśa* of Śrī Brahmā, celebrated the marriage (*vivāha*) of Śrī Trailokanātha. And so the procession (*yātrā*) took place. With the water of Śrī Gaṅgā in a conch (*śaṅkha*) the ocean was made to come. With the *kalaśa*, it was bathed (*snāna*); with the *pañcāmṛta* its great bath (*mahāsnāna*) was given. Music (*vādya*) was played, (sweet) smelling incense (*sugandha dhūpa*) was lit, bells (*ghaṇṭa*) were shaken. This was done with (the help of ?) Śrī Bhīma Bharo. All that was done for the great bath of Śrī Trailokanātha.

Notes

* First published in: *BEFEO* (Bulletin de l'Ecole française d'Extrême Orient) LXXIV, 1995

1. Wright, D., ed., *History of Nepāl* (1st edition 1877), 1966 (3rd edition), Calcutta, Ranjan Gupta, pp. 167-8; Regmi, D.R., *Medieval Nepal*, Calcutta, Firma K.L. Mukhopadhyay, 1966, Part II, pp. 283-7.
2. Shepherd Slusser, M., *Nepal Mandala: A Cultural Study of the Kathmandu Valley*, Princeton, Princeton University Press, 1982, Vol. 1, p. 372.
3. Pal, P., *The Arts of Nepal, Part 1: Sculpture*, Leiden, E.J. Brill, 1974, chapter: "Buddhist Sculpture": the pages on Avalokiteśvara, pp. 114-20.
4. Locke, John K., *Karunamaya: The Cult of Avalokiteśvara Matsyendranāth in the Valley of Nepal*, Kathmandu, Sahayogi Prakashan, 1980, describes the monastery of Jana Baha and two other temples of white Avalokiteśvara at Nāla and at Chobar, pp. 345-73.
5. Shepherd Slusser, M., *op. cit.*, p. 369: "The historians of the Gopālarāja

Vaṃśāvalī invariably refer to him as Vugama Lokeśvara or a variant thereof. From their time until the mid-eighteenth century, all sources identify the deity as Avalokiteśvara by such names as Bunga Lokeśvara, Lokanātha, Āryāvalokiteśvara, Karuṇāmaya or Padmapāṇī. But suddenly, with a Patan inscription of A.D. 1748, the deity is named "Śrītin Macchendranātha", thrice illustrious Matsyendranātha. Following the Gorkhali conquest the new name of the Bungamati deity became increasingly common. It is regularly employed in the Brahmanical versions of the nineteenth-century chronicles. The older name Bungadyo endured among those persons most intimately associated with this cult, the Newars of Bungamati and Patan, and in Buddhist recensions of the chronicles."

6. Locke, J.K., *op. cit.,* chap. XIII "Avalokiteśvara becomes Matsyendranāth", pp. 405-45 and Shepherd Slusser, M., *op. cit.*, pp. 367-78.
7. Foucher, A., *Etude sur l'iconographie bouddhique de l'Inde d'après des documents nouveaux,* Paris, E. Leroux, 1900, First Part, p. 99.
8. Roerich, G., *Biography of Dharmasvamin,* Patna, 1959, pp. 54-5. The dates of Dharmasvamin's stay in Nepal are 1228-34. The Tibetan author Chos-kyi Nyi-ma, in the eighteenth century still speaks of A-Kham and Bu-Kham in A.W. Macdonald and Dvags-po Rin.po.che, 'Un guide peu lu des Lieux-saints du Népal', 11e Partie, in *Tantric and Taoist Studies in Honour of R.A. Stein* (ed. by M. Strickmann), Bruxelles, 1981, p. 258.
9. Shepherd Slusser, M., *op. cit.*, p. 368.
10. Shepherd Slusser, M., *ibid.*: In his first metamorphosis, the indigenous Bungadyo become identified with Avalokiteśvara, a syncretic form he would keep for a millennium or more. This paralleled the transformation of certain local *māīs, ajimās,* and similar godlings into divinities of more respectable international standing, Buddhist or Brahmanical . . . In any event, whenever the transformation took place, the curious little godling of Bugayumi Bungmati for many centuries played a dual role as Bung Lokeśvara p. 368. Lévi, S. *Le Népal: étude historique d'un royaume hindou,* Paris, E. Leroux, 1905, Vol. I, pp. 347-57.
11. Locke, J.F., *op. cit.,* p. 209. Vergati, A., "Social Consequences of Marrying Viṣṇu Narayana: Primary Marriage among the Newars of Kathmandū Valley", in *Contributions to Indian Sociology* (NS), Vol. 16, No. 2 (1982), pp. 271-87.
12. Getty, A., *The Gods of Northern Buddhism,* Oxford, Clarendon Press, 1928. Mallmann, M. Th. *Introduction à l'étude d' Avalokiteśvara,* Paris, PUF, 1967.
13. Locke, J. F., *op. cit.*, chap.," The Jawalakhel Festival and the showing of the bhoto", pp. 273-8.
14. Locke, J.F., *ibid.*, pp. 405-45. Unbescheid, G. *Kānphaṭā. Untersuchungen*

zu Kult, Mythologie und Geschichte Śivaitischer Tantriker in Nepal. Wiesbaden, F. Steiner Verlag, 1980. Beiträge zur Südasien Forschung Sudasien-Institut, Universitat Heidelberg.

15. Vergati, A., "Taleju Sovereign Deity of Bhaktapur", *Asie du Sud. Traditions et changement,* Paris, Adrien-Maisonneuve, 1979, pp. 163-9.
16. Vergati, A. "Le culte du Buddha Dīpaṅkara dans la vallée de Kathmandu", *Arts Asiatiques,* tome XXXVII (1982), pp. 22-7.
17. Pal, P., *op. cit.,* Vol. 1, *Sculpture,* pp. 140-2 describes several stone sculptures which illustrate the antiquity and the popularity of the cult of Nāgarāja: the most ancient dates from the fourth century and is in the courtyard of Kumbheśvaṛa at Patan.
18. Greenwold, S.M., "The role of the priest in Newar Society", in *Himalayan Anthropology. The Indo-Tibetan Interface,* ed. J. Fisher, The Hague, Paris, Mouton, 1978.
19. Vergati, A., *A Sketch Book of Newar Iconography,* New Delhi, International Academy of Indian Culture, 1982. On p. 53, we see the drawing of Varuṇa's *maṇḍala.* Mitra, R., *The Sanskrit Buddhist Literature of Nepal,* Calcutta, Sanskrit Pustak Bhandar, 1971 reprint, gives the description of the *maṇḍala* of Varuna according to the *Svayambhū Purāṇa.* "There was a continuous drought for seven years in Nepal. The drought brought on a famine. The people were dying of starvation. At the request of the King Gunakamadeva, Santikara undertook to allay the famine. He drew the figures of a lotus with eight petals, and invoked the Nagas. They came. In the centre of the lotus sat Varuna, of a white colour with two hands and seven hoods. On the eastern petal, came the blue coloured Ananta; on the southern petal, Padmaka of the colour of a lotus stalk, with five hoods; on the western petal, the saffron coloured Takshaka with nine hoods; on the northern, Vasuki, green, with seven hoods; on the south-west, Sandkha, green; on the north-west, Kulka, white, with thirty hoods; on the north-east, the gold-coloured Mahapadma with as many hoods. But the blue coloured Karkata, who was to have sat on the sourth-eastern petal, did not come. At the command of Śāntikara, King Guṇakāmadeva brought him against his will from his retreat in the Lake Adhara, to the south of the Gandhavati, by main force. Santikara worshipped these Nagas, and they sent a copious shower. Santikara, with the blood extracted from the bodies of serpents, painted the figures of these Nāgas as seated on lotus and placed the picture in a city, named Nag-pura founded on the occasion, and consecrated it. The worship of the Nagas in this form was declared to be an antidote to famine and droughts," p. 253.
20. Lienhard, S., *Die Legende vom Prinzen Viśvantara. Eine nepalesische Bilderrolle aus der Sammlung des Museums für Indische Kunst, Berlin,* Berlin, Museum für Indische Kunst, 1980.
21. Pal, P., "Paintings from Nepal in the Prince of Wales Museum", in

Bulletin of the Prince of Wales Museum, No. 10 (1967), pp. 1-26 mentions the paintings concerning Avalokiteśvara (pp.10-11) without analysing their content and without translating the captions they bear.

22. *Les Royaumes de l'himālaya* (ed. A.W. Macdonald) Paris, Imprimerie Nationale, 1982, p. 204, ill. 31 and p. 207, ill. 35.
23. Locke, J.F., *op. cit.*, p. 314.
24. *Pūrṇimā* 12, aprakasit Thyasaphu, No. 12, pp. 31-3 and Locke, J. F., *op. cit.*, pp. 317-18.
25. Pal, P., *op. cit.*, Vol. II, chapter: "Narrative Paintings", pp. 94-114, publishes several scrolls from the seventeenth and eighteenth centuries where the scenes are separated by bands with flowers or trees: each part concerns one theme (ill. 140, 142, 145, 150). This technique is very old in Nepal: it was used already for painting book-covers in the eleventh century (ill. 22 and ill. 39).
26. Mallmann, M.-Th. de, *Introduction à l'iconographie du Tântrisme bouddhique*, Paris, Adrien-Maisonneuve, 1975, pp. 95 and 106.
27. Pal, P., "The Iconography of Amoghapaśa", in *Oriental Art*, XII, 4 (1966), pp. 234-9 and XIII, 1 (1967), pp. 20-7.
Mallmann, Marie Thérèse, *Introduction à l'étude d' Avalokiteśvara*, Paris, PUF, 1967, pp. 168-70 gives a good description of the iconography of Amoghapāśa Lokeśvara.
28. Mallmann, *op. cit.*, p. 105.
29. Lévi, S., *op. cit.*, pp. 325-9.
30. Locke, J.F., *op. cit.*, p. 259.
31. Macdonald, A.W. and Vergati Stahl, A., *Newar Art: Nepalese Art during the Malla Period*, Warminster, Aris and Phillips, 1979, p. 42, ill. 108 and ill. 109.
32. *Critical Pali Dictionary* S.V. The Pali word *iṣi* (Skt. *ṛṣi*) is a respectful way of designating certain persons close to the Buddha and sometimes the Buddha himself. Tibetan dictionaries give as the equivalent of the Skt. word *ṛṣi*, Tib. *dren-sron* and glose: "lama who offers a *homa*". It is clear that the word is in this case only the equivalent of the Skt. word *ācārya* and that the Tibetan explanation of the word is witness to an Indian and Nepalese habit of calling the *vajrācārya*, when they celebrate a *homa*, *ṛṣi*.
33. In popular Newar imagery dogs and ravens are the messengers of death of Yamarāja. Every year in the month of October (*Kartik*) a *pūjā* is celebrated for dogs and another one for ravens. Dogs are identified with Bhairava. See Nepali, G.S., *The Newars, An Ethno-Sociological Study of a Himalayan Community*, Bombay, United Asia Publications, 1965, p. 329.
34. Biardeau, M. Etudes de mythologie hindoue IV, *BEFEO* LXIII, 1976, pp. 151-2.
35. Lévi, S., *op. cit.*, Vol. II, p. 172.
36. Shepherd Slusser, M., *op. cit.*, p. 291. "In his role as defender and

guardian, Mahākāla is one of the chief protectors of all the other Valley gods, a task he shares with Sankata Bhairava of Te-bahal, Kathmandu . . . . conceptually related to Bhairava, from whom he probably derives, the Buddhist deity is teamed with Bhairava in practice, shares aspects of his iconography, and the name Mahākāla, one of Bhairava's epithet."

37. Lévi, S., Vol. II, pp. 164-5.
38. Snellgrove, D., *Buddhist Himālaya,* Oxford, B. Cassirer, 1957, chap. "Buddhism in Nepal", pp. 91-120.
39. This painting was published in Pal, P., *op. cit.,* Vol. II, p. 157 and ill. 220, and in *Les Royaumes de l'Himalaya,* p. 206, ill. 33.
40. Lévi, S., *op. cit.,* Vol. II, pp. 330-46.
41. Locke, J.F., *op. cit.,* pp. 152-3.
42. Regmi, D., *op. cit.,* Vol. II, p. 77.
43. *Biography of Dharmasvamin,* XII, p. 37 "bharo" signifies in Nepali "rich" (Tibetan *phyug -po*). The word is not to be found in the dictionary of Jørgensen, H., *A Dictionary of the Classical Newārī,* Copenhagen, Levin and Munksgaard, 1936.
44. Locke J.F., *op. cit.,* p. 224, ill. 33
45. Locke, J.F., *op. cit.,* pp. 262-73.
46. Unbescheid, G., *op. cit.,* chap. III, "Der Kult zu kanphaṭa yogis im Kathmandu", pp. 82-129.

Select Bibliography

Allen, M., Girls' Pre-puberty Rites amongst the Newars of Kathmandu Valley, Unpublished Manuscript.

Allen, M., 1973, "Buddhism without Monks: The Vajrayana Religion of the Newars of Kathmandu Valley", *Journal of South Asian Studies,* No. 3 (University of Western Australia Press).

Allen, M., 1976, "Kumari or Virgin Worship in Kathmandu Valley", *Contributions to Indian Sociology,* 10, 2, pp. 293-317.

Anderson, M.A., 1971, *The Festivals of Nepal,* London, George Allen and Unwin.

Auer, G. and Gutschow, N., 1974, *Bhaktapur. Gestalt, Funktionen und religiöse Symbolik einer nepalischen Stadt im vorindustriellen Entwicklungs Stadium,* Darmstadt, Technische Hochschule.

Barré, V., Berger, P., Feveile, L., Toffin, G., 1981, *Panauti, une ville au Népal,* Paris, Berger Lavrault.

Bennett, L., 1979, *The Status of Women in Nepal,* Vol. I, Pt. 2, Kathmandu, Tribhuvan University.

Bhattacharyya, N.N., 1973, *History of Śakta Religion,* New Delhi, Munshiram.

Biardeau, M., 1981, *Etudes de mythologie hindoue,* 2 vols., Paris, E.F.E.O.

Bista, K.B., 1972, *Le culte de Kuldevata au Nepal,* Paris, Editions Nove.

Bose, A., 1942, *Social and Rural Economy of Northern India,* Calcutta, University of Calcutta.

Briggs, G.W., 1938, *Gorakhnath and the Kanphata Yogis,* Calcutta, Y.M.C.A. Publishing House. Reprinted by Motilal Banarsidass, Delhi, 1973.

Caplan, L., 1975, *Administration and Politics in a Nepalese Town,* London, Oxford University Press.

Chambard, J.L., 1961, "Mariages secondaires et foires aux femmes en Inde centrale", *L'Homme* 1, 2, pp. 52-88.

Dumont, Louis, 1953, "Définition structurale d'un dieu populaire tamoul: Aiya Nar, le Maître", *Journal Asiatique,* pp. 255-70.

Dumont, Louis, 1966, *Homo Hierarchicus. Essai sur le système des castes,* Paris, Gallimard.

Dumont, Louis, 1969, "Marriage in India: The Present State of the Question", *Contributions to Indian Sociology* 7, 3, pp. 77-90.

Dumont, Louis, 1975, *Une sous-caste de l'Inde du Sud. Organisation sociale et religion des Pramalai Kallar,* Paris, Mouton.

Eck, D.L., 1982, *Banaras, City of Light,* Princeton, Princeton University Press.

Foucher, A., 1900, *Etude sur l'iconographie bouddhique de l'Inde d'après des documents nouveaux,* Paris, E. Leroux.

Fuller, C.J., 1976, *The Nayars Today,* London, Cambridge University Press.

Fürer-Haimendorf, Chr. von, 1956, "Elements of Newar Social Structure", *The Journal of the Royal Anthropological Institute of Great Britain and Ireland,* 86:2, pp. 15-38.

Gaborieau, M. 1977, "Les gens de caste ou l'Inde omniprésente", in *Le Népal et ses populations,* Bruxelles, Editions Complexe.

Gellner, D., 1992, *Monk, Householder and Tantric Priest: Newar Buddhism and its Hierarchy of Ritual,* Cambridge, Cambridge University Press.

Getty, A., 1928, *The Gods of Northern Buddhism,* Oxford, Clarendon Press.

Greenwold, S.M., 1981, "Caste: A Moral Structure and a Social

System of Control", in A.C. Mayer, ed., *Culture and Morality: Essays in Honour of C. von Fürer-Haimendorf*, Delhi, Oxford University Press, pp. 84-106.

Gupta, S. and Gombrich, R., 1986, "Kings, Power and the Goddess", *South Asia Research*, No. 2, pp. 122-38.

Gutschow, N., 1982, *Stadtraum und Ritual der newarischen Stadte im Kathmandu-Tal. Eine architekturanthropologische Untersuchung*, Stuttgart, Verlag W. Kohlhammer.

Gutschow, N. and Kölver, B., 1975, *Ordered Space, Concepts and Functions in a Town of Nepal*, Wiesbaden, F. Steiner Verlag.

Hasrat, B.J., 1970, *History of Nepal as Told by its Own and Contemporary Chronicles*, Hoshiarpur, V.V. Research Institute Press.

Höfer, A., 1979, *The Caste Hierarchy and the State in Nepal. A Study of the Muluki Ain of 1854*, Innsbruck, Universitatsverlag Wagner.

Jha, N.H., 1970, *The Licchavis*, Varanasi (Chowkhamba Sanskrit Studies, Vol. 75).

Jørgensen, H., 1936, *A Dictionary of the Classical Newārī*, Copenhagen, Levin and Munksgaard.

Kane, P.V., 1974, *History of Dharmaśāstra*, Vol. II, Pt. I, Poona, Bhandarkar Oriental Research Institute.

Karmakar, A.P., 1950, *The Religions of India*, Vol. I, Lonavla, Mira Publishing House.

Kathmandu Valley: The Preservation of Physical Environment and Cultural Heritage. A Protective Inventory, Vol. I, Vienna, A. Schroll, 1975.

Kölver, B., 1976, "A Ritual Map from Nepal", in *Folia Rara*, Wiesbaden, F. Steiner Verlag, pp. 68-80.

Kölver, B., 1978, "Aspects of Nepalese Culture: Ancient Inscriptions and Modern Yatras", in *Proceedings of the First Symposium of Nepali and German Sanskritists*, Dang/ Kathmandu, Institute of Sanskrit Studies, pp. 157-72.

Korn, W., 1976, *The Traditional Architecture of the Kathmandu Valley*, Kathmandu, Ratna Pustak Bhandar.

Kulke, H., 1980, "Legitimation and Town Planning in the

Feudatory States of Central Orissa", in *Ritual Space in India, Studies in Architectural Anthropology*, edited by J. Pieper, London, AARP, pp. 30-40.

Les Royaumes de l'Himālaya (ed. A.W. Macdonald), Paris, Imprimerie Nationale, 1982.

Levi, R.I., (with the collaboration of Kedar Raj Rajopadhyaya), *Mesocosm: Hinduism and the Organization of a Traditional Mewar City in Nepal*, Berkley, University of California Press, 1990.

Lévi, S., 1905, *Le Népal: étude historique d'un royaume hindou*, 3 vols, Paris, E. Leroux.

Lévi, S., 1932, *Mahākarmavibhaṅga* (La grande classification des actes) *et Karmavibhaṅgopadeça*, Paris, E. Leroux.

Lienhard, S., 1978, "Problèmes de syncrétisme religieux au Nepal", *Bulletin de l'École Française d'Extrême-Orient* 65, pp. 239-70.

Lienhard, S., 1980, *Die Legende vom Prinzen Viśvantara. Eine nepalesische Bilderrolle aus der Sammlung des Museums für Indische Kunst, Berlin*, Berlin, Museum für Indische Kunst.

Locke, John K., 1980, *Karunamaya: The Cult of Avalokiteśvara Matsyendranāth in the Valley of Nepal*, Kathmandu, Sahayogi Prakashan for Research Centre for Nepal and Asian Studies, Tribhuvan University.

Macdonald, A.W., 1975, *Essays on the Ethnology of Nepal and South Asia*, Kathmandu, Ratna Pustak Bhandar.

Macdonald, A.W. and Vergati Stahl, A., 1979, *Newar Art: Nepalese Art during the Malla Period*, Warminster, Aris and Phillips.

Madan, T.N., 1965, *Family and Kinship: A Study of the Pandits of Rural Kashmir*, Bombay, Asia Publishing House.

Malamoud, Ch., 1976, "Village et forêt dans l'idéologie de l'Inde brahmanique", *Archives Européennes de Sociologie* 17, pp. 3-20.

Mallmann, M.-Th. de., 1975, *Introduction à l'iconographie du Tântrisme bouddhique*, Paris, Adrien-Maisonneuve.

Mitra, Rajendralala, 1971, *The Sanskrit Buddhist Literature*, Calcutta, Sanskrit Pustak Bhandar (revised edition).

Nepali, G.S., 1965, *The Newars, An Ethno-Sociological Study of a Himalayan Community*, Bombay, United Asia Publications.

Oldfield, H.A., 1880, *Sketches from Nipal*, I, London, W.H. Allen.

Pal, P., 1966/1967, "The Iconography of Amoghapaśa", in *Oriental Art*, XII, 4 (1966), pp. 234-39, and XIII, 1 (1967), pp. 20-7.

Pal, P., 1967, "Paintings from Nepal in the Prince of Wales Museum", in *Bulletin of the Prince of Wales Museum of Western India*, No. 10, pp. 1-26.

Pal, P., 1974, *The Arts of Nepal, Part 1: Sculpture*, Leiden, E.J. Brill.

Pal, P., 1975, *Nepal, Where the Gods are Young*, New York, Asia House Gallery.

Pandey, R.B., 1965, *Hindu Saṃskāras*, Delhi, Motilal Banarsidass.

Parry, J.P., 1979, *Caste and Kinship in Kangra*, London, Routledge and Kegan Paul.

Petech, L., 1984, *Medieval History of Nepal*, Roma, Is.M.E.O.

Pott, P.H., 1966, *Yoga and Yantra: Their Interrelation and their Significance for Indian Archaeology*, The Hague, M. Nijhoff.

Ray, A., 1968, "The Paśupatinātha Temple: Nepal", *Man in India*, 49, pp. 10-23.

Regmi, D.R., 1965/1966, *Medieval Nepal*, Calcutta, Firma K.L. Mukhopadhyay, 2 vols.

Regmi, M., 1968, *Land, Tenure and Taxation in Nepal. Religious and Charitable Land Endowments, Guṭhi Tenure*, Vol. 4, Berkeley, University of California.

Regmi, M., 1976, *Landownership in Nepal*, Berkeley, University of California.

Renou, L. and Filliozat, J., 1947, *L'Inde Classique. Manuel des Etudes Indiennes*, 2 vols., Paris, Payot.

Riccardi, Th., 1980, "Buddhism in Ancient and Early Medieval

Nepal", in *Studies in History of Buddhism*, ed. by A.K. Narain, Delhi, B.R. Publishing Corporation, pp. 265-81.

Rosser, C., 1966, "Social Mobility in the Newar Caste System", in *Caste and Kin in Nepal, India and Ceylon*, edited by Chr. von Fürer-Haimendorf, London, Asia Publishing House, pp. 68-140.

Seneviratne, H. L., 1978, *Rituals of the Kandyan State*, Cambridge, Cambridge University Press.

Sircar, D.C., 1973, *The Śākta Pīṭhas*, 2nd edition, Delhi, Motilal Banarsidass.

Slusser Shepherd, M. and Vajrācārya, Gautama Vajra, 1973, "Some Nepalese Stone Sculptures: A Reappraisal within their Cultural and Historical Context", in *Artibus Asiae*, Vol. XXXV, Nos. 1/2, pp. 79-138.

Slusser Shepherd, M. and Vajrācārya, G., 1974, "Two Medieval Nepalese Buildings: An Architectural and Cultural Study", in *Artibus Asiae*, Vol. XXXVI, No. 3, pp. 169-218.

Slusser Shepherd, M., 1982, *Nepal Mandala: A Cultural Study of the Kathmandu Valley*, Princeton, Princeton University Press.

Snellgrove, D., 1987, *Indo-Tibetan Buddhism: Indian Buddhists and their Tibetan Successors*, London, Serindia Publications.

Stevenson, S., 1971, *The Rites of the Twice Born*, New Delhi, Oriental Books, Reprint Corporation.

Stürbecher, K., 1981, *Bhaktapur. Architektur und Stadtentwicklung im Kathmandutal.* Saarbrücken, Verlag Breitenbach.

Teilhet, J.H., 1978, "The Tradition of the Nava Durgā in Bhaktapur, Nepal", in *Kailash*, Vol. VI, No. 2, Kathmandu, pp. 81-98.

Thurston, E., 1907, *Ethnographic Notes*, Madras, Government Press.

Toffin, G., 1975, "Etudes sur les Néwar de la vallée de Kathmandu: *Guṭhi*, Funérailles et Castes", *L'Ethnographie*, 70, pp. 205-25.

Toffin, G., 1977, *Pyangaon, une communauté néwar de la Vallée de Kathmandu: la vie matérielle,* Paris, Éd. du C.N.R.S.

Toffin, G., 1981, "Culte des déesses et fête du Dasāī chez les Néwar (Népal)", *Puruṣārtha,* 5, pp. 58-81.

Toffin G., 1984, *Société et Religion chez les Néwar du Népal,* Paris, C.N.R.S.

Tucci, G., 1969, *Théorie et pratique du mandala,* Paris, Fayard.

Vajracarya, D. and Malla, K.P., 1985, *The Gopālarājavaṃśāvalī,* Wiesbaden, F. Steiner Verlag.

Vergati, A., 1982, "Le Népal. Les Royaumes de la vallée de Kathmandu", in *Les Royaumes de l'Himalaya,* éd. par A.W. Macdonald, Paris, Imprimerie Nationale (Collection Orientale), pp. 164-208.

Vergati, A., 1986, "Quelques remarques sur l'usage du mandala et du yatra dans la vallée de Kathmandu, Népal", in *Mantra et diagrammes rituels dans l'hindouisme,* éd. par A. Padoux, Paris, Éd. du C.N.R.S., pp. 11-31.

Vergati, A., 1993, "Narrative Paintings in Nepal and in Rajasthan", in *Nepal, Past and Present,* éd. par G. Toffin, Paris, Éd. du C.N.R.S., pp. 195-204.

Vergati, A., 1994, "Bouddhisme et caste dans la vallée de Kathmandu", in *Bouddhisme et cultures locales: Quelques cas de réciproques adaptations,* Actes du colloque franco-japonais de septembre 1991, éd. par F. Fukui et G. Fussman, Paris, E.F.E.O., pp. 53-68.

Waldschmidt, 1969, *Nepal, Art Treasures from the Himalaya,* Calcutta, Oxford Publishing Co.

Wiehler, S. and H., 1980, "Nevar Musical Instruments", *Journal of the Nepal Research Center,* 4, pp. 67-133.

Wiesner, U., 1978, *Nepalese Temple Architecture: Its Characteristics and its Relations to Indian Developments,* Leiden, E.J. Brill.

Witzel, M., 1976, "Zur Geschichte der Rajopadhyaya von Bhaktapur", in *Folia Rara,* Wolfgang Vogt LXV Diem Natalem Celebranti, Wiesbaden, F. Steiner Verlag, pp. 159-79.

Wright, D., ed., 1877, *History of Nepāl,* translated from the Parbatiyā by Munshī Shew Shunker Singh and Pandit Shrī Gunānand, with an introductory sketch of the country and people of Nepāl, Cambridge, Cambridge University Press.

Index